Part I

Foundations

We start this book with an introduction to positioning in Chapter 1. In Chapter 2, we go deeper into the content of the concept of positioning and its relationship with other concepts such as image, identity, and reputation. We end this chapter with a description of the positioning process.

Brand Positioning

Brand Positioning is an English translation of an exceptionally well-renowned Dutch textbook, which provides a practical approach to analysing, defining and developing a brand's positioning strategy.

Divided into three key parts, the book works step-by-step through the creation of an effective marketing strategy, combining an academic approach with the strategic and operational guidelines, tools and techniques required. Unlike other textbooks, it has a unique focus on the relationship between branding, marketing and communications, exploring brand values, brand identity and brand image, and analysing how these can be transformed into a successful positioning strategy, using international case studies, examples and practical exercises.

This textbook will be core reading for advanced undergraduate and postgraduate students of marketing strategy, branding, marketing communications and consumer behaviour. It will also be of great value to marketing and communications professionals looking to develop and maintain their company's brand.

Erik Kostelijk is Associate Professor of Marketing at the Amsterdam School of International Business of the Amsterdam University of Applied Sciences, the Netherlands. He has teaching, research and professional experience in China, USA, Lithuania, France, Spain and Italy. He is the designer and author of the Value Compass, a method to assess the influence of values on branding.

Karel Jan Alsem is Professor in Marketing at Hanze University of Applied Sciences in Groningen, the Netherlands, and is Lecturer in Marketing at the University of Groningen, the Netherlands. He is also a brand consultant. He has published in several academic journals and has written multiple marketing books, including *Applied Strategic Marketing* (Routledge, 2019).

Brand Positioning

Connecting Marketing Strategy and Communications

Erik Kostelijk and Karel Jan Alsem

Routledge
Taylor & Francis Group

LONDON AND NEW YORK

First published 2020
by Routledge
2 Park Square, Milton Park, Abingdon, Oxon OX14 4RN

and by Routledge
52 Vanderbilt Avenue, New York, NY 10017

Routledge is an imprint of the Taylor & Francis Group, an informa business

© 2020 Erik Kostelijk and Karel Jan Alsem

The right of Erik Kostelijk and Karel Jan Alsem to be identified as authors of this work has been asserted by them in accordance with sections 77 and 78 of the Copyright, Designs and Patents Act 1988.

All rights reserved. No part of this book may be reprinted or reproduced or utilised in any form or by any electronic, mechanical, or other means, now known or hereafter invented, including photocopying and recording, or in any information storage or retrieval system, without permission in writing from the publishers.

Trademark notice: Product or corporate names may be trademarks or registered trademarks, and are used only for identification and explanation without intent to infringe.

British Library Cataloguing-in-Publication Data
A catalogue record for this book is available from the British Library

Library of Congress Cataloging-in-Publication Data
Names: Kostelijk, Erik, author. | Alsem, K. J., author.
Title: Brand positioning : connecting marketing strategy and communications /
Erik Kostelijk, Karel Jan Alsem.
Description: New York : Routledge, 2020. | Includes bibliographical references and index.
Identifiers: LCCN 2019044289 (print) | LCCN 2019044290 (ebook) |
ISBN 9780367250119 (hardback) | ISBN 9780367250195 (paperback) |
ISBN 9780429285820 (ebook)
Subjects: LCSH: Branding (Marketing) | Strategic planning.
Classification: LCC HF5415.1255 .K67 2020 (print) |
LCC HF5415.1255 (ebook) | DDC 658.8/27—dc23
LC record available at https://lccn.loc.gov/2019044289
LC ebook record available at https://lccn.loc.gov/2019044290

ISBN: 978-0-367-25011-9 (hbk)
ISBN: 978-0-367-25019-5 (pbk)
ISBN: 978-0-429-28582-0 (ebk)

Typeset in Times New Roman
by codeMantra
Printed and bound by CPI Group (UK) Ltd, Croydon, CR0 4YY

Contents

Part III: The implementation of the brand positioning strategy

Chapter 1

Relevance of brand positioning

1.1 An introduction to brand positioning

This book is about brand positioning. The concept of positioning has become internationally known because of the famous book by Ries and Trout (1986): *Positioning, the Battle for Your Mind*. **Positioning** essentially is about two things (Laforet, 2010):

1. First you decide what kind of message and image you want to convey to a target group. This concerns the strategic choice of a distinctive position in the market.
2. Then you ensure that you achieve that position. This is done through tactics: orchestrating the marketing mix (the five P's: product, price, place, promotion, and personnel).

This book focuses on the first of these two things. The second item involves the implementation of the positioning: the operational marketing plan.

It may seem rather trivial to write a separate book about positioning. Because it might seem that it is nothing more than a small element of marketing. And what about its role in communication? And there are countless books about marketing and communication. All right. Here we have the first (theoretical) issue. Positioning belongs to both marketing and communication. And as a result, it is undervalued in both fields!

A second problem is the professional reality. Marketing and communication practitioners do not devote enough attention to brand positioning. This is because marketers are mainly occupied with all sorts of tactical marketing aspects; in the heat of the moment, they often don't pay enough attention to the essence of the brand. This creates the risk that all kinds of activities are initiated that actually do not fit the brand, which leads to ambiguity. In turn, communication people often are also more concerned with operational matters such as making brochures or discussing the web site design with the agency. Or they are active on social media without strategically considering whether everything is in line with what the essentials of their brand.

The consequence of all this: consumers do not really know anymore what the brand stands for. The result is that it becomes difficult to create customer loyalty.

Red Bull illustrates how effective a good brand positioning can be (Example 1.1). The Red Bull brand consistently emphasizes values such as "extreme" and "energy." In this way the brand aims at customers who consciously or unconsciously associate with these values or at least desire to have an energetic feeling.

Example 1.1 The consistent branding of Red Bull

Red Bull stands for "extreme sports." Because it stands for "energy." And not just that. Red Bull shows in all possible ways that "extreme challenges" completely match with the brand. Red Bull sponsors Formula One races, organizes spectacular flying shows, and sponsors the highest individual free fall from space to earth. Partly because of this, Red Bull receives a lot of media attention. One of the energetic consequences: Sampling among students during the exam period. Wake up!

Photo 1.1 Red Bull stands for extreme performance. Source: istockphoto.com.

1.2 The increasing importance of brand positioning

There are several reasons (or actually trends) that make a clear brand positioning very important. These reasons are:

1. increasing competition
2. online growth leading to increasing market transparency and more powerful customers
3. increasing power of intermediaries
4. a lot of low involvement among consumers

5. the paradox of choice
6. the importance of the subconscious in decision-making

Ad 1 Increasing competition

A trend that has been going on for decades is the increase in **competition** in many markets. Competitors know each other more and more and it is therefore increasingly difficult to gain, let alone maintain, an advantage over the competition. Related to this, we also observe a decreasing "time to market" for innovations: if an organization has a product innovation, it should not wait too long with the actual introduction, because before you know it, the competition will enter the market and you lose your "first mover advantage." And if you are the first one, the competition will not wait long to introduce the same, or even an improved version, so your advantage will be brief and not as big as expected. The life cycle of new technologies is therefore becoming shorter and shorter. This can be seen, for example, in the smartphone market where new, better, faster types quickly follow up and a smartphone is – even after only a year – no longer up-to-date.

Ad 2 Increasing market transparency and more powerful customers

The **internet** is the main cause of an enormous availability of information about brands and markets. Online you can actually find everything about brands: what brands communicate about themselves, experiences of customers, tests of independent organizations, etcetera. If there has ever been a complaint, it probably can still be found online. And with the growth of **social media** the power of the customer has actually increased exponentially. After all, a tweet is enough to reach a huge amount of people. And if that tweet is also picked up by a journalist, an even stronger flood of publicity is created. The use of social media and internet stimulated another trend: the availability of enormous quantities of data. We refer to this as **big data**. For both practitioners and academics it is the challenge to obtain useful information out of these data.

Ad 3 Increasing power of intermediaries

There are several important trends in the distribution of products and services. We mention the following developments:

- **Increasing power of retailers**. This trend has been going on for decades, mainly in the food sector. For instance in The Netherlands only two retailers occupy more than half of the market: the chains Albert Heijn and Jumbo jointly have approximately 55% (2019) of the food market in their hands.
- **Growth of online sales**. The possibility for online shopping (and communication) is the biggest breakthrough in the history of marketing. It leads to fundamentally new consumer behavior and therefore also to new digital business models (Verhoef, Bijmolt, 2019), especially the growth of new digital platforms such as

Amazon, Alibaba, Booking.com, Uber and AirBNB. These new intermediaries have generated an enormous power and strongly affect the retailing value chain (Reinartz et al., 2019).

These trends emphasize that you, as a supplier / brand, have to make new fundamental choices about your positioning. What is your role in delivering customer value? How do you cope with the new competition? What channels will be used? This has also to do with what is sometimes referred to in marketing as 'push versus pull'. *Push* means that as a provider you try to promote the product to the intermediary ('through the chain'). *Pull* means that your brand mainly stimulates the final demand, i.e., the needs of end users, to 'force' intermediaries to pay sufficient attention to your brand. Nowadays in most markets it is not a choice between push or pull, or online or offline, you have to do all.

Ad 4 A lot of low involvement among consumers

Due to the previous two developments, consumers could become more critical when making purchasing decisions. After all, an average consumer can compare alternatives relatively easily and then choose the brand that fits him best.

Yet this is probably not the case. Precisely because there is so much competition, and the development of new products is fast, many consumers get the impression that "all brands will be equally good," which means that it does not really matter what you buy. This creates **low involvement**. Suppose a consumer has to choose a laundry detergent in a supermarket, facing a shelf full of different brands, sizes, types, and variants. This overload can lead to an "arbitrary" choice determined by, for example, the colour of the packaging or by a possible promotion. See also the next issue.

Ad 5 The paradox of choice

It has been argued that the multitude of choices creates a form of "choice fatigue." This is also called the "**paradox of choice**": you would expect that a greater choice for consumers is positive, because then there is really something to choose. But it could also lead to greater uncertainty because you can never be sure that you have actually chosen the best brand. This leads to **cognitive dissonance**: the feeling that you are less satisfied after your choice. The decision-making process thus becomes more complex, while the importance of the choice becomes smaller: almost all products on the market are in principle good enough to meet the needs.

This phenomenon has been investigated in a large number of studies. In a meta-analysis of the studies they investigated, Scheibehenne, Greifeneder, and Todd (2010) found, on average, no correlations in the number of brands and the choice motivation or the satisfaction afterwards. So, they did not find support for the existence of "the paradox of choice." This does not mean that the paradox of choice never occurs, and perhaps it does in some circumstances, but more research is needed on this point.

Ad 6 The importance of the subconscious in decision making

A trend that is not so much related to consumer behaviour but more central to the field of psychology (and marketing) is the "discovery" of the importance of the unconscious. Many psychological experiments show that many decisions of people are often taken unconsciously (Dijksterhuis, 2007). This finding is at odds with the idea of the "homo economicus," often used in economics: that people use rational, "economic" considerations when making choices. This point is important for positioning because it means everything has to be right from the first impression. Every detail from the first to the last brand contact contributes to the image.

All the above-mentioned developments increase the need for brands to distinguish themselves in one way or another from other brands. And when we talk about "distinguishing," we are talking about positioning.

1.3 The importance of brand positioning according to theory

It goes without saying that brands receive attention in marketing and communication science. In this section we want to focus on the following topics around brands:

- the question of when a brand is strong
- brand associations
- brand awareness and the Sharp studies
- the importance of reputation in communication

We end this chapter with a conclusion about the importance of positioning.

1.3.1 When is a brand strong?

In marketing science, David Aaker can be regarded as the first major brand expert. Aaker wrote two interesting books about building brands (Aaker, 1991, 1995) and did his own experimental studies on the effects of brand extensions. In his classic paper in *Journal of Marketing* (with Kevin Lane Keller, 1990) on the latter topic, the conclusion was drawn that brands have to be careful with the introduction of brand extensions that do not fit with the mother brand. Subsequently, there have been dozens of follow-up studies by other authors who have made refinements and expansions in the study of brand extensions.

The same Keller also specialized in brands and in 1995 issued the first edition of *Strategic Brand Management*. In this book Keller knows how to combine scientific insights about brands with practical recommendations and models. Here we outline the central principle that Keller uses in relation to building a **strong brand**. He states that "a brand is strong when consumers have a more positive reaction to the brand's actions because of the knowledge they have about the brand than if they had less

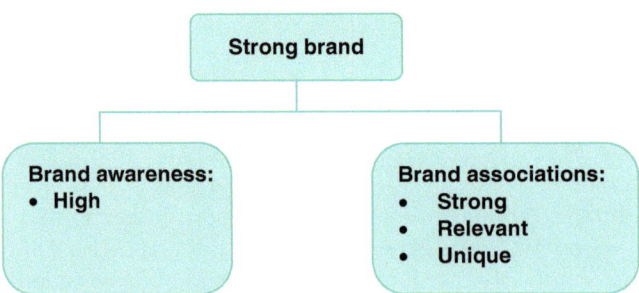

Figure 1.1 **Strong brands according to Keller**

knowledge about the brand." That knowledge aspect has two components according to Keller (Figure 1.1):

1. Brand awareness: consumers have heard about the brand; they know that in a certain product category the brand is one of the suppliers.
2. Brand associations: consumers have not only heard about the brand but also know something about it. They have strong, relevant, and unique associations with the brand.

In fact, Keller opts for a so-called "cognitive" approach, namely knowledge leads to preference: "Known makes loved." Knowledge then concerns both brand awareness and knowledge about what the brand stands for (associations).

The connection with our focus on brand positioning is mainly in the second knowledge dimension: the realization of associations with consumers. We will now go further into these associations.

1.3.2 Brand associations

The word "image" is often used in relation to brands. The **image** of a brand is the complete set of associations that the consumer has with the brand. These associations are the added value of the brand: consumers see or hear a certain brand name, and this evokes certain images or memories in the consumer's mind. **Brand positioning** aims to provide the brand with strong, favourable, and unique associations. But the marketer does not have the exclusive right to realizing brand associations. The brand image is influenced every time the consumer hears about the brand, uses the brand, or is in touch with the brand in a different way. This can be positive, with pleasant experiences, but it can also be negative.

Brands must be careful in the prevention of negative experiences or negative publicity. In this connection it is sometimes said: "Reputation is hard to gain but easy to lose." This proverb is only partly true. It is true that building a good image takes time. But a negative experience does not always push the brand out of favour immediately. Research shows that strong brands are more resistant to a knockout. It also depends on how brands deal with errors. It is important to win trust. See Example 1.2.

Example 1.2 Volkswagen

Until the autumn of 2015, Volkswagen was known as a reliable, solid brand. This changed suddenly when it became known that Volkswagen had been cheating in emission tests by making its cars appear far less polluting than they are. The brand had installed software that could detect whether a car was tested. If a test was detected, the car would be set in the "fuel-efficient and environmentally conscious" mode. As soon as the car was used normally again, the normal settings were re-installed after which the car became much less environmental-friendly. Because of this "dieselgate" the reputation of the brand was strongly affected in a negative way. So indeed ... Volkswagen's reputation was easily lost here. This was partly because the Volkswagen management did not respond quickly and openly. Only after a few days there was a reaction from the company, and the CEO had to resign. A couple of months later (October 2015) Volkswagen offered its apologies in full-page ads and promised to do everything to regain confidence.

Remarkably, the sales of Volkswagen was hardly affected by the reputation problem. 2018 was the best year ever for Volkswagen. This might be due to the brand power Volkswagen already had.

Positive associations add value to the brand. This added value, defined by Keller (2012) as **brand equity**, occurs when the consumer is familiar with the brand and when the brand evokes positive associations with the consumer, associations that match with this brand and not with competing brands. Positive associations lead to consumers appreciating the brand, developing a preference for the brand, or deciding to buy or keep buying the brand. Coca-Cola, for example, is in essence a dark-coloured soft drink with a lot of added sugar. However, thanks to marketing activities, this brand now represents happiness, and this – conscious or unconscious – association encourages people to buy Coca-Cola.

Photo 1.2 Coca-Cola. Happiness. Cozy. Christmas. Source: istockphoto.com.

Brand awareness and brand associations can be described as an associative network (Keller, 2012). The **associative network model** (Anderson, 1983) is a psychological model that describes how information is stored in our memory. In this model, memory is seen as a network of associations. This network consists of a number of nodes and the connections between these nodes. Each node represents a certain information. By means of connections that can vary in strength, this information is linked to other information in our memory. Figure 1.2 gives an example of an associative network that a certain consumer can have about the brand 7UP.

If this consumer thinks about 7UP, he automatically thinks about the soft drink. The "node" 7UP contains information. Seeing a bottle of 7UP, or the thought of this soft drink, activates this node and connections to other nodes in the memory. These connections represent the associations with – in this case – the brand 7UP. These associations may consist of characteristics of the brand (7UP is transparent), or aspects that are independent of the physical characteristics of the brand such as benefits (refreshing), previous experiences (I do not like it), or values associated with the brand (pure).

In the associative network in the example of Figure 1.2 also conflicting associations are visible. Depending on the strength of the connections with "sweet" or with "no colouring or flavouring agents added," the brand is seen as predominantly healthy or predominantly unhealthy. It is quite possible that different people have different associations with the same brand. After all, associative networks are individually determined. If different consumers were asked about their associations with 7UP, this would lead to different associative networks.

As mentioned earlier, brand positioning is aimed at creating, changing, or strengthening a brand image. Positioning activities therefore aim to change the network of brand associations by strengthening associations or making them less important, or by adding certain associations.

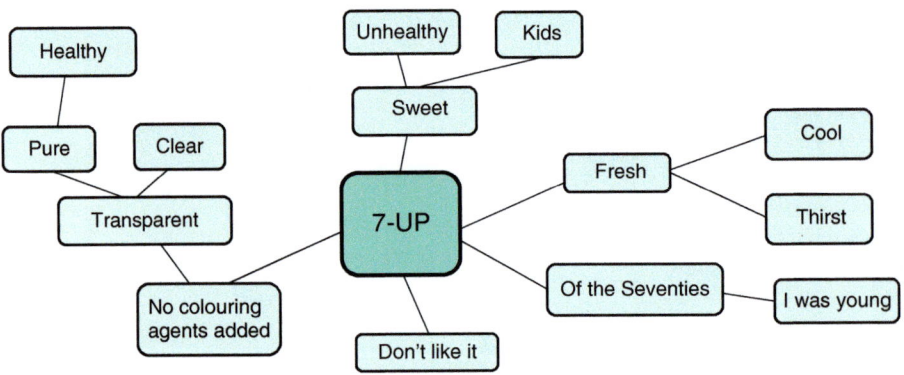

Figure 1.2 **Associative network**

1.3.3 The Sharp studies and the importance of positioning

In his very accessible book *Why Brands Grow?*, Sharp (2012) summarizes various studies that have been done at the London Business School on brand choices, based on large databases with real purchase data. The most important conclusion from all these studies is the big importance of **brand awareness**. Sharp shows that consumers have a strong preference for well-known brands. It also appears that information about, for example, quality plays a much less important role. Sharp shows, for instance, that brands that resemble each other in the perception of consumers are much less directly competing with each other than you would expect on the basis of these perceptions. The size of a brand (basically: the number of times people hear about the brand or are confronted with the brand) also plays a dominant role in the preferred position that a brand has in the minds of consumers. In fact, Sharp seems to question the importance of brand positioning to a certain extent. In terms of Keller, Sharp actually seems to prove that the brand awareness dimension is especially important for consumers and not the associations dimension!

An explanation for the findings of Sharp is in the low involvement that consumers generally have when purchasing products. We mentioned this already in Section 1.2 under ad 4. And then it makes sense that in their brand choices consumers are mainly guided by brand awareness. With presumably as thought: I know that brand and if it is so well-known, it is probably good. A good example of such a brand is Heineken (Example 1.3).

Example 1.3 Brand awareness of Heineken

Heineken probably has a huge global reputation as a beer brand, almost 100% in many countries. The question, however, is about Heineken's "unique associations." The point is that Heineken has had quite different campaigns over the years. And some campaigns were also rather generic, profiling the name Heineken more than what the brand represents. The question is how consistent and unique Heineken is in its brand communication. Nevertheless, Heineken is a global market leader in beer production and sales. A reason could be that it is "just the tastiest beer." In the beer category, however, it has been shown that emotion is much more important for brand choice than the actual characteristics and taste of the product. A simple blind test demonstrates this: when people see the brand name there are totally different preferences than without seeing a brand name. The explanation is probably that Heineken has both a very high brand awareness and a "positive feel" resulting from all visible behaviours of the brand. That good feeling apparently matches the unconscious choices that consumers make when choosing beer.

Photo 1.3 Heineken has high brand awareness. Photo © Moktarama (cc-by-3.0), with permission of Heineken

Sharp's findings are sometimes but not always in line with a large number of other scientific studies into the effects of marketing on the sale of products. In 2015, a second edition of Hanssens' (2015) *Empirical Generalizations in Marketing* was published, in which he summarizes many hundreds of studies on the effects of marketing. One striking conclusion is that out of the three market instruments, i.e. price, distribution, and advertising, the strongest effects can be expected from an intensive distribution. Price reductions also have a strong influence on sales, but that is often temporary. Advertising seemed to have only a small influence: the mean advertising elasticity is only about 0.1, which does not suggest that strong media pressure (and thus awareness) strongly affects sales. The strong effect of distribution can be explained by the fact that if a brand is available in many places, it is also sold a lot. Physical availability apparently has a strong influence on purchasing behaviour: if something is available, you buy it faster. This is in line with Sharp's emphasis on availability. The limited effect of advertising cannot be unambiguously linked to the results of Sharp, because higher brand awareness can also be achieved through strong communication, so by spending a lot on advertising. And Pauwels and Ewijk (2013) show that ("soft") attitudinal measures (so brand image) as well as ("hard") online behaviour tracking data are a good prediction of sales. So, brand image does matter.

Our conclusion from the "relevance-of-image"-debate is that both brand awareness and brand associations are important.

1.3.4 Positioning in communication science

We will suffice on this site with a brief comment about positioning in communication literature. In communication science, the word "positioning" is less common than in marketing. A concept that is strongly connected with this is **reputation**. We will discuss this further in the next chapter. However, it can be said at this location that there is a lot of literature about reputation (Van Riel, 2010). The importance of a good reputation for an organization is evident. Hallahan et al. (2007) also speak of "strategic communication" as being all purposeful communication that contributes to fulfilling the mission of an organization. Management, marketing, and communication disciplines play a role in this strategic communication.

1.3.5 Importance of positioning – conclusion

At the end of this chapter we conclude that consciously choosing a strategic position for an organization is of great importance. If we follow Keller's model, we see that it is about creating visibility and associations. Distinction and recognizability need not necessarily lie in substantive associations, but they can also lie in performance aspects such as the appearance of a brand and/or – more in emotional aspects – as sympathy and humour. As we said earlier, the unconscious processes – the instinctive impressions that people have with a brand – are very important. In fact, this also applies in human relationships: it is not for nothing that it is sometimes said that an employer already knows whether or not it is suitable when an applicant comes in.

Summary

Brand positioning is choosing a distinctive position for the brand. This is becoming increasingly important. This is partly because choice processes of customers happen largely unconsciously and also often under low involvement. This means that every element in the profile of the brand should fit. Due to the growth of online media, many brands have less grip on the final customer. That too requires strong branding. A brand is strong if the reputation is high and strong, with distinctive and relevant associations. A strong brand should be clearly visible.

Chapter 2

Essentials of brand positioning

2.1 The brand positioning concept

In Chapter 1 we already saw that positioning has everything to do with marketing and also with communication. In this chapter we will try to explain the relationship between these three concepts. But first we define positioning itself. After the definition of this concept, we discuss the relationship of positioning with branding, the requirements for positioning, and the relation with other concepts. We conclude this chapter with the positioning process, which also forms the guideline for the rest of this book.

2.1.1 Definition of positioning

Positioning comes from the verb to position, which simply means something like "to give a position." That does not help us too much in the context of brands. But what if we realize that it is the mental position in the head of a consumer! **Positioning** is indeed primarily determining which "position" a brand has to take in relation to competing brands in the head of a customer. And that "position" then is a mental position or an image of a brand. In other words what associations a customer should have with a brand. For example what kind of image should a customer have when we say "Mercedes?" Durability? Luxury? Man with a cigar? Expensive? Positioning is the determination of the desired associations that a consumer should have with a brand. The positioning is then "the desired brand image."

It is important to realize that this is a mental "brain position." Positioning has everything to do with associations with brands. This matches with the model of Keller as described in the previous chapter: the purpose of positioning is that people link knowledge and feelings to a brand (name). If these knowledge elements are positive (and unique), then positive opinions and reactions to the brand will be generated.

2.1.2 Relationship between branding and positioning

In Subsection 2.1.1 the word **brand** was used several times. *Brand* and *positioning* are closely related. In fact, they have a very unambiguous relationship. A brand (name) can only have one positioning and vice versa a positioning always belongs to a brand name. Take the Mercedes example that includes a certain desired image. It could well be that the brand Mercedes wants to evoke a different picture with one target group (for example, business people) than with a different target group (private drivers). After all, needs and desires of consumers differ, which is also the reason to segment and to serve different segments in different ways. The obvious problem in reality is that communication about brands cannot be strictly separated between target groups. Suppose that a brand would use a different positioning and would communicate differently to young people and to the elderly; then each target group will undoubtedly also see the communication messages intended for the other target group, after which confusion occurs. The ultimate consequence of this reasoning is that a brand can only represent one image.

In essence, this also applies to people. Everyone has a name, which we could call a personal "brand name." And everyone has a certain personality. A difference with brands is that people do not "consciously" have to choose their own positioning, although this may be the case, for example, in job interviews. Brands need to be more aware of positioning because they consciously communicate to the world, with commercial interests. In addition, many different people in an organization are involved in this communication. All these people must be aware of the positioning of the brand they're working for.

Because positioning is unambiguously associated with a brand and vice versa, we can also speak of **brand positioning**.

2.1.3 Requirements for positioning

We have defined positioning as determining the desired associations with a brand. There are three important requirements for those associations:

1. The positioning must match the brand itself. The brand should be able to deliver the promise and the position should be in line with the strengths of the brand; this is a form of consistency.
2. The positioning must be "relevant" for the target group. There is no point in creating a brand image that is of no interest to potential customers.
3. The desired brand image should preferably be distinctive, i.e. different from the image that of competing brands. This is in fact the essence of creating a brand: finding a distinctive position!

The three requirements for positioning can be summarized in the positioning triangle (Figure 2.1).

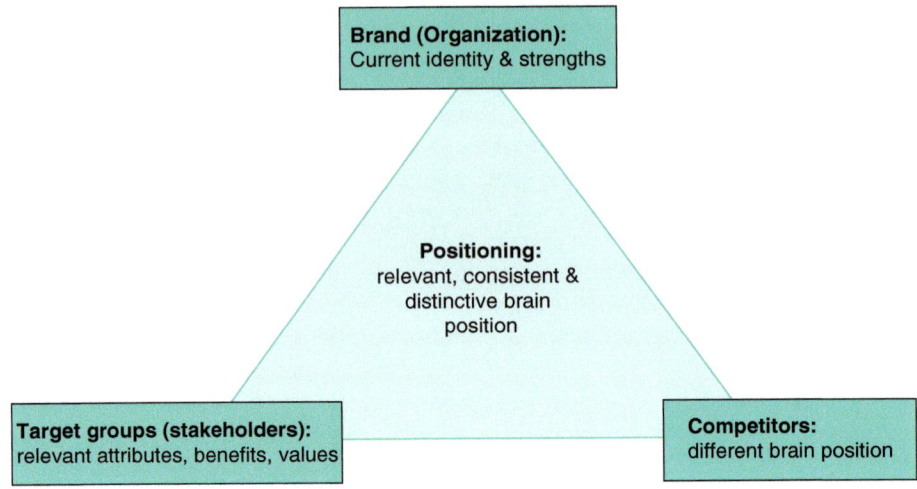

Figure 2.1 **Positioning triangle**

2.1.4 Relationship with other terms

There are many other concepts in marketing and communication that are related to the concept of positioning, but that are not the same. We discuss the following concepts: image, reputation, identity, mission and vision, proposition, Unique Selling Points (USPs) and Unique Buying Reason (UBR), and "branding."

Image

As mentioned in Section 1.3, the word image or **brand image** is often used in relation to brands. The image is the set of associations that people have with a brand. The big difference with positioning is that a brand image is the set of associations as *realized* in the target audience whereas positioning is the *desired* set of associations.

The word image is sometimes interpreted in a negative way, namely as if it were an artificial image created by marketing. In a way, the word image has an image problem. This sometimes also applies to image research. Sometimes companies do not want to do image research, while on the other hand they find it useful to know what associations people have with them!

Reputation

The term reputation is closely linked to image. Reputation usually refers to an organization as a whole. Fombrun, Gardbert, and Sever (2000) introduce the following six dimensions of reputation in the so-called **Reputation Quotient**:

1. emotional attractiveness (such as trust and appreciation)
2. products and services (quality and innovation)
3. vision and leadership (degree of strong leadership)

4.   work environment (such as being a good employer)
5.   social responsibility
6.   financial performance

The six dimensions are measured by means of questionnaires among various external stakeholders. Example 2.1 exhibits some brand rankings on the Reputation Quotient for 2018.

Example 2.1 Brand rankings with the Reputation Quotient (Source: Reuters, March 13, 2018)

Apple, Inc. and Alphabet, Inc.'s Google corporate brands dropped in the annual Harris Poll Reputation Quotient poll while Amazon.com, Inc. maintained the top spot for the third consecutive year, and electric carmaker Tesla, Inc. rocketed higher after sending a red Roadster into space.

IPhone maker Apple dropped to 29th from its previous position of No. 5, and Google dropped from 8th to No. 28. Apple had ranked No. 2 as recently as 2016, according to the Reputation Quotient released on Tuesday.

The poll, conducted since 1999, surveyed 25,800 US adults from December 2011 to January 2012 on the reputations of the "most visible" corporate brands.

John Gerzema, CEO of the Harris Poll, told Reuters in an interview that the likely reason Apple and Google fell was that they have not introduced as many attention-grabbing products as they did in past years, such as when Google rolled out free offerings like its Google Docs word processor or Google Maps and Apple's then-CEO Steve Jobs introduced the iPod, iPhone, and iPad.

"Google and Apple, at this moment, are sort of in valleys," Gerzema said. "We're not quite to self-driving cars yet. We're not yet seeing all the things in artificial intelligence they're going to do."

Meanwhile, Amazon.com held on to the No. 1 spot, which it has held for five years with the exception of 2015, when it slipped to No. 2. Gerzema attributed Amazon's ranking to its expanding footprint in consumers' lives into areas like groceries via its Whole Foods acquisition.

Elon Musk's Tesla climbed from No. 9 to No. 3 on the strength of sending Tesla Roadster into space aboard a SpaceX rocket – despite fleeting success delivering cars on time on earth, Gerzema said.

"He's a modern-day carnival barker – it's incredible," Gerzema said of Musk. "This 'The Right Stuff' attitude is able to capture the public's imagination when every news headline is incredibly negative. They're filling a void of optimism."

For its part, Facebook, Inc.'s reputation improved in the 2018 study, despite being the target of questions from US lawmakers about the role of social media in Russia's efforts to influence the US presidential election in 2016. Facebook ranked 51st, its best showing since 2014 when it ranked 38th, the highest the firm ever ranked in the poll.

Some say the difference between image and reputation is that image is the impression of people from an organization without having any experience, while reputation is the perception of people who do have experience with the organization. As such, reputation would be a kind of purer picture. In our opinion this is incorrect. Image also applies to people who have experience with an organization.

Reputation seems to be comparable with the concept "**corporate image**": the image that stakeholders have of the organization as a whole. The aforementioned Reputation Quotient then operationalizes that with six specific dimensions.

In short: image is the same as the brand image realized in a target group. This can relate to a product/brand but also to a company. In the latter case it concerns the corporate image, which corresponds to reputation.

Identity

Many books have been written about the concept of **identity**. There are also different definitions of it. For example, identity is sometimes related to the visual identity of a brand; then it mainly concerns matters such as house style, logo, and way of communicating. Identity in a broader sense relates to the essence of the brand, which is, as it were, the own personality of the brand. The concepts identity and personality are so closely related that they can be used interchangeably.

It is possible to make a distinction between realized identity and desired identity. The disadvantage of this distinction is that it gives the impression that a brand or organization can "choose" another identity. That is of course not the case. The identity is trapped in people and culture in an organization. You cannot change an identity just like that. The identity can be changed, but that is a slow process. For example, the culture of a supply-oriented organization can be adjusted to a more customer-oriented orientation, but that is a comprehensive process.

The difference between identity and positioning is that identity is more concerned with the personality and values of an organization, while positioning more concretely indicates what is distinctive about the organization/brand. Competition and the customer play an important role in positioning, not with identity.

Mission and vision

The terms mission and vision are often used interchangeably, partly because different definitions are used. Following Alsem (2019) we define:

- the **mission** as: the delineation of the current activities
- the **vision** as: the ambition of the company, that what the company wishes to achieve in the future

In the mission the aforementioned aspect of Marketing Myopia plays a role: how is the market demarcated?

Three components can be included in the vision:

1. the opinion of the company (or the CEO/director)
2. the identity of the company, for example on the basis of its value strategy
3. the long-term goals of the company

The relationship with positioning is mainly in the interpretation of the vision. A statement can be made about the identity of the company, which – as we have already seen – is the starting point for positioning.

Proposition

A concept strongly linked to positioning is proposition, also referred to as **value proposition**. Different definitions of this concept exist. And there are also different views on the relationship between proposition and positioning. In our opinion the most logical and simple definition of a proposition is: "the promise to the customer," the ultimate short, distinctive, and customer-formulated reason why the customer has to buy your brand. For instance, for Volvo, that could be: "a safe car."

With proposition, the word "value" is often added. Then it is about the value for the customer. The value of a product or brand for a customer is by definition the difference between the revenues and the costs. The revenues are the advantages of the brand for the customer. These can be functional and emotional. In Part II of this book we will come back to this point in detail. The costs for the customer can be monetary costs (the price), but also non-monetary costs such as waiting time or the effort to buy the product.

The relationship between proposition and positioning is that the proposition is the translation of the positioning into a concrete promise. For example, a positioning shows the difference with the competition and also who is the main competitor. A positioning statement can be summarized into a concrete promise.

USP and UBR

The USPs of a brand are the **Unique Selling Points**. The UBR is the **Unique Buying Reason**. The difference between these two indicators is that the USP focuses on the product, while the UBR reflects the motivation of the customer: the idea that a product should be a solution to a "problem" of a customer. This idea matches well with the well-known Marketing Myopia idea that was put forward decades ago by Levitt (1960), namely that companies should not define their business in terms of products but in terms of needs. A classic example is Kodak that has become "out of business" because its product (materials for traditional photography) was replaced by electronics. The Kodak company focused on its traditional product for which there is no market anymore, whereas its business in terms of customer needs (something like "capturing memories") still exists.

The relationship between USP and UBR and positioning is that both elements together form the positioning. As we shall see in Part II of this book, the positioning must include both the unique characteristic of the product and the customer's need.

Branding

Finally, it is also good to establish a relationship with branding. There is often confusion between the terms "branding" and "positioning." Literally branding refers to "applying a brand (name)." But branding refers to a broader process, namely

Figure 2.2 **The relation between brand identity, brand positioning, and brand image**

the creation of a unique and favourable brand image (associations) in the minds of consumers. Although branding focuses more on the process than on the outcomes, the words branding and positioning are often treated as synonyms.

We have summarized the relationship between a number of concepts in Figure 2.2.

2.2 Brand positioning and marketing

In this section we outline the relationship between marketing and positioning. First, we indicate what marketing entails. This concept exists at three levels in an organization (Subsection 2.2.1). Then in Subsection 2.2.2 we go deeper into the concept of "marketing as culture" because that is the core meaning of marketing. We will see that it is the connection between customer needs and brand identity. In Subsection 2.2.3 we show that these two variables influence each other. In Subsection 2.2.4 we focus on the relationship between positioning and the market instruments.

2.2.1 Marketing hierarchy

In order to be able to properly interpret the relation between marketing and positioning, we must first establish that the concept of marketing itself can be interpreted in various ways (Webster, 1992, 2005). Marketing can be understood as (see Figure 2.3):

1. Organizational culture (the **marketing concept**): the commitment of an organization to meet the needs of the customer in order to be profitable in the long term, in short putting the customer first.
2. Strategy: this involves choosing target groups and positioning the products and services. For the **marketing strategy** the acronym **STP** is often used:
   - Segmentation ("Segmenting")
   - Target group choice ("Targeting")
   - Positioning
3. **Tactics** and activities: this relates to the daily activities around the five market instruments product, price, distribution/channel selection ("place"), communication ("promotion"), and personnel.

These three interpretations of marketing can be seen as a hierarchy in the marketing concept. The essence of this hierarchy is that the core concepts at higher levels result in activities at lower levels. This hierarchy can be interpreted both from a theoretical and an applied perspective. We will discuss the applied perspective below.

Figure 2.3 **Marketing hierarchy**

Ad 1 Organizational culture (the marketing concept)

A company that considers marketing to be of paramount importance is fully aware of central importance of the customer. According to theory the target group needs to be examined first and only then the desired products can be designed. This is clearly different from a sales orientation that states that a company first makes products (without looking at the customer) and then tries to sell them, with a lot of effort if necessary. Traditional marketing theory suggests that a sales orientation would not work. Yet that is not completely right. In reality, entrepreneurs also come up with innovations that are not directly requested by customers, but still sell well afterwards. And the insights of Sharp (Subsection 1.3.3) tell us that a brand's physical and mental visibility has a major impact on sales. So "intensive selling" certainly helps.

In fact, the essence of marketing is that a customer does not buy products but solutions ("benefits"). For example, he does not buy toothpaste but a "fresh breath." And he does not buy Axe (or Lynx; the brand uses two different names globally) deodorant but "attraction to women." Marketing is therefore primarily about being able to empathize with customers and thinking meeting their conscious or subconscious needs. Having a customer orientation is a normal approach for many organizations, but this is not the case in sectors where the market-oriented thinking was only recently introduced.

Recently, some authors state that "marketing 3.0" is not only about delivering value to customers but also to society. So, issues like sustainability are then incorporated in the marketing concept. Kumar (2018) introduces the word "transformative marketing" to show the need to address important long-term trends such as online behaviour of people and also the need for sustainability. In our view, however, these important trends do not affect the marketing concept but marketing activities.

Ad 2 Marketing strategy

If a company wants to be truly customer-oriented, it needs to choose a marketing strategy. The company will then choose a target group and position itself in the market. By means of this positioning the company aims to give a certain image (certain associations) to the brand. The challenge is to choose those brand associations that are relevant to the target group and unique to the brand, so different from the competition.

Ad 3 Marketing tactics and activities

The next step is to translate the marketing strategy into the marketing tools. A product positioned as high quality, for example, will then have a relatively high price, possibly be limitedly available and be communicated as a top product.

Of these three interpretations, the marketing tactics receive most attention in professional practice. This is understandable because, for example, daily (offline and online) communication needs attention from moment to moment. But it is evident that marketing tactics are driven by the choice of the marketing strategy: target group and positioning. Only a clear interpretation of these two components gives a clear direction to the content and shape of the marketing instruments. A central premise of this book is our impression that too little attention is paid to marketing strategy. The absence of sufficient marketing strategy is perceptible in many small and medium-sized companies, who are mainly engaged in "day to day" activities. But the lack of a long-term marketing strategy is also visible in larger companies and brands. As a result, implementation of the marketing instruments will be untargeted and without strategic direction. See Example 2.2.

Example 2.2 Change of corporate design

Sometimes a company decides to change the corporate design because "it has been the same for a long time." Subsequently, an agency is commissioned to develop a more modern design for the company. The agency then presents with a number of alternatives for a new visual identity and the most beautiful is chosen. What goes wrong here is the motivation for the change of design. The question must be whether the corporate design still fits with the desired positioning of the company. And not whether the design is "old-fashioned." It is possible that a somewhat classic visual identity matches very well with the years of experience and quality of the company concerned. A new, modern design could then detract from the desired quality image.

Other examples of inadequate strategic management concern the introduction of products that do not fit the brand, thereby affecting the image of the brand. For example, shower gel and deodorant brand Sanex failed when introducing a toothpaste a couple of years ago, and 7UP was not successful with the introduction of the confusing "7UP Ice Cola."

In short every decision related to branding and communication or any of the other marketing instruments can only be taken after a clear decision has been made about brand positioning.

2.2.2 Marketing as culture

We now consider the highest level of marketing: marketing as a concept or culture. This is in fact the essence of marketing.

In marketing, the customer traditionally comes first. Marketing is about customers. A good illustration is the mission statement of Walmart, which literally puts the customer first. Example 2.3 features how this mission was stretched to an online retail environment with Walmart.com.

Example 2.3 The mission of Walmart.com (Source: Walmart.com)

The secret of successful retailing is to give your customers what they want. And really, if you think about it from your point of view as a customer, you want everything: a wide assortment of good-quality merchandise; the lowest possible prices; guaranteed satisfaction with what you buy; friendly, knowledgeable service; convenient hours; free parking; a pleasant shopping experience.

(Sam Walton, founder of Walmart).

Walmart.com is a lot like the neighbourhood Walmart store. It features a great selection of high-quality merchandise in combination with Walmart's famous Every Day Low Prices. Walmart.com also has another goal: to bring the customer the best shopping experience on the Internet.

Founded in January 2000, Walmart.com is a subsidiary of Wal-Mart Stores, Inc. Walmart.com's headquarters is on the San Francisco Peninsula near Silicon Valley, where it has access to the world's deepest pool of Internet executive and technical talent.

But Walmart thinks of itself, first and foremost, as a retailer. So the ties to Bentonville, Arkansas – where Sam Walton opened the first store that bore the Walton name and where Wal-Mart Stores, Inc., is still based – give the company its foundation. Walmart.com fosters the ideals of its parent company.

From modest beginnings in north-western Arkansas, Walmart has grown to become a worldwide household name. At the heart of Walmart's growth is the unique culture that Sam Walton built. His business philosophy was based on the simple idea of making the customer No. 1. He believed that by serving the customer's needs first, his business would also serve its associates, shareholders, communities, and other stakeholders. The goal at Walmart.com is to bring this culture and philosophy to the Internet.

With Bentonville's support, Walmart.com taps into many things that have made Walmart a universally known brand – like excellent supplier relationships, highly efficient systems, an unswerving commitment to Sam Walton's "Always Low Prices" philosophy, and unrivalled retailers who strive to make the customer No. 1.

This is combined with another Walmart.com goal – providing easy access to more of Walmart. This is evident in the more than 1,000,000 products available online and in the innovative businesses that Walmart.com develops, such as Music Downloads and 1-Hour Photos, which gives customers the convenience of ordering products online and picking them up at a local Walmart.

In short, Walmart.com is passionate about combining the best of two great worlds – technology and world-class retailing – to give customers a wide assortment of their favourite products, Every Day Low Prices, guaranteed satisfaction, friendly service, convenient hours (24 hours, 7 days a week), and a great online shopping experience.

We should raise the question, both from a theoretical perspective and from professional reality, whether an exclusive focus on customer needs provides sufficient guidance for companies to develop a marketing strategy. Most companies choose to position themselves exclusively within their mission. This implies that companies do not only consider customers and their shifting needs in the company's strategy but also their own strengths and wishes as specified in their mission statement. The example of Walmart.com illustrates this: "Walmart.com taps into many things that have made Walmart a universally known brand – like excellent supplier relationships, highly efficient systems, an unswerving commitment to Sam Walton's 'Always Low Prices' philosophy." A well-known theory from strategic management, the so-called resource-based view (Wenderfeldt, 1984), also says that a strategy must be based primarily on what a company is good at, i.e. on its core competencies (Prahalad & Hamel, 1990).

These core competencies, in turn, are related with the concept of **brand identity**. It is obvious to base the brand identity on what the organization is really good at. In this context, the term DNA can be used nicely: both the brand identity and core competencies have to do with the DNA of the brand. A mission statement often reflects the DNA of a company.

Thus, the **essence of marketing** is the aim to find a match between the company's own strengths and the desires of target groups.

We conclude that marketing does not mean that companies have to focus exclusively on meeting the needs and desires of customers, but that they have to find a balance between the desires of target groups and their own desired brand identity. A company will have to ask itself what its own "passion" is and then has to put this passion at the service of a specific customer group. In short, the question is not so much "What does the customer want?" but more "What can I do for the customer?" The essence of marketing is summarized in Figure 2.4.

A good example is the slogan of Philips: *Innovation and you.* Philips represents innovation and this brand value is the core with which customers must be attracted and retained. With this slogan, the company emphasizes that it wants to serve the interests of its customers through this identity.

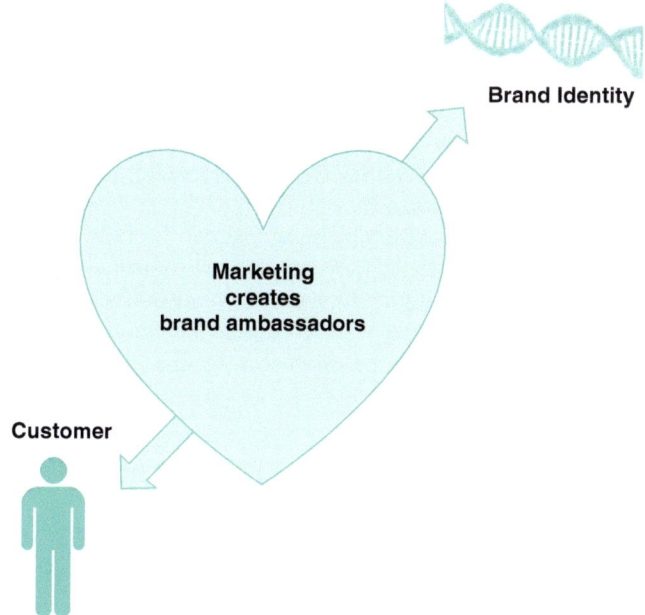

Brand Identity

Marketing
creates
brand ambassadors

Customer

Figure 2.4 The essence of marketing

2.2.3 Dynamics between brand and consumer

The identity of an organization and the desires of customers are often described as separate constructs for this, but it is important to determine how they influence each other (Figure 2.5).

Needs and identity influence each other both ways. First, consumers learn about new products from companies. Apparently, consumers sometimes even do not need certain products at all, but as soon as they are there, everyone wants them! The most obvious examples are in electronics. Market research in the nineties of the last century showed that there was no need for being accessible anytime and anywhere. But nowadays nobody can do without a smartphone. Similar studies also showed that having your own computer was not important for consumers. But now almost

Brand
Identity

Brand builds trust and loyalty by
creating awareness and consistent associations

Brand follows the customer needs and tries to
connect its identity to these needs

Customer
Needs

Figure 2.5 Brand identity and customer needs

everyone has a PC, laptop, iPad, or whatever. It may have been Steve Jobs' strength that he "sensed" which potential needs people have without being aware of it. In conclusion brands (or their products) influence the needs of consumers.

At the same time there is a reverse influence. New needs may arise to which companies have to respond. For example, people increasingly seem to need convenience. As a consequence, organizations can try to make life easier for people. Sometimes the division between who influences who is difficult to clarify. Example 2.4 illustrates: there is a growth in electronics with which parents can literally follow their babies from second to second. For example, they can be kept informed of the temperature and heart rate of the baby, measured with a chip in baby clothes, with an app. There is an undeniably trend that parents want to check their children more and more intensively, but that trend may also be reinforced by the increasing availability of electronic possibilities.

Example 2.4 From quantified self to quantified baby

Anyone who has just entered parenthood knows that the first emotion after birth is not an overwhelming experience of unconditional love, but rather stress. "Does he drink well?", "Does he grow fast enough?", "Why is he crying?", "Will he ever walk?"

There was already the "quantified self": measuring all kinds of things about your own body. With smart technology we can register how much we eat, sleep, or run, or what our heart rate is, our mental state, or our need of medication. And now there is also the "quantified child." Once, there were baby monitors to monitor your baby from a distance. Then baby monitors with cameras and thermometers appeared. But now there is much more: smart rompers, diapers that measure urinary infections, a sock that continuously measures heart rate. On slightly older children you can stick motion monitors with motivational games for the child and activity graphs for the parents. Manufacturers like to pamper over-anxious parents.

Source: NRC Next, July 31, 2014

We take a moment here to look at the relationship between positioning and other business decisions. There is an explicit distinction between corporate strategy and marketing strategy (Alsem, 2019). **Corporate strategy** concerns the choice of product-market combinations, or the portfolio decision of a company. This is also referred to as the issue of "where (on which markets) will the company compete?" The **marketing strategy** is then the choice of the points of difference, or the answer to the question "how (with which differential advantages) will the company compete?" Because positioning is about distinctive character, positioning is part of the marketing strategy.

In itself, the distinction is justified. But in reality, they cannot be always clearly separated: in the end the choice for a certain product-market combination is also determined by the possibility to gain a competitive advantage on a market. Similarly, priorities for product innovation will be guided by the core competencies and therefore the brand identity of the organization. For example, Walmart will always look for innovation in retail whereas Apple is looking for innovations in user-friendly electronics.

2.2.4 Elaboration of positioning in marketing

Concluding from our previous discussion target group choice and positioning are part of the marketing strategy.

Marketing strategy is a prominent element of the **marketing plan**, the plan that describes what objectives the manager has in mind for his brand, and how he intends to achieve these objectives. The planning process used to arrive at this marketing plan is central to strategic marketing literature. This planning process is schematically shown in Figure 2.6. For a detailed description we refer to specialized literature, such as the book *Applied Strategic Marketing* (Alsem, 2019).

Positioning is used in the planning process as the start for developing the **marketing mix**. The marketing mix consists of the instruments that are used to shape

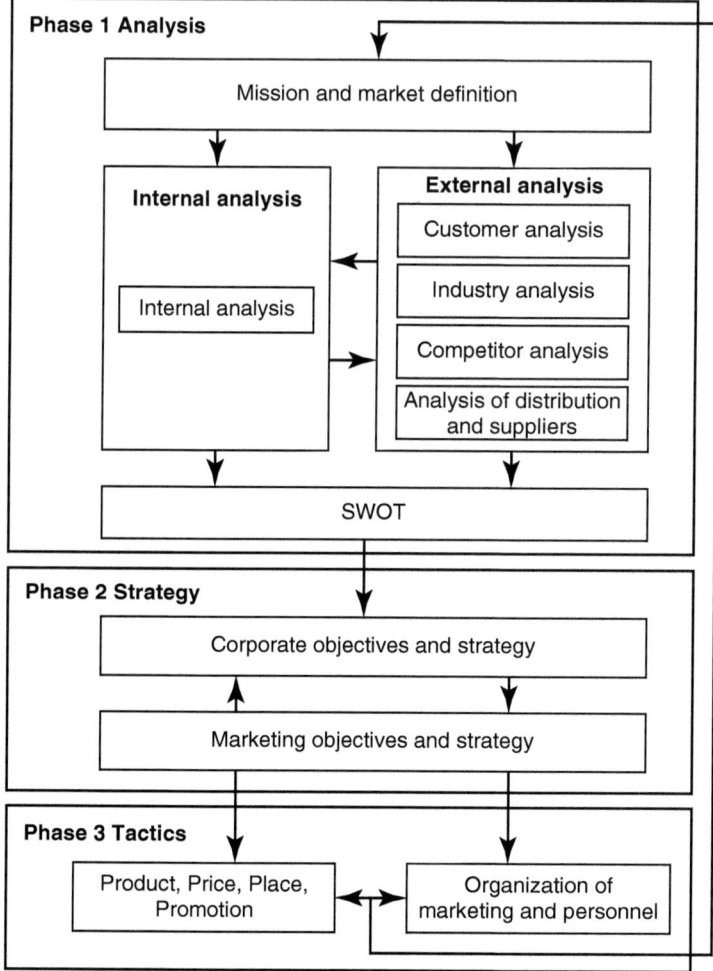

Figure 2.6 The strategic marketing planning process (Alsem, 2019)

a brand. Four marketing instruments are usually distinguished in marketing, the so-called four Ps:

1. *Product*: this relates to the goods, services, or ideas that are made to meet the needs and desires of the consumer. Product decisions relate to the composition and design of the physical product, but also to matters such as the packaging, the guarantee, or the service that is offered.
2. *Price*: the amount of money requested for the product. In addition to determining the exact level of the price, pricing policy also relates to determining the price level that matches the desired positioning, for example a price higher or lower than the price of the direct competitor.
3. The *place* where a product is available must also match the desired positioning. Distribution decisions include the choice of the distribution channel and the desired distribution intensity, the standards set for the sales points, and the relationship between online and offline distribution.
4. *Promotion* or communication refers to the way in which the brand communicates with the target group (and with other stakeholders). A communication strategy matching the brand positioning must be developed, communication messages or commercials need to be developed, communication via website and social media must be designed, as well as choices with respect to the use of offline media (such as television, radio, or newspaper). An important factor for promotion is the budget: theoretically, everything about the brand can be communicated, but the communication budget is not endless. Choices must be made. The criterion for these choices is the positioning that has been set for the brand: which way of communication contributes most to the realization of the desired positioning?

Especially in service organizations, a fifth P is often added. The P of **personnel** concerns issues such as how should current and future personnel be deployed to serve the brand in the best possible way? What capabilities should our staff have? Chapter 10 gives more attention to the P of personnel.

From the point of view of positioning, the four (or five) Ps should be seen as instruments. Product, price, distribution, and promotion policies are aimed at realizing the desired positioning. Brand values therefore need to be translated in detail into every market instrument. Suppose an amusement park wants to position itself with values such as emotion, share, care, and joy; then it is the creative challenge to express these experiences to every detail, up to and including the way in which bicycles in the park can be rented or bottles of cola in the park are sold. In short try to see the Ps as the tools you can use to realize the desired brand positioning.

In addition to the five Ps, there are other decisions in the organization that are based on the brand positioning. Then we are talking about matters that are closely related to the brand itself:

- the brand architecture: the combination of brand names in the organization
- the brand name itself
- the visual appearance of the brand (the corporate design or house style)

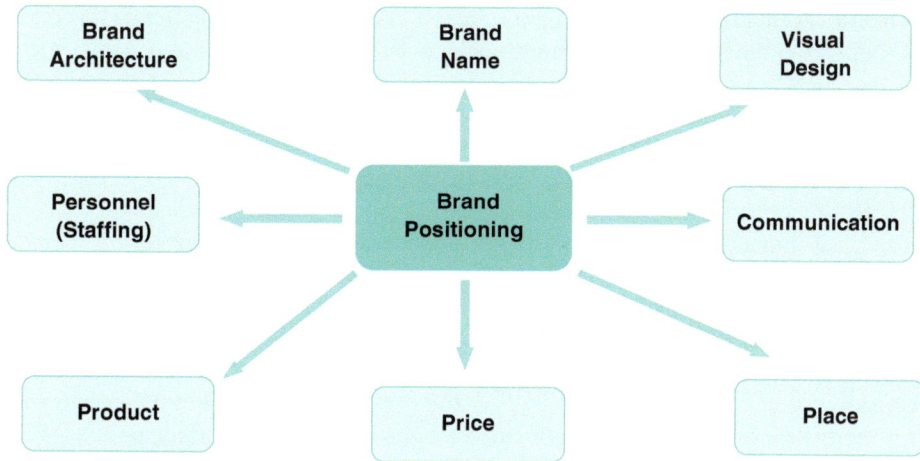

Figure 2.7 Positioning and other decisions in the organization

Figure 2.7 summarizes the most important relationships between positioning and other decisions in the organization.

2.3 The brand positioning process

The relation between the concepts of marketing, brand positioning, and communication can be derived in part from Figure 2.3 in which the three levels of marketing were outlined. The most important relation is the logical relationship between the second and third level of marketing: marketing as a strategy is decisive for marketing as a tactic.

Marketing as a strategy concerns the choices of target groups and positioning. Marketing as a tactic relates to daily activities. The market instruments (the four or five Ps) give substance to these daily activities. These Ps are thus logically derived from the characteristics of the target group and the chosen positioning: the marketing mix is a consequence of the marketing strategy.

However, the creation of the positioning of a brand is not described in Figure 2.3. For a first insight we use the **positioning triangle** from Figure 2.1, which states that the positioning is – by definition – a combination of:

- the brand's strengths
- the needs of the target group
- the (relative) weakness of the competitor

This emphasizes that three components from the well-known strengths, weaknesses, opportunities, and threats (SWOT) analysis are important for positioning decisions: the internal analysis, the customer analysis, and the competitor analysis. In this book we do not describe all these phases in detail; for that we refer to Alsem (2019). Instead, we emphasize in this book the **positioning process**. This process describes the building blocks needed to design a brand positioning (Subsection 2.3.1). In Subsection 2.3.2 we describe the structure of the remainder of this book.

2.3.1 Building blocks for designing brand positioning

The positioning process indicates which information must be collected in order to create a successful brand positioning. A key role here is played by the identity and the image of the brand. Positioning is namely – as indicated in Section 2.1 – determining the desired associations with a brand. Positioning activities therefore aim to adjust the **current brand image** among the target group, i.e. the current brand image, in the direction of the brand image desired by the organization. This desired image will normally be close to the identity of the brand as defined by the organization. After all, most managers prefer the target group to interpret the brand in the same way as the ideal that he himself has in mind with the brand.

The difference between (current) brand image and (**desired) brand identity** actually forms the catalyst for the positioning process: the need for positioning activities increases as the difference between image and identity increases. However, positioning is more than moving the brand image in the direction of the desired brand identity. The consumer must be able to continue to recognize himself in the image that the brand evokes. After all, the core of marketing is finding the balance between the wishes of the target group and the desired identity of the brand. For positioning decisions, knowledge of the needs of the consumer in the target group is and remains indispensable.

The positioning is thus derived from the combination of identity, image, and needs of the target group. If – on the basis of these three factors – a choice has been made for a specific brand positioning, it will then have to be materialized. In order to do so, the organization has access to an extensive range of marketing and communication tools: the five Ps of the marketing mix and the communication tools and media of the communication mix and media mix.

Figure 2.8 gives the schematic representation of the positioning process described here. This figure illustrates the phases that are central to the development of the brand positioning:

1. needs assessment and target group choice: "Who do we want to serve with our brand?"
2. determining the current brand image: "How does the target group see our brand and the competing brands?"
3. the brand identity: "What does our brand stand for?"
4. the positioning itself: the choice of the positioning strategy and the concrete description of this strategy in the right images and wording
5. the development of the positioning: the translation of the positioning in marketing and communication activities

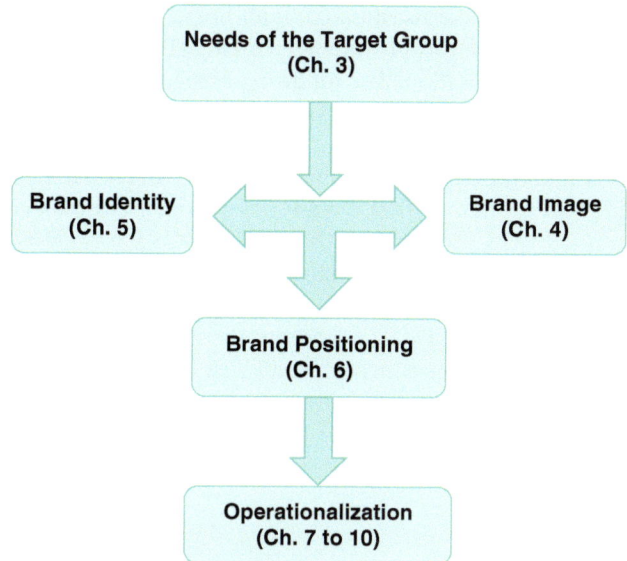

Figure 2.8 **Stages in the positioning process**

2.3.2 Structure of this book

The remainder of this book is structured on the basis of the positioning process described earlier.

Part II describes the brand positioning as the result of brand image, brand identity, and needs of the target group. The needs of the target group are discussed in Chapter 3. In this chapter we also look at the benefits the target group is looking for and at the customer values that guide the choices that the target group makes.

Chapter 4 pays attention to the brand image. In line with the discussion about the importance of brand awareness dimensions and association dimensions, a distinction is made between the extent to which the brand is known to the target group and is relevant to the target group (*mindshare*) and the associations that the target group has with the brand (*heartshare*). In this chapter we also describe the methods by which mindshare and heartshare can be mapped.

Chapter 5 focuses on brand identity. First, we describe what brand identity actually is. A distinction is made between real identity and desired identity. Then an overview is given of what is involved in defining a brand identity. An important principle here is that the identity must be consistent with the strong points of the brand, without promising things that the brand cannot deliver.

The next step is to establish the brand positioning itself. Chapter 6 describes the positioning strategy and also discusses how the positioning can then be "written down."

Once the positioning has been established, all brand-related activities will have to be worked out in line with this positioning. In Part III of this book, we will give ample attention to this elaboration. The following aspects are discussed here:

- Communication (Chapter 7): out of the five Ps, the relationship between promotion/communication and positioning is the strongest.
- Brand architecture (Chapter 8): this is a very fundamental strategic choice in the company.
- Brand names and visual design (Chapter 9): these brand elements should be strongly linked to positioning decisions.
- Personnel (Chapter 10): the staff is perhaps the most important of the five Ps, especially in services. We note here that staff cannot actually be called a marketing tool: it is part of the corporate activity human resource management, although a strong connection with the marketing function is recommended.

Summary

The positioning concept is closely related to concepts such as image, identity, vision, reputation, and USP. The term "branding" is in fact the same as positioning. A company that wants to make a marketing plan must go through three main phases. First the analysis of "strengths, weaknesses, opportunities and threats" (SWOT analysis). Then it needs to capture this in the marketing strategy: target group choice and positioning. Choice of marketing strategy determines the five Ps: product, price, place/distribution, communication/promotion, and personnel/staffing. At the same time, the brand architecture needs to be chosen as well as brand name and visual design. The relation between marketing and positioning is therefore that positioning (and target group choice) is the core of the marketing strategy. The relation between communication and positioning is that positioning is the starting point for all brand communication.

Case material for Part I

Strongbow tries to put masculinity into cider

In 2013, the cider category was booming. Fuelled by sunny weather and the urge for a sweeter, more drinkable summer beverage, consumers couldn't get enough of bottled fruit cider. But trends fade, and cider is no longer as popular as it used to be.

But even today, as much of the cider industry is slumping, Strongbow continues to shine. Strongbow is known as a reliable favourite, harvesting from traditional apple orchards. That's a good fit for the modern millennial, who is seeking beverages with history, authenticity, and natural roots. The brand is currently the No. 1 cider brand globally.

The Dutch Heineken company, owner of the well-known beer brand Heineken, became the parent company of Strongbow in 2008, when the company bought Scottish & Newcastle.

"Nowadays, millennials are eager to know more about the product," says Nuno Teles, Heineken USA's CMO, who believes that authenticity can't be faked. "These millennials, they google everything. And rightfully so! They want honesty."

Strongbow has pushed the narrative of craft and quality. While the brand has launched new flavours, it has emphasized that the new flavours are all based in traditional cider-production methods, continuously strengthening the authenticity of the brand. The exhibit below showcases an example of a Strongbow campaign.

> **Strongbow connects with nature**
> Strongbow Apple Ciders launched its "Nature Remix" campaign in April 2017 as it seeks to extend its appeal among millennials on a global scale by positioning itself as a brand "with a positive point of view."

The campaign included experiential activity, as well as a new TV ad, digital films, and social media amplification. All activity focused on the brand's range of nature-inspired flavoured ciders. The TV ad showed how Strongbow Apple Ciders had created an orchard in central Johannesburg, South Africa, by allowing local gardeners to plant apple trees in a derelict urban space. All trees used in the campaign were donated to the university fruit garden in a bid to "leave a tangible legacy." The brand planned similar experiential activity in Toronto, Bucharest, Bratislava, Prague, Lisbon, and Vietnam.

At the campaign introduction, Jiri Rakosnik, global marketing manager of cider at Strongbow parent Heineken at that time, emphasized the importance of the campaign in getting Strongbow noticed outside of the United Kingdom where brand awareness is not as high, as well as allowing the cider brand to take a more emotional route: "Instead of using traditional pictures of apples and orchards as a way of explaining the category, we wanted to create [a campaign] that cider drinkers could get emotional about. So we needed to have a positive point of view."

Rakosnik added that the brand also desires to fit in with a current trend among millennials to connect with nature. "We come from the orchard, but mainly talk to a young generation that lives in the cities. If you look at what makes them tick, they are the first generation since the 1960s to have a positive attitude towards the world," he explained.

> Nature seems to be a big topic across art, architecture, fashion and pop culture. As people try to reconnect with nature, it seemed like a match made in heaven for the brand. It's not so much about sustainability as about inspiring young people to get their hands dirty and make cities more enjoyable and fun to live in.

Rakosnik, however, believed that the campaign is more than a piece of "experiential" activity and will have wider positive consequences. He concluded:

> It's not just about creating something nice for the sake of it or for shooting the ad. It is about doing things first before talking about it. We want to do something with the local community for the local community.

But even with this authenticity-focused narrative, trends change. And so do consumers' tastes. A successful company needs to follow, but at the same time stick to its roots. Strongbow's answer to changing preferences: Strongbow Dark Fruit.

Heineken allowed Strongbow to be introduced in 2014. In that year, it launched Strongbow Dark Fruits in 10 pubs. The results were beyond expectations. Emma Sherwood-Smith, cider marketing director at Heineken, still can't quite believe it: "People went absolutely crazy. The success and speed at which it grew penetration and distribution completely took us by surprise so we are now in 26,000 pubs in the UK bearing in mind we started with 10."

Over time Strongbow Dark Fruit has become a firm favourite and the brand has learnt to lean into the brand love it managed to establish – including engaging with its most extreme fans: "We set up our own tattoo pop-up in Shoreditch where you could get your own Strongbow tattoo and we thought what if no one showed? We had 20 places and they were gone within a couple of hours."

Consumers competing for a brand's attention are something Sherwood-Smith says is "unusual for a mainstream brand." In more recent years Dark Fruit has been using social media more heavily to capitalise on the love that has made it a "become a cultural phenomenon" she says. Despite the joy the team gets from engaging with super-fans on social and at events, Sherwood-Smith is adamant TV remains crucial.

Since its launch in 2013, Strongbow Dark Fruit has become the second best-selling draught cider in the United Kingdom, behind Strongbow Original but Sherwood-Smith believes there will be a day that the fruit variant will overtake its parent brand:

> *The question is, if Dark Fruit continues on this trajectory there could be a time when it will be bigger than Strongbow original and that will present a whole new set of challenge which we'll then have to deal with.*

For now the brand is feeling pretty smug about the anniversary and its success: "If we could bottle what we did with Dark Fruit we could probably sell it on to marketers around the world."

The origins of success

For years, consumers had been putting blackcurrant in their cider to sweeten the taste so Strongbow decided to do the same. Sherwood-Smith says: "Right from the start we reached out into culture and asked what are people doing. What is the current behaviour and how can you bring the [Strongbow] in the world effect to that?"

"Our business objective was 'how do you recruit people into mainstream cider when what they're interested in is flavours and sticky sweet?'. That doesn't really fit with the masculine Strongbow brand and ethos," added Sherwood-Smith.

So the brand had two jobs to do: it needed to bring people into flavoured cider but it also needed to rejuvenate the Strongbow master brand. "It couldn't dilute [Strongbow original's] identity but it had to breathe new life into it for a new generation. It was quite tricky in getting that balance right in the early days," Sherwood-Smith explains.

From its inception, differentiating Strongbow Dark Fruit through marketing has been crucial. Competing flavoured ciders as well as Strongbow

Original were offering sun-filled orchard settings for their campaigns in a bid to recruit women. But for Strongbow Dark Fruit the opposite was decided. Sherwood-Smith says:

> When the competition zigs you zag and it was really juxtaposed to all the traditional summer blue sky images of cider at the time… [we had to be] true to the infrastructure of the Strongbow brand and not be tempted to make it feminine.

The result: Strongbow Dark Fruit is now the second best-selling draught cider in the United Kingdom, which its marketing director puts down to sticking to the master brand's masculine roots rather than being "tempted to make it feminine." And, despite the reluctance for feminine marketing the brand has worked hard to get more female drinkers and Sherwood-Smith now estimates that 45% of its clientele are women.

So, in the end it was all a matter of smart brand positioning!

Sources: Marketingweek.com, Businessinsider.com

- https://www.businessinsider.com/heinekens-strongbow-cider-not-a-trend-2016-4?international=true&r=US&IR=T; April 2, 2016
- https://www.marketingweek.com/2016/04/07/strongbow-focuses-on-local-community-work-in-bid-to-attract-and-inspire-younger-generation/; July 4, 2016
- https://www.marketingweek.com/2019/04/01/strongbow-dark-fruit/; April 1, 2019

Questions

1. Design an associative network for the Strongbow brand, by using the information in the case.
2. Use the information in the case to describe the brand positioning of Strongbow.
3. The book defines three requirements for a successful brand positioning. Discuss to what extent these requirements have been met in the branding of Strongbow.
4. Sharp emphasizes brand awareness whereas Keller focuses on brand equity and the importance of brand associations. Which point of view seems to be followed in the marketing of Strongbow: Sharp's point of view or Keller's point of view? Explain your answer.
5. The book emphasizes the need for a brand to find a balance between following consumer needs and staying true to its brand identity. How did Strongbow deal with this balance?
6. The book distinguishes between marketing as a concept, marketing as a strategy, and marketing as a set of tactics. Give examples of each of these by using the information in the case.

Part II

The creation of the brand positioning strategy

Part II of this book describes the stages of the brand positioning process. Chapter 3 highlights methods to classify consumers into target groups. This chapter also discusses customer needs, and how these relate to brand benefits and brand values. Chapter 4 deals with the second stage of the positioning process: mapping the current brand image. This chapter discusses a number of techniques that can be used to determine the brand image. Chapter 5 focuses on the third stage: this chapter highlights brand identity and the DNA of the brand. Finally, Chapter 6 provides an in-depth discussion of the actual brand positioning: the creation of a strong brand with a consistent brand image, relevant to the consumer and distinctive from the competitor's offer.

Chapter 3

Customer needs and customer values

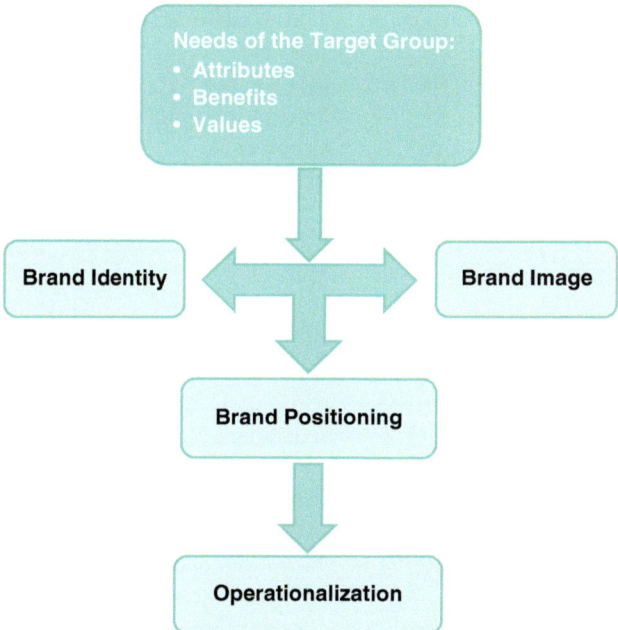

3.1 An introduction to the needs concept

Consumers have needs. For example, in the bicycle market, some people need a bicycle to go to work, while others want to indulge in mountain biking in the forest. It is even possible that someone has both needs; such a person belongs to different target groups at different times. The first stage in brand positioning is that the brand needs to determine its target market and target group (the mountain biker or the commuter in the city) and what the needs of this target group are.

In this first chapter of Part II we look at the needs of the consumer. Because "the" consumer does not exist, we first examine methods to divide consumers into market segments. This is discussed in Section 3.2. Next, in Section 3.3 we address consumer needs and the role that needs play in brand choice. We will see that consumers only become interested in a particular brand if they believe that this brand can meet their needs. The central question here: to what extent does the consumer believe that by buying a certain brand he is able to achieve his goal (fulfilling a certain need)? In Section 3.3, extensive attention is paid to a model that links product characteristics and consumer "goals," the so-called means-end chain. Two important elements of the means-end chain are benefits and customer values. Benefits are discussed in detail in Section 3.4 and customer values in Section 3.5.

3.2 Segmentation

Consumers can be divided into market segments. In **segmentation** we make the following distinction in ways to divide potential customers in groups (segments):

1.   geographic segmentation (geographics)
2.   demographic and socio-economic segmentation (demographics)
3.   psychographic segmentation (psychographics)
4.   behavioural segmentation (product- or brand-related)

Ad 1 Geographics

Geographics classify consumers based on geographic criteria. The starting point is that there are differences in needs that have to do with the country or region where people live, or because they live in the city instead of the countryside. There are some practical reasons for this type of difference. For example, there is more need for winter clothing in Northern Europe than in countries such as Spain or Portugal. But availability and accessibility can also play a role. In the city, retail locations are often within walking or cycling distance. Consumers in a suburb or the countryside often have to travel more for their purchases. So they have to plan their activities better or order more online. This leads to different living patterns, in which other needs and products will fit.

Ad 2 Demographic and socio-economic segmentation

Consumers can also be classified on the basis of such things as age, income, profession, education, or ethnicity. **Demographic and socio-economic factors** are widely used for segmentation. This has to do with the fact that needs, desires, and product use are often directly related to demographic and socio-economic variables. For example, because of their height, children need different clothing than adults, and because they go to school they need school supplies. An interesting demographic variable is the **family life cycle**. During your life you experience different phases, from being a baby, nursery, and childhood, from living at home with your parents to living on your own (in rooms) for the first time, from living with your partner to having a family with children. These children are gradually getting older again and eventually leave the house, after which you, as an aging couple, initially enjoy the extra free time and then are increasingly confronted with defects. Each stage of life brings its own needs, and a brand can position itself towards a certain stage of life.

Demographic variables are often easy to define, and this explains a significant part of their popularity. But often these variables form a derivative for something else. If people between the ages of 20 and 25 lead an irregular life, get up quite late, go out with friends, and often party until late, is it because of their age (between 20 and 25 years) or is it because they are students and lead a suitable lifestyle? Probably the last. And in that case, it is recommended to segment on the basis of lifestyle

Photo 3.1 **Lifestyle is often a better indicator for behaviour than demographics (age). Photos released under Pixabay license: free for commercial use, no attribution required**

(psychographics) and not on the basis of age. Lifestyle segmentation takes into account that a 22-year-old with a full-time job and children leads a different kind of life than a 22-year-old student.

Ad 3 Psychographics

Psychographics classify consumers according to the lifestyle they lead. Lifestyle is often defined on the basis of so-called **AIO** variables: the activities, interests, and opinions that consumers have. A lifestyle says something about the way someone spends the day, and therefore also about the needs that that entails.

An interesting example of psychographic segmentation is used by the research agency Motivaction. This agency has developed the Mentality model. In this model, the Dutch population is divided into eight so-called mentality segments based on a number of background variables and lifestyle characteristics. Examples of these segments are the postmodern hedonists (independent, highly educated young people, who focus on having stimulating experiences) and the traditional bourgeoisie (strongly conservative middle class with strong family values and a stay-at-home mum; Figure 3.1).

Marketing often uses personas when describing lifestyle. A **persona** is a "typical" representative of a group of consumers with a certain lifestyle. A good description of a persona visualizes the description of this group of consumers, so that the

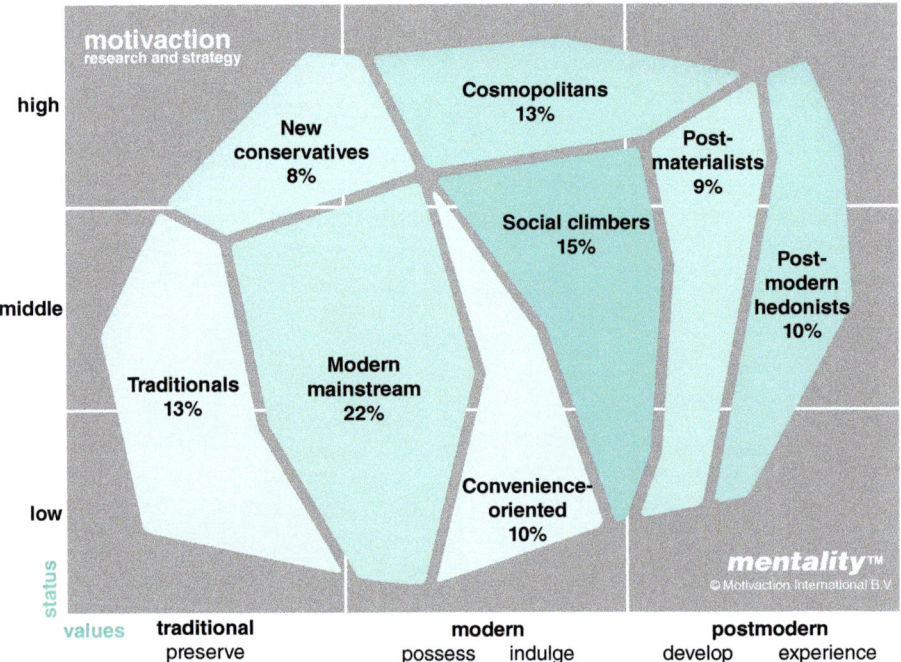

Figure 3.1 **The Mentality model (percentages refer to the part of the Dutch population that belongs to a certain segment)**

segment becomes more tangible for the responsible marketer. It is of course a way of stereotyping, but this ultimately applies to every form of segmentation: individuals are unique, but in segmentation you try to arrive at a common denominator that gives a good description of the whole. Example 3.1 is an example of a persona description.

Example 3.1 The ambitious student

Claire studies Law in New York. She enjoys life, and because of that, her first year was not very productive. Campus activities and many cheerful evenings with her sorority friends have taken a lot of her time. However, she is ambitious; good study results are considered important in her family. And her boyfriend Bernard, business student, also encourages her.

Claire's way of life is quite expensive. Fortunately, her parents pay her tuition fees, but she has to pay for her evening fun herself. Occasionally she earns some pocket money with some jobs for her father, partner in a big law firm. After all, like that she earns more than with serving beers in some bar.

Ad 4 Behavioural segmentation

Behavioural segmentation classifies consumers on the basis of their knowledge, opinions, or preferences for a product or brand, or the reason why they buy this brand. Marketers often see this as the best way of segmenting, because there is already a relation between consumer and brand when segmenting.

An important form of behavioural segmentation is **benefit segmentation**. Consumers are classified according to the reason why they use the product. The idea behind this is that different groups of consumers can be distinguished because they use the product for different reasons. The toothpaste market provides a good example of benefit segmentation. We have already indicated in Subsection 2.2.1 that there are various benefits for the use of toothpaste such as preventing tooth decay or getting a fresh breath or radiant white teeth. These motives play a part for everyone to some extent, but for some consumers prevention will be a major reason, while for others the radiant white teeth are much more important.

In addition to benefit segmentation, segmentation can also be based on usage frequency (light users versus heavy users), usage situation (for example at home in front of the tv or with friends in the pub), familiarity with the brand (people who do not know a brand need a different marketing approach than people who do know the brand), or degree of brand loyalty.

3.3 Fulfilment of needs: the means-end chain

After dividing consumers into segments, we can zoom in. After all, we need to know what the needs within a particular market segment are. Choices have to be made: a brand usually cannot fulfil the needs of everyone in the market. Therefore, a target group is chosen. The **target group** consists of the segment (s) on whose needs the brand specifically targets. Target groups are often chosen on the basis of a number of strategic considerations. An important element here, however, is the extent to which the brand is able to respond to certain needs. To stay with the example of the toothpaste: some brands of toothpaste are good at fighting cavities, while other brands have more influence on bacteria in the mouth (and are therefore better at creating a fresh breath).

Consumers are only interested in a certain brand if a number of conditions are met. First, they have to feel a certain need. For example, they need good oral care. To meet this need, they want to buy an oral care product, for example toothpaste. They have certain requirements for this care product such as fresh taste, effective in the fight against tooth decay, or reasonably priced. When consumers buy a certain brand, they must therefore believe that this brand contributes to fulfilling their needs. This "belief" is connected with the brand image: if the brand is associated with a desired product characteristic or benefit, then that brand is potentially interesting for the consumer. In our example, oral care products are only eligible if the consumer believes they are effective, fresh, and reasonably priced. In summary, the following conditions apply before consumers become interested in a brand:

1. Consumers feel a certain need.
2. Consumers believe that the brand can meet this need.

We first briefly discuss human needs. We then discuss the relationship between consumer needs and brand associations. In this evaluation, also the means-end chain is discussed.

3.3.1 Needs

Human behaviour, including consumer behaviour, stems from human needs. Needs motivate the consumer to take action, for example in the form of a purchase of a product or service, that is why needs are central to marketing. According to the classic definition of the marketing concept, needs are the starting point of all activities of an organization: marketers try to respond to **consumer needs** with products and services that match these needs. According to our own definition of marketing, a company can also start with their own ideas about potential needs, and develop a product that will fulfil future needs. But before going into this further, it is good to give a little more attention to the concept of needs: what is actually a need?

A familiar way of looking at needs is Maslow's **hierarchy of needs** (1954). Maslow was an American psychologist who saw needs as the main driver for human behaviour. Maslow distinguished between different types of needs; he also provided a hierarchy. According to him, certain basic needs must first be met before people start focusing on meeting needs at a higher level. At the bottom of his hierarchy are the innate, primary needs that are necessary to survive. This concerns needs for food, drinks, and sexuality. Although some of our behaviour is certainly related to this, according to Maslow, other needs are also important. His theory distinguishes a total of five types of needs:

1. primary, physiological needs (food, water, sexuality)
2. the need for safety and security
3. social needs: the need for love and friendship
4. the need to be appreciated by others
5. the need for self-actualization

In Maslow's theory there is a clear sequence in fulfilling these needs: only when the needs of a lower level are fulfilled, someone is interested in fulfilling needs of a higher level. That is why we also speak of a hierarchy of needs: see Figure 3.2. The highest level in this hierarchy is **self-actualization**. At this level people allow themselves to be guided by their own ambitions and ideals, regardless of what is needed to survive or what others think of it. This can take various forms, from attending a Master's program as the start of an ambitious career to running a marathon as a personal challenge.

In reality, the order of needs is not always so strict, and people will experience needs at different levels at different times of the day, depending on their situation at that time. A marathon runner also needs love occasionally.

Needs create a buying motive, a reason for the consumer to take action. A model like that from Maslow can be helpful in giving these needs a name.

There are more theories that try to give insight into human needs. We will not go further into these models here. It is important for the marketer to understand that there are different types of needs. Brand positioning gives the marketer the

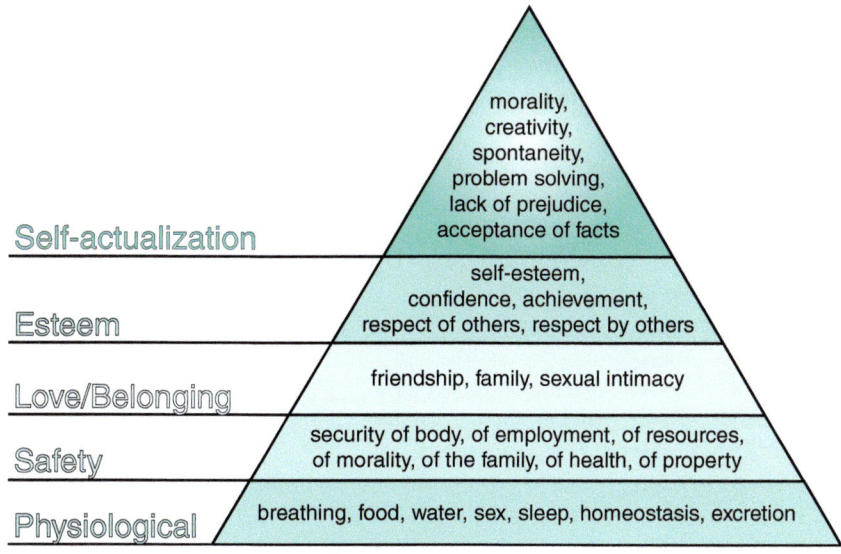

Figure 3.2 **Maslow's need hierarchy (Maslow, 1954)**

opportunity to address these needs in the right way. For the positioning of a brand, it is very important to know the basic needs of the target group: after all, the marketer needs to know which buying motives his customers have and where these motives come from.

3.3.2 The means-end chain

The extent to which the consumer is convinced that a brand can meet a particular need is related to the associations that the consumer has with that brand. Analysis of the associative network of a brand is therefore of great importance.

The relationship between brand associations and consumer behaviour is described in the so-called **means-end chain** model (Gutman, 1982). According to this model, people opt for behaviour that provides benefits and at the same time has as few negative consequences as possible. Of course, this also applies to consumer behaviour: consumers choose those products that give them the most benefits. Of course, not every benefit is equally important to everyone. The assessment of benefits depends on what consumers think is important in their life, or the central values in their life. For example, the benefits of a car can consist of comfort, safety, low environmental impact, or the prestige that the car brand gives to the driver. Similarly, oral care results in benefits such as fresh breath, counteracting tooth decay, or radiant white teeth. If a consumer attaches great importance to his or her own health, then he will attribute the benefit of "preventing tooth decay" to a greater importance. Consumers for whom giving a good impression to others is an important value will find a fresh breath or radiant white teeth more important.

In short, the mean-end chain thus describes the following relationship (Figure 3.3):

1. Brands have certain attributes (properties).
2. Consumers connect benefits to these attributes.
3. Benefits are seen as more favourable the more they match the central values of the consumer.

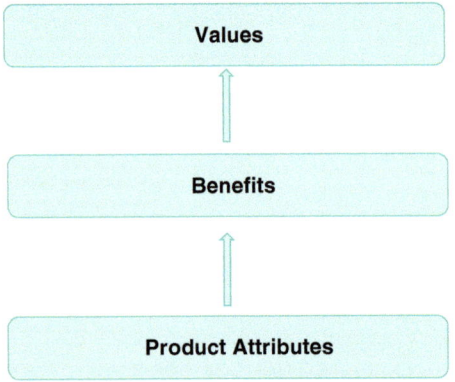

Figure 3.3 **Schematic representation of the means-end chain**

The means-end chain represents the structure of meanings connected to a brand. A commonly used technique to get this structure of meanings is **laddering** (Reynolds & Gutman, 1988). In this technique, the means-end chain is filled from top to bottom by constantly asking the consumer what he thinks is important: "Why do you think that's important?" In this way, an attempt is made to start with the product attributes, determine the benefits the consumer is looking for, and the underlying pattern of values that makes these benefits so important for a certain consumer or for a specific target group. By applying laddering, it becomes possible to position a brand on the basis of certain product attributes, on the basis of the resulting benefits, or on the basis of the underlying values.

Figure 3.4 presents the means-end chain for toothpaste, as an example. Some consumers are preoccupied with healthy teeth and thus wish to prevent tooth decay, whereas others are looking for fresh breath or radiant white teeth. A toothpaste brand can meet these needs by providing certain benefits such as the possibility to prevent cavities or the promise of the desired fresh breath. These benefits can be provided because toothpaste consists of certain **attributes**. For example, toothpaste contains fluoride. Fluoride strengthens teeth and helps in cavity prevention.

Products therefore offer benefits and these **benefits** are made possible because the product consists of certain ingredients. Product attributes thus indicate **HOW** a certain benefit can be realized.

Not every benefit is equally important. Some consumers are focused on cavity prevention, while others consider fresh breath a more important benefit of toothpaste. The importance of certain benefits depends on the values of the consumer. These **values** determine why someone considers a benefit important. If health is a central value for the consumer, then this explains the importance of cavity prevention. If love and friendship are important values, then fresh breath or radiant white

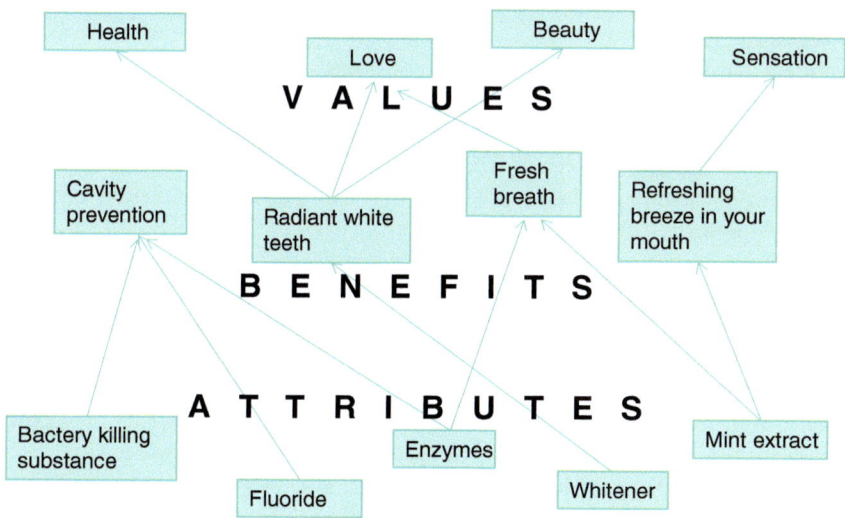

Figure 3.4 **Means-end chain for toothpaste**

teeth becomes more relevant benefits. At least, if the consumer is convinced that a fresh breath makes a good impression on his partner, and thus reinforces his love life. In this way, the values of a consumer explain **WHY** he finds certain benefits important.

In the positioning of a brand, attributes, benefits, or values can be emphasized. Positioning can therefore be aimed at each of the three levels in the means-end chain of a brand, but also at the relationships between these levels. Examples include:

- Changing the importance of certain product attributes: for example, showing that there are many different bacteria in your mouth, some of which are very harmful to your teeth. A bactericidal toothpaste is important in the fight against these bacteria.
- Changing the importance of certain benefits: emphasizing that healthy teeth are more important than a fresh breath.
- Emphasizing the relationship between product characteristics and benefits: a bactericidal substance not only prevents tooth decay but also contributes to fresh breath.
- Establishing a relationship between certain benefits and consumer values: a fresh breath makes you more attractive to your friends and loved ones (commercial with a kissing couple, a voice-over, for example: "For me, passion in a relationship is very important. My love means everything to me and since I use toothpaste X, I just feel that she kisses me again as intensely as in the beginning" followed by a close-up of brand X toothpaste and the pay-off: "Everything for a fresh breath").

In the following sections we give extensive attention to benefits and values.

3.4 Benefits

Consumers have needs. Needs motivate consumers to act to meet these needs. Organizations exist because they create products and services that contribute to fulfilling these needs (or that evoke future needs). These products or services provide certain benefits, **benefits** that result from the consumption of the product or service. For example, in the previous section we saw that using toothpaste results in benefits such as "white teeth," "fresh breath," or "fighting cavities."

Different types of benefits have been distinguished in marketing literature. Holbrook and Hirschman (1982) assume two views on consumer behaviour. On the one hand, the consumer can be seen as a rational being, looking for functional solutions. For instance, someone has to get from A to B quickly, and a car does exactly that. In order to fulfil this need it does not matter whether a car is beautiful or ugly, as long as it can drive. This vision emphasizes tangible benefits of products and services: products have functions. As a consequence, a purchase decision should be assessed on the basis of **instrumental criteria**: consumers evaluate products or services based on whether it does what it is supposed to be doing.

Table 3.1 Instrumental (functional) and hedonic (emotional) aspects of consumer behaviour (Voss, Spangenberg & Grohmann, 2003)

Instrumental aspects	Hedonic aspects
Effective ⇔ ineffective	Not fun ⇔ fun
Useful ⇔ not useful	Dull ⇔ exciting
Functional ⇔ not functional	Not delightful ⇔ delightful
Necessary ⇔ unnecessary	Not thrilling ⇔ thrilling
Practical ⇔ unpractical	Unpleasant ⇔ pleasant

The **experiential view** opposes this. This view focuses on the importance of the experience and the extent to which consumption contributes to the experience: brands provide fun, entertainment, excitement, or emotion. **Hedonic consumption** is defined as consumer behaviour aimed at the experience, the fantasy or the emotion that consumers will feel by consuming products or services: is the car "cool" or does the car give pleasure in driving? Table 3.1 provides an overview of a number of instrumental and hedonic aspects of consumer behaviour.

Hedonic consumption indicates how the brand responds to the psychological and social needs of the consumer. Here psychological needs relate to the pleasant experience that a consumer feels by using the brand, while social needs relate to the way the consumer wants to be seen by others. By dividing hedonic benefits in a social component and an experiential component, we create a division into three types of benefits (Park, Jaworski & MacInnis, 1986):

1. A brand with *functional benefits* is designed to solve consumption-related needs, for instance, solve a current problem, prevent a potential problem, resolve conflict, or change a frustrating situation.
2. *Experiential benefits.* These benefits create the desire for products that make the consumer experience something or have him enjoy it. A brand providing experiential benefits is designed to fulfil these hedonic desires. This type of brand was emphasized in the influential book *The Experience Economy* by Pine and Gilmore (1999). In this book, the central point is that brands must offer an experience to people by entertaining or stimulating them, and by connecting with the consumer in a personal way by delivering lasting pleasant memories.
3. *Symbolic benefits* are outer-directed. These benefits enable people to express how they relate to each other: a brand expressing symbolic benefits is designed to give the consumer a certain image, or by associating him to a certain group or role. Consumers may value the prestige, exclusivity, or fashionability of a brand to express a certain status position. Think of brands like Gucci, Dolce & Gabbana, or Aston Martin. Brands can also be purchased because they strengthen the relationship between the consumer and someone else, or because they show that the consumer cares about someone else. The rose for Valentine's Day or Christmas gifts belong to this category.

Photo 3.2 **Gucci: a brand with symbolic benefits. Photo by Godisable Jacob, released under Pexels license: free for commercial and non-commercial use**

Some product categories are associated with one of these three categories. For example, insurance is usually related to functional benefits, perfume often provides symbolic needs, and a festival usually seems to be visited for the experience. Brands can, however, in principle be positioned in each of these three categories of benefits. For example, a car can be profiled as functional ("safe from A to B"), but also as an experience ("fun to drive") or related to symbolic needs (the exclusivity or prestige of a certain brand). Figure 3.5 shows that toothpaste can also be positioned on the basis of various benefits: fighting cavities is a clearly functional benefit, but white teeth can also have an important symbolic meaning – "a beautiful appearance."

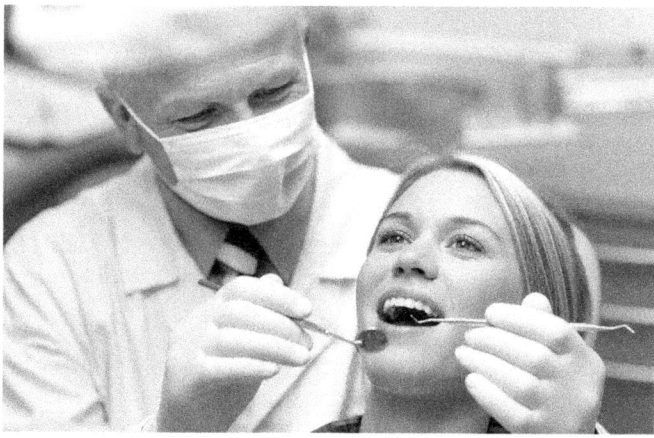

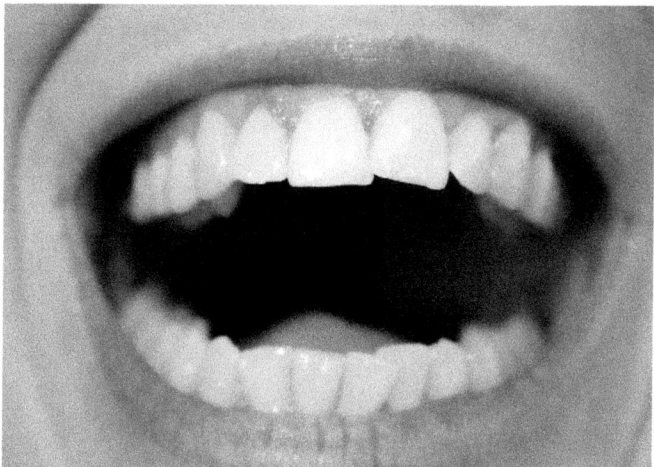

Photo 3.3 Two different benefits of using toothpaste: healthy teeth and sparkling white teeth healthy teeth. Photos Pxhere.com: CC0 public domain

3.5 Values and the Value Compass

At the highest level in the means-end chain are the (consumer) values. **Values** are deeply rooted in the personality of the consumer. Therefore, they can hardly be influenced by marketing or communication activities. Nevertheless, values are an important factor for brand positioning. They determine to a large extent why a consumer makes certain choices: values determine the buying motives of the consumer.

Psychological research has shown that the human value system is built up systematically. This value system is discussed in Section 3.5.1. This subsection demonstrates that this way of thinking about values is of great importance for marketing.

However, psychological value systems often remain fairly abstract, and therefore they are not always directly applicable for describing and explaining consumer behaviour.

Therefore we present a value system specifically designed to apply values to consumer behaviour (Kostelijk, 2016). This value system was developed by investigating for a large number of brands which values fit for these brands and to what extent these values are used by consumers in their selection process. This is discussed in Section 3.5.2.

3.5.1 Values in psychology

Values can be defined as a consistent belief that a particular behaviour or situation is preferred over another behaviour or situation. This belief can be a social belief ("freedom and equality are central values in our society"), but for marketing it is often more interesting to look at individual values (for example "For me my career is more important than having a family"). Values are used by people to judge other people, events, or objects (e.g. brands). Values are also used to make choices and then justify these choices.

Here we discuss two psychological value theories that are important for marketing: the value theory of Rokeach and the value theory of Schwartz.

Value theory of Rokeach

An important role in the development of value theory was played by the American psychologist Rokeach. For him, values were central to understanding and interpreting all forms of human behaviour (including consumer behaviour). The following quote makes it very clear:

> The value concept, more than any other, should occupy a central position in all the social sciences... able to unify the apparently diverse interests of all the sciences concerned with human behaviour.
>
> (Rokeach, 1973, p. 3)

Rokeach (1973, 1979) developed a list with 36 values that is still widely used in marketing. He makes a distinction between terminal values and instrumental values (see Table 3.2). Terminal values are items that people find important in their lives. It concerns matters such as happiness, friendship, or freedom. Instrumental values indicate how an individual should behave to realize certain terminal values. Examples of instrumental values are fair, ambitious, or obedient. In reality, the distinction between terminal values and instrumental values is sometimes difficult to make. A more important problem, at least for the marketer, is the somewhat abstract level of the **value theory of Rokeach**. This is because Rokeach defined his values by means of a survey asking about important matters "as a guideline for his/her life." This has led to fairly broad and often somewhat abstract descriptions, such as "inner harmony" or "self-respect." This can be very important in someone's life, but for the positioning of a brand these terms are less useful.

Table 3.2 **Values according to Rokeach**

Terminal values	Instrumental values
A comfortable life (a prosperous life)	Ambitious (hard-working, aspiring)
An exciting life (a stimulating, active life)	Broadminded (open-minded)
A sense of accomplishment (lasting contribution)	Capable (competent, effective)
A world at peace (free of war and conflict)	Cheerful (lighthearted, joyful)
A world of beauty (beauty of nature and the arts)	Clean (neat, tidy)
Equality (brotherhood, equal opportunity for all)	Courageous (standing up for your beliefs)
Family security (taking care of loved ones)	Forgiving (willing to pardon others)
Freedom (independence, free choice)	Helpful (working for the welfare of others)
Happiness (contentedness)	Honest (sincere, truthful)
Inner harmony (freedom from inner conflict)	Imaginative (daring, creative)
Mature love (sexual and spiritual intimacy)	Independent (self-reliant, self-sufficient)
National security (protection from attack)	Intellectual (intelligent, reflective)
Pleasure (an enjoyable, leisurely life)	Logical (consistent, rational)
Salvation (saved, eternal life)	Loving (affectionate, tender)
Self-respect (self-esteem)	Obedient (dutiful, respectful)
Social recognition (respect, admiration)	Polite (courteous, well-mannered)
True friendship (close companionship)	Responsible (dependable, reliable)
Wisdom (a mature understanding of life)	Self-controlled (restrained, self-disciplined)

Value theory of Schwartz

Like Rokeach, Schwartz (1992) considers values decisive for behaviour: values are central to the choices people make. In his value theory, Schwartz defines six important **features of values**:

1. Values are the beliefs that something is important in someone's life. For example, if *independence* is an important value to someone, then he has the conviction that independence is important in his or her life.
2. Values motivate action to achieve this conviction. A person who values independence will engage in activities that make or keep him independent.
3. Values are choice criteria. People make choices based on the extent to which a certain choice contributes to a certain value. With independence as central value, someone in a choice situation will opt for the alternative that ultimately yields the most independence.
4. Values transcend specific situations. Independence as value is important in someone's work, but also in family relationship, for a person's political opinion or for the individual as a consumer.
5. Values can be arranged in order of importance: some values are more important than other values. And this differs from person to person (or from consumer to consumer).
6. The relative importance of values determines behaviour. Since the importance of values differs from individual to individual, different individuals will also make different choices.

Schwartz studied human value patterns in a large number of countries. This research shows that values of people all over the world can be described in the same way. This of course does not mean that all those values are equally important in every culture. For example, values such as performance or prestige occur in every culture, but these values may be more important in masculine cultures such as the United States than, for instance, in the more feminine Scandinavian cultures.

Two dimensions are central to the **value system of Schwartz**:

- *Openness to change versus conservation.* This dimension represents that, on the one hand, people can be motivated to follow their own emotional and intellectual interests and want to change things (values such as stimulation and self-direction), but, on the other hand, we also have values that actually prevent us to change: values stimulating us to stick to the current situation and the certainty it offers (security, conformity, tradition).
- *Self-enhancement versus self-transcendence.* This dimension symbolizes the conflict between, on the one hand, values that emphasize individual interests (self-enhancement means putting yourself first: achievement, power, hedonism) and, on the other hand, more social values, with a focus on the welfare of others (self-transcendence means "to rise above yourself" and to care for the interests of others).

Schwartz emphasizes the way values relate to each other. A central element in his value theory is the assumption that some values reinforce each other, sharing similar motivations, whereas other values conflict with each other. For example, an individual for whom power is an important value will probably also appreciate leadership, or other values that emphasize the ability to influence others. A value like equality, on the other hand, will conflict with these values and will have an opposite effect on behaviour. According to Schwartz, behaviour is the result of the entire individual pattern of mutually reinforcing and conflicting values.

Use of values in marketing

We all have inside us all the values of the value system, but the importance attached to these values differs from person to person. Human behaviour, including consumer behaviour, is stimulated by the sum of all these values together, where some values reinforce each other and others conflict with each other. For example, people with strongly developed power and achievement values in combination with a great importance to security might want to aspire a good career, in a job with a permanent contract. But if a major security interest is combined with highly developed altruistic values, then one probably looks for certainty in the social context, for example, paying much attention to family life and friends.

By focusing on human psychology in general, Schwartz's value model, as well as Rokeach's classification, is not directly applicable for the marketer. It is quite possible that some values from Schwartz's model are not really important for consumer behaviour. On the other hand, it is also possible that some values are specifically relevant for consumer behaviour and therefore not mentioned in the psychological models. Finally, abstract descriptions such as altruism, obedience, or self-direction are perhaps important building blocks for human behaviour, but they might not be the readily applicable descriptions that the marketer needs when he tries to develop a brand positioning.

However, these models do have a major impact on how we view consumer behaviour and brand positioning. An important insight is that we have to consider values in mutual connection. The consequence is that for brand positioning, the brand cannot be simply loaded with a number of values. Selected values have to be consistent, so that they reinforce each other. Schwartz's model indicates how this consistency can be achieved.

3.5.2 The Value Compass: the value system of the consumer

Consumers are guided by their values; after all, these are connected in the means-end chain to the benefits that consumers are looking for. Following Chapter 1 where we discussed the relevance of unconscious decisions, the influence of values on behaviour can be both conscious or unconscious. This makes values an important construct for the analysis and prediction of consumer behaviour. Recent empirical research (Kostelijk, 2016) demonstrates that there is a specific set of values that influence consumer behaviour. These values appear to be related to each other in a value system with a circular structure comparable to the structure found in Schwartz's psychological research (1992). This value system, the **Value Compass**, is a representation of all values that are relevant for consumer behaviour, and thus also shows the interrelationships between these values (see Figure 3.5).

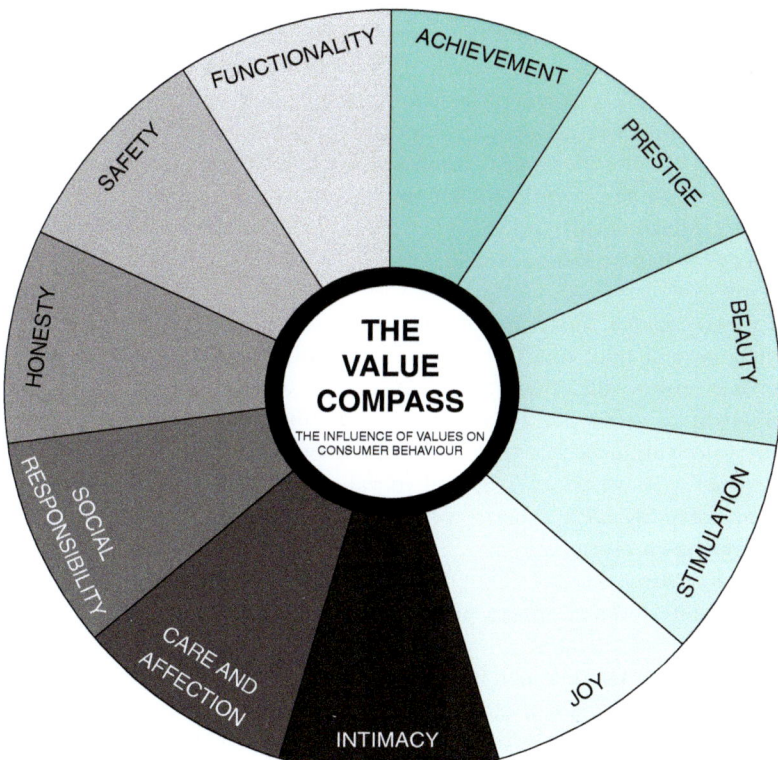

Figure 3.5 **The Value Compass (Kostelijk, 2016)**

Table 3.3 **The value types of the Value Compass**

Value type	Corresponding value items
Prestige & reputation	Leadership, power, status, being successful
Beauty & appearance	Beauty, elegance, good-looking, sense of beauty
Stimulation	Adventure, being active, being sportive, courage
Enjoying life	Enjoying life, excitement, fun, pleasure
Intimacy	Cosiness, intimacy, romance, sensuality
Care & affection	Caring for someone, family life, friendship, harmony
Social responsibility	Being environment-friendly, providing for a better world, recycling
Honesty	Honesty, keeping a promise, loyalty
Safety	Feeling of security, protection, safety
Functionality	Efficiency, functionality, precision, reliability
Achievement	Innovation, intellect, progress, smart solutions

The Value Compass consists of 11 **value types**, each of which refers to a certain consumer motivation. Each value type actually consists of a number of related values that can be described under this header. For example, the value type *enjoying life* contains values such as enjoying the moment, having fun, or indulging oneself. Table 3.3 gives a complete overview of the value types of the Value Compass, with their respective values.

Some values in the Value Compass reinforce each other, while other values represent conflicting motivations. This can be seen in Figure 3.5 by looking at the mutual distance between values. Values with a more similar meaning such as *care & affection* and *intimacy* are shown as close to each other or next to each other. Values that have less in common are placed on greater distance, and values with a conflicting meaning such as *functionality* and *enjoying life* oppose each other in the Value Compass. You can try to create your own Value Compass at www.valuecompass.nl.

Just as the compass points of a compass indicate which direction to follow (North, East, South, West), the Value Compass also offers directions. The following **value dimensions** can be distinguished:

■ *Fun versus function.* This dimension represents values motivating people to improve their quality of life by making hedonic choices, as opposed to values motivating people to improve their quality of life by making utilitarian (functional) choices.

■ *Promotion of self-interests versus care for others.* This dimension represents values motivating people to promote their own personal interests, to make a difference with others, as opposed to values motivating choices aimed at living in harmony with others, caring for others, and taking care of others. Among the care-oriented values, a distinction can be made between, on the one hand, caring for and taking care of close others, and, on the other hand, sustainability-oriented values, promoting a sense of responsibility for the future.

The structure of the value system is the same for every consumer: for everyone, *stimulation* and *enjoying life* are related values, and *stimulation* and *safety* are opposite values. The extent to which values are considered important, however, differs from consumer to consumer: for some people *stimulation* is a core value, while for others *safety* is a core value. These differences make it possible to segment consumers on the basis of dominant value patterns.

Consumers are not always directly aware of their values. But, consciously or unconsciously, they will influence their behaviour. See Example 3.2.

Example 3.2 Influence of values on behaviour

Let's look at the core values of two people: Jack and Jill. Jill's core values are related to safety and care & affection, while for Jack stimulation is an important value. Both Jack and Jill are potential visitors to Disneyland, but the underlying considerations are very different. Jill wants to go to Disneyland to have quality time with her family; she probably figured out in advance how to drive to Disneyland, which attractions are suitable for the whole family, and how to get to the parking lot. After all, safety means avoiding risks. Jack, however, will want to focus on the latest attractions and probably also wants to try them out. If Jack and Jill are a couple, you can imagine that the visit to Disneyland could be a disappointing experience for both.

Because of the influence that values have on behaviour and on brand experience, they are important for the marketer. Therefore, we now discuss each of the values of the Value Compass and their underlying consumer motivations.

Prestige & reputation

People have a natural need for respect and appreciation. These needs are also in Maslow's pyramid. But for some people this need is more developed than for others. If ***prestige & reputation*** are core values of consumers, then they have a strongly

Photo 3.4 **Conspicuous consumption: expensive brands give status. Photo Pxhere.com: CC0 public domain**

developed need to leave a good impression on others, to show status, to stand out or to be well-known, recognized or famous, or to dominate others.

A certain type of consumer behaviour that is stimulated by these values is described in marketing as **conspicuous consumption** (Bagwell & Bernheim, 1996): the desire to radiate a certain status or wealth through consumption. This applies to certain luxury brands such as Dior, Gucci, Louis Vuitton, Moët Hennessy, or Ferrari.

Beauty & appearance

People for whom this value is important would like to make a difference with others by **appearance**. This can be done by means of external beauty (looking good), but also elegance or stylish behaviour is in line with this value, as well as wanting to follow a certain etiquette. Consumer behaviour that is driven by this value is often symbolic in nature. Consumers look for brands that bring a certain appearance: they want to look elegant, stylish, beautiful, or attractive, and in that way impress others, or even be appreciated by others. Producers of fashionable clothing, jewellery, perfume, cars, or watches often connect to this value, but also low calorie food, fitness centres, or dance schools can try to appeal to this value.

For a jewellery brand, it is not immediately distinctive to connect with appearance in general. After all, competing brands will do this too. Such a brand has to empathize with the target group, and then try to make it plausible that wearing this brand gives the owner in the target group exactly the look that he or she wants.

Photo 3.5 **Fashion helps to make people feel beautiful. Photo © Garry Knight (cc-by-2.0)**

Stimulation

Central to the value ***stimulation*** is the experience of stimulating sensations. This includes values such as adventure, courage, being active, or being sportive.

In essence, the search for stimulating experiences is a generic human need: everyone needs a certain level of stimulation. But consumers for whom looking for such sensations is a core value can be distinguished by their active search for this type of experience and their preparation to take certain risks. After all, this value opposes safety-related values. An activity like mountain climbing fits very well here, but also certain rides in the funfair or going off the beaten track during holiday trips are stimulated by this value type.

Photo 3.6 Iceland inspires for stimulating holidays. Source: Karel Jan Alsem.

The influential book *The Experience Economy* (Pine & Gilmore, 1999) emphasizes that every brand must bring a certain degree of stimulation. It can be created, for instance, by making the brand itself an experience: both Guinness (the Guinness Factory Tour in Dublin) and Heineken (the Heineken Experience in Amsterdam), for example, have turned the process of beer making into an experience. Another example is the effort that shopping malls make to attract customers: the experience of "real" shopping can be an important motive to attract the consumer to go shopping in the mall and not from behind the laptop. Brand experience is relevant for all brands, but the correct dosage is important. If things like socializing ("cozy with friends to the Summer Week") or having fun ("fun shopping in the city") are important motives, then any event must also be linked to these values, and not only to the experience aspect.

Enjoying life

Fun shopping is an activity that fits well with the value *enjoying life*. If a shopping mall profiles itself as the place for an afternoon of fun and enjoyment, then it focuses on that part of the shoppers for whom enjoying life is an important value. Also variety seeking ("striving for a varied life") and pleasure fit well with this value type. This value type is opposed to functional values such as convenience or usefulness: people that value enjoyment will be guided by pleasure or the extent to which they can enjoy their purchase, and less by their functional aspects. Pleasure can be found in such things as enjoying a relaxing holiday or an afternoon of shopping in the city, but also in enjoying a moment for yourself with a Magnum or with a bottle of Coca-Cola. Everyone wants to enjoy once in a while, of course, but consumers for whom this value is central will use this as a key choice criterion in many situations. Consider, for example, the choice of an amusement park: if fun and enjoyment are central values for you, then you want to go to an amusement park for a different reason than when good family life is an important value.

Photo 3.7 Coca-Cola: the pleasure of a moment for yourself. Source: istockphoto.com.

Intimacy

The previous value, enjoying life, focuses on individual enjoyment. The value *intimacy* is about being able to enjoy life together with others. Central to this value is the importance of a warm, intimate relationship: the warm, happy feeling you get from the relationship with your loved ones. This can be the relationship with your partner, but also the bond with your child or with your friends. Values such as love, romance, and sensuality match well here. The combination of pleasure together with others places this value between the value types enjoying life and care & affection.

The importance of this value is also recognized in branding. The advertising agency Saatchi & Saatchi uses the Lovemarks concept to describe brands that manage to touch the customer in their hearts (Roberts, 2005). Saatchi & Saatchi emphasizes the importance of intimacy and the related values sensuality and mystery: according to the advertising agency, a brand without these brand values cannot create strong bonds with their customers.

Photo 3.8 The intimate relation between parent and child is often used for brand positioning purposes. Photo released under Pexels license: free for commercial and non-commercial use

Care & affection

The value type *care & affection* represents the importance of attention for the well-being of others. This includes valuing friendship, as well as a good family life, having respect for each other, or living in harmony with each other. Consumer behaviour that is stimulated by this value type emphasizes the importance of fulfilling the needs of others, for example by buying gifts for birthdays or Christmas. Product categories varying from baby care to dog food frequently associate with care-related values, as well as health care associations or insurance companies. Creating a cozy homely atmosphere also matches with these values and is used for instance by brands like IKEA or home improvement shops: the interior design of the house makes a good family life possible.

Photo 3.9 Christmas: important for people that value care & affection. Photo © Sigismund von Dobschütz (cc-by-sa/4.0)

Social responsibility

The value type ***social responsibility*** emphasizes the responsibility that one bears for the life and well-being of everyone on our planet, for now and for future generations. Consumers for whom this is an important value will consider sustainability

Photo 3.10 The circular economy and sustainability are important elements of corporate social responsibility. Photo released under Pixabay license: free for commercial use, no attribution required

and environmentally friendly behaviour important. These consumers will feel more attracted by campaigns that emphasize these issues.

Corporate social responsibility (CSR) receives a lot of attention. Many organizations use concepts such as CSR, responsibility, or sustainability in their profiling. These terms are often used in the context of the corporate image of the organization. In Chapter 2 social responsibility has already been referred to as one of the six dimensions of reputation (Subsection 2.1.4). Incidentally, different concepts are often used interchangeably. CSR is the collective name for the whole of social goals that an organization has. Various facets can be distinguished within CSR such as:

- *Sustainability*. That means doing business in an environmentally friendly way. The Brundtland Commission of the United Nations defined sustainable development as "development that meets the needs of the present without compromising the ability of future generations to meet their own needs" (World Commission on Environment and Development, 1987).
- *Social projects*. This can relate to various charities. Examples are the Ronald McDonald House Charities, the co-financing of anti-alcoholism campaigns by beer companies, or funding of micro-credit projects in India by financial corporations.
- *Internal social policy*. Think of HR (Human Resources) policies with respect to the protection of women, elderly workers, or employees from specific ethnic backgrounds.

The consumer value social responsibility refers to the importance that consumers attach to the well-being of society as a whole. Different facets can be distinguished: some consumers attach greater importance to sustainability, whereas others consider social activities in the neighbourhood to be more important.

Honesty

Values that fit well with the value type of **honesty** also include loyalty, trust, and keeping promises. The value type honesty indicates the importance of trust in the intentions of others. This can refer to other people, but it also applies to being able to trust promises made by a brand. Examples of consumer behaviour stimulated by this value type include have a preference for "honest" products (for example sustainably produced, without child labour and without the abuse of scarce raw materials) or a tendency to have a preference for suppliers who show genuine commitment. Brand loyalty also matches with this value: loyal consumers are looking for a sincere bond with the brands in which they believe and in which they have confidence. This illustrates that some consumers are brand-loyal by nature, while loyalty to other consumers does not belong to their nature.

Photo 3.11 **Honesty is a core value for Fairtrade products. Photo © Juliamh123 (cc-by-sa/4.0)**

Safety

The value type *safety* relates to the safety needs in the Maslow pyramid. This value type is the opposite of the value type stimulation, as indicated earlier. If this is one of your central values, you consider it important to avoid uncertainty and to exclude risks. A safety seeker will check traffic reports and rain radar before going to the beach, and then preferably chooses a beach where he has been before and where he knows exactly where to park the car. Safety is broader than physical safety: a person buying dandruff shampoo might experience an "emotional risk." Brands can meet security seekers by offering extended service or warranties, or by showing testimonials from users who had a good experience with the brand.

Photo 3.12 **Insurances are important when you score high on safety values. Photo © Money, July 30, 2014 (cc-by-2.0)**

Everyone needs a certain degree of security; safety is also an essential feature in some product categories. For example, safety is important for all cars. A brand can, however, choose to explicitly link this value to the brand. A brand like Volvo does this. In one Volvo advertisement, this was explicitly linked to the history of the brand: "Volvo has distinguished itself with its attention to safety since 1959." By the way, in the same ad the word fashion was explicitly used, in combination with sleek design of the ad and an explicit connection with a fashion brand; all these features hint that also beauty & appearance is essential to the brand values of Volvo.

Functionality

The value type ***functionality*** emphasizes that a brand does what it should do: "performance according to specifications." Consumers who are guided by this are sensitive to concepts such as efficiency, usefulness, expertise, professionalism, reliability, or usability. If functionality is important to you, you pay more attention than others to the practical aspects of a possible purchase, and less attention to the pleasure that such a purchase can bring. You go into the city because you need a pair of trousers, not because shopping is a fun activity. And for lunch you opt for a sandwich with cheese or ham, because that is easy to prepare and gives enough energy to get you through the day. Much attention is therefore paid to functional benefits, in contrast to the symbolic or experience-oriented benefits that are linked to other values.

Essentially, many product categories have functional origins. Cars are used to drive from A to B, phones are used to communicate, fruits and vegetables are healthy, and banks enable us to save or borrow money. Functional foods are an example of products that explicitly aim at functional values. For instance, dairy products such as Yakult or Danone Actimel distinguish themselves by making health claims: these products contain the *Lactobacillus casei* bacteria that are supposed to have positive effects on our inner constitution.

Photo 3.13 The *L. casei* bacteria in Danone Actimel are supposed to be good for us. Photo provided by Danone Actimel

Achievement

The value type ***achievement*** stimulates choices where progress is an important motivation. If you score high on this value type then you attach great value to matters such as intellect, innovation, product improvement, and expertise. Having a good education is probably important for you, as well as brands that help you to perform better. You may also be sensitive to product innovations or product claims such as "completely renewed," "now better than ever," etc.

Both the value type achievement and the value type prestige emphasize the importance of a high performance. For example, there is an important career drive in both values. But if the career motivation results from prestige considerations, then you want to perform better than others, so that others will recognize and esteem your performance. Achievement values, on the other hand, motivate a good career because it is important to get ahead in life, or because you want to challenge yourself.

Photo 3.14 **Elon Musk's Tesla symbolizes innovation. Photo © Maurizio Pesce, October 1, 2011 (cc-by-2.0)**

Summary

Consumers have needs. Brands want to meet these needs. They do this by positioning the brand as well as possible towards the consumer in the target group: the brand tries to match the benefits and values of the brand as closely as possible to their target customers. In the description of the means-end chain, we have looked extensively at an essential component: the benefits that the consumer is looking for. People buy products or services because of the benefits promised by these products or services. Three types of benefits were distinguished:

- functional benefits
- experience-oriented benefits: offering a certain "experience"
- symbolic benefits, through which the consumer can express himself to others

Benefits are a central part of the structure of meanings of a brand. Benefits offered by a brand are important for the consumer if they match the central values that the consumer strives for in his life: the consumer's value system determines which benefits are important for the consumer. We have described this value system on the basis of the Value Compass. Often, personality dimensions are used to describe brands. We believe that values are in fact more important because "what you find important" has a stronger relationship with buying behaviour than "who you are."

The means-end chain expresses two things: the means and the end. The "means" are formed by the brand; after all, the brand delivers product characteristics that enable the benefits that consumers are looking for. Just think of toothpaste that contains (among other things) whiteners to deliver the benefit "radiant white teeth." The "end" consists of the values that the consumer aims for: for example, consumers might want radiant white teeth when the beauty ideal of a perfectly groomed appearance is an important value for them.

Different types of consumers pursue different values, and consequently are looking for different benefits. That is why markets are divided into segments. A segment is a group of people with more or less the same needs, so a group of people who are looking for more or less the same benefits. In this chapter, therefore, attention was also paid to the segmentation criteria that can be used to classify the market.

Chapter 4

Brand image and brand values

4.1 An introduction to brand image

Marketing has been described as conquering "share of minds, share of hearts and share of markets." Share of markets refers to market share: the portion of total category sales (or turnover) for the brand. **Market share** is a commonly used indicator of the market position of a brand; marketing objectives are often expressed in terms of a market share that has to be achieved. Managers are then held accountable for the market share that they realized.

Positioning relates to conquering mindshare and heartshare. **Mindshare** is the extent to which the brand is "top of mind," i.e. the extent to which consumers think about the brand or are reminded of the brand when they feel a certain need. **Heartshare** refers to the extent to which the brand image fits the desires and preferences of the consumer: do the brand associations hit the right emotion with the consumer? The "three shares" are logically related: as mentioned in Chapter 1, large shares of mind or shares of heart lead to higher intentions to buy and thus to higher market shares.

The way in which a brand has to be positioned depends on the current brand awareness and the current brand image in the target group. Both mindshare and heartshare must therefore be mapped before a brand starts with any (re) positioning activities.

This chapter starts with a discussion about brand image, and how mindshare and heartshare contribute to this image. Subsequently, extensive attention is paid to methods for measuring brand awareness and brand image. Brand awareness is discussed in Section 4.3. In the subsequent sections we look at brand image and brand associations. Many methods have been developed to measure the image of the brand among the target group. A distinction is made between qualitative methods (Section 4.4) and quantitative methods (Section 4.5).

A favourable brand image should lead to brand preference, which then translates into the intention to buy the brand or to talk positively about the brand with others. Brand preference is discussed in Section 4.6 and indicators to measure behaviour (purchase intent and client ambassadorship) in Section 4.7.

4.2 Brand image: a combination of mindshare and heartshare

The **brand image** is the image that the target group has with a brand. This image is made up of all the associations that the target group has with the brand. Section 3.4 already stated that these associations can be functional, symbolic, or experience-oriented in nature and that they can relate to product attributes, product benefits, or values.

A distinction can be made between the image of a brand (brand image) and the image of an organization (**corporate image**). This distinction is important insofar as there is an organization that markets its brands under a different name than the name of the organization.

On the corporate level, Van Riel (2010) prefers the word reputation to corporate image. **Reputation** then relates to the image of an organization in its totality, and brand image on the representation of aspects of that organization. Take, for example, the company Heineken, manufacturer of brands such as Heineken, Amstel, or the cider brand Jillz. Heineken's reputation then relates to the Heineken company, while Heineken's brand image relates to the Heineken beer brand. The reputation of an organization will also be of importance to other stakeholders such as employees, environmental groups, the government, or financial stakeholders.

As mentioned earlier, a distinction between the reputation of a company and the image of the individual brands of that company is particularly important if the company and the brand have a different name. If brand name and company name are the same (as in the case of Philips and Heineken), the image at brand level and the reputation at the corporate level – at least in the eyes of the consumer – are difficult to separate. The importance of the corporate brand is increasing for the consumer market. For example, in television commercials for Unilever brands, Unilever's logo is now visible. The intention of this form of **endorsement** is that the reputation of the company Unilever becomes linked to the separate brands (this is discussed in more detail in Chapter 8).

With respect to brand imagery, regardless of whether there is a corporate brand or an individual brand, the consumer associates with the image related to the brand name he encounters on the packaging of the product or on the facade of the service provider. The question we raised in the introduction is whether the consumer is mainly influenced by mindshare or heartshare. This is discussed in more detail in the following subsections.

4.2.1 Mindshare: recording in the evoked set

The **purpose of creating mindshare** is to make the brand part of the evoked set. The **evoked set** is the group of brands that the consumer considers and from which he will ultimately make his choice (Nederstigt & Poiesz, 2014). A brand is only included in this evoked set if the consumer thinks about the brand during his decision-making process. The brand is therefore, as it were, "in the mind of the consumer": the consumer thinks of the brand when he feels a certain need. There are two conditions for inclusion in the evoked set:

1. Awareness: the consumer must know the brand.
2. Salience: the brand must be connected to the need felt by the consumer.

The first step is **awareness**. Consumers have to know about the existence of the brand. This means on the one hand **brand recognition** and on the other hand brand recall. Brand recognition or aided brand awareness means that the consumer knows what type of product is involved when they hear or see the brand name. So when the consumer hears Lay's,[1] he knows that it is about potato chips. With **brand recall** or unaided brand awareness, it is about consumers thinking about the brand when they think about a specific product category. So, if he has to buy potato chips, then Lay's is one of the brands that comes to mind.

Brand salience is one step more than brand awareness. Salience starts when the consumer thinks "automatically" about the brand in a given situation or a specific need. Brands must therefore be connected to needs or situations. Take, for example, someone who organizes a party. A party includes snacks. If the Lay's brand is a salient brand for this person, Lay's chips would automatically be considered: the Lay's brand is in the mind of this person an inseparable part of a party. Inclusion of the brand in the evoked set is therefore fundamental. The image of a brand can

---

1 Lay's is the brand name in most countries. In the United Kingdom and Ireland, the brand is called Walkers.

be perfect, but if the brand is not in the evoked set, it will not be chosen. According to Sharp (2010), brand positioning should therefore focus primarily on connecting brands with certain needs or situations, and thus to get the brand in the evoked set. If we follow the example: Lay's chips is an inextricable part of a successful party in the mind of the consumer and brand positioning is necessary to realize this association.

Sharp (2010) draws attention to the importance of brand salience: the extent to which the brand is linked to the needs of the target group. In other words: does the consumer think of the brand when he feels a need? Sharp emphasizes mindshare, because according to him the role of the brand image is limited. He indicates that in most markets there is low involvement. As a result most brands are interchangeable from the point of view of the consumer. In the logic of Sharp there are actually two possibilities. The first possibility is that a shopping list is made with the words "beer, potato chips, peanuts." In the supermarket, then a brand of potato chips is chosen. Comparison of Lay's chips with any other brand based on brand image does not take place; the brand of potato chips that the consumer thinks of in the supermarket – i.e. the brand that is most prominent in the evoked set – is bought, without considering any other brands. Sometimes, this can even boil down to buying the brand that is literally the most visible and the most "up for grabs" in the supermarket. The second option is that, as discussed earlier, the Lay's brand is inextricably linked to the situation "organizing a party." If the situation and the brand are so closely linked, the brand name Lay's will end up on the shopping list. In this second situation, the brand image of Lay's and competing brands is also irrelevant according to Sharp; the purpose of brand positioning then is to strengthen the salience of the brand, as indicated earlier.

4.2.2 Heartshare: strong, relevant, and unique brand associations

In fact, in a situation of mindshare as described in the previous section, the evoked set consists of only one brand, namely the brand that is chosen. However, if the consumer has multiple brands in the evoked set, he has to make a choice. He will then choose that brand of which he has the most positive image. The brand image then plays a crucial role in selecting a brand from the evoked set. Brand image relates to all associations the consumer has with the brand, both functionally and emotionally. We refer to this as heartshare: the consumer develops a preference for the brand that in his eyes has the best image, so the brand that he holds closest to his heart. The **purpose of creating heartshare** is to establish strong, positive, and distinctive **brand associations**. These associations can be based on their own experiences with the brand, but also on other characteristics, benefits, or brand values associated with the brand. We would like to emphasize that heartshare can be realized through both functional and emotional associations: preference can be the result of a feeling about a brand, but also of facts about the brand.

While Sharp emphasizes the importance of brand awareness and brand salience, authors like Keller and Kotler focus on the importance of brand image. Kotler and Armstrong (2008) emphasize the importance of establishing unique brand associations: they see positioning primarily as the means to distinguish the brand from competing brands. Kotler, Kartajaya, and Setiawan (2010) explicitly emphasize the importance of heartshare: "Marketers should target consumers' minds and spirits simultaneously to touch their hearts." In other words, a brand image provides added value to the target group by differentiating on the emotional level.

According to Keller (2012), brand positioning is essential for the development of a marketing strategy. Like Kotler, he emphasizes the importance of a strong brand image: "The power of a brand lies in the minds and hearts of customers." According to Keller, associations are of great value to the brand. A strong brand is in his reasoning a brand with a great reputation and with strong, relevant, and distinctive associations. Keller speaks about **customer-based brand equity**. This is defined as the added value that brand awareness and brand associations give to a brand, as compared to the same product without brand name. Put in simple words: consumers want to pay more for a product with a brand because they know the brand and because this brand evokes positive images and feelings.

Keller distinguishes four stages that contribute to the realization of brand equity:

1. *Salience*. This is the brand awareness and brand salience as described in Section 4.2.1: the extent to which the consumer thinks of the brand in certain situations.
2. *Brand meaning*. This relates to the associations that the brand evokes. Keller's model distinguishes:
    - Brand performance – functional associations about the function, reliability, or quality of the product: *laundry detergent X washes cleaner than other detergents.*
    - Brand imagery – band associations based on personal experiences, brand values, and the like: *My mother always washes with detergent X.* An example is chocolate bar KitKat that uses imagery to relate to a usage situation: "Have a break, have a KitKat."
3. *Brand response*. This relates to the thoughts and feelings that these associations evoke. Again, a distinction is made between:
    - Brand judgements about product quality: *Detergent X is simply the best detergent.* For instance, Carlsberg beer advertises with "Probably the best beer in the world."
    - Brand feelings that relate to the emotional experience of the brand: *A good mother washes her clothes with detergent X.* Perhaps detergents are not directly a product category that evokes a lot of emotions, but also think of feelings of care and affection (Dove), fun (Disney), or safety (Volvo). McDonald's "I'm loving it" fits with this category as well.
4. *Resonance*. Thoughts and feelings result in brand preference or a certain bond with the brand (for example in the form of brand loyalty or actively participating in the brand community of the brand on Facebook). Ultimately, brand preference determines the choices the consumer makes: brand preference can lead to a purchase intention.

Photo 4.1 An emotional brand response: Disney aims for heartshare. Photo used with permission of Disney; © Disney

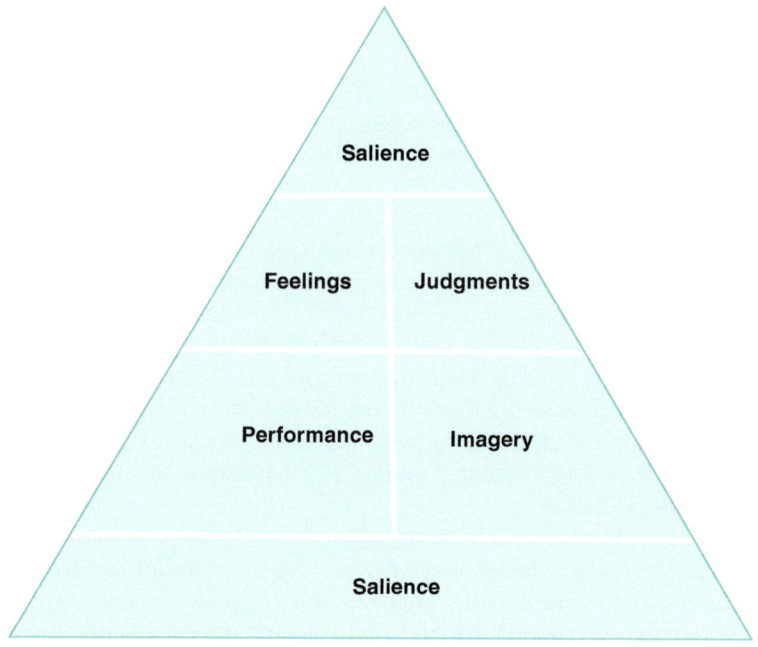

Figure 4.1 Customer-based brand equity. Source: Keller, 2012.

The four stages of the customer-based brand equity model can be represented in the form of a pyramid (see Figure 4.1).

Salience in the Keller model is actually the same as what we call mindshare. Heartshare refers to the positive thoughts and feelings that the brand evokes in the consumer. Keller's model clearly shows that heartshare can be the result of both emotional associations (imagery) and functional associations (performance).

According to Keller, salience is an important first step in building brand equity, but usually not enough. Brand meaning and brand response are essential to building a strong brand and thus to achieve brand preference. In the words of Keller: "The strength, favorability and uniqueness of brand equity play a critical role in determining the differential response to brand equity." Keller thus places a central role on brand associations, so on heartshare. In this respect the opinion of Keller is clearly different from that of Sharp.

4.2.3 A strong brand has mindshare and heartshare

Summarizing the previous discussion, we can see that building a **strong brand** involves a number of factors:

- mindshare and heartshare
- brand preference
- brand behaviour (purchase intent or word-of-mouth (WOM))

A strong brand is prominently present in the consumer's mind; as a result, the consumer thinks of the brand when he feels a certain need (mindshare). But a strong brand also evokes strong and positive associations that distinguish the brand from competing brands (heartshare). It seems a matter of taste which of these two is more important. Sharp emphasizes that most choices occur under low involvement, and that mindshare is essential, while for Keller the importance of heartshare is central. Pauwels and Ewijk (2013) show that ("soft") attitudinal measures as well as ("hard") online behaviour tracking data are a good prediction of sales. So, brand image does matter.

As is often the case, the truth is somewhere in between. Depending on the situation (for example the level of involvement), mindshare or heartshare will be the dominant factor in the consumer's choice process, so for a strong brand both mindshare and heartshare are important. It is up to the marketer to determine which of the two receives priority in the positioning strategy. We will discuss this in the chapter on brand positioning (Chapter 6).

A strong brand, so a brand that managed to realize a certain degree of mindshare and/or heartshare, leads to **brand preference**: the consumer wants to have the brand, and prefers this brand to competing brands. Brand preference therefore increases the probability that the consumer will buy the brand. With mindshare, brand preference is largely irrelevant, especially in a situation of low involvement, as the evoked set consists of only one brand: you organize a party, and that includes potato chips. In the supermarket you see Lay's chips, the brand you know, and you buy that without any further consideration.

The relation between brand image, brand preference, and brand behaviour is presented schematically in Figure 4.2: strengthening the brand image leads to more

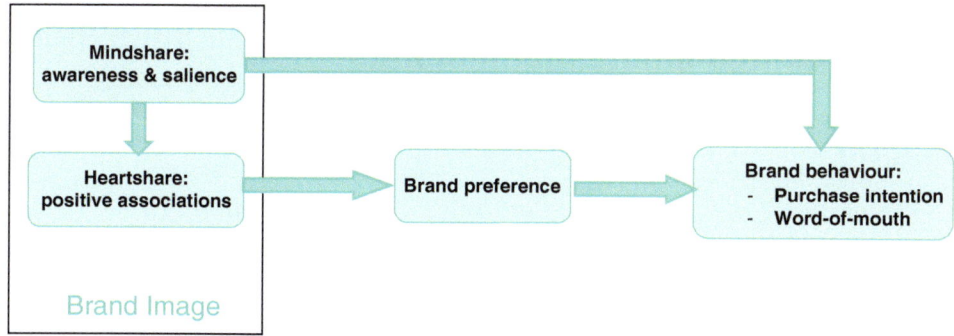

Figure 4.2 **Relation between brand image, brand preference, and purchase intent**

brand preference, and this, in turn, leads to a stronger purchase intent or a greater probability of positive WOM.

Insight into the current brand image and brand preference and the current intentions of the target group is important. The current situation largely determines how the brand should be positioned in the future. We therefore need to measure the current brand image, current brand preference, and the current purchase intentions. That is why we discuss in detail in the following sections how these indicators can be measured.

4.3 Mindshare: measuring brand awareness and brand salience

In the previous section we indicated the importance of mindshare: the inclusion of a brand in the evoked set. Two types of indicators were named for this: brand awareness and brand salience. Four levels can be distinguished with regard to brand awareness:

1. Unfamiliarity: the brand is not known.
2. Aided brand awareness or **brand recognition**. A positive answer to the question: "Have you ever heard of brand X?"
3. Unaided brand awareness or **brand recall**. This is measured with the question: "Which brands in product category Y do you know?"
4. **Top of mind awareness (TOMA)**. The first brand that is mentioned as a reply to the question "Which brands in product category Y do you know?" is the brand with the highest TOMA.

Brand salience relates to the extent to which the consumer thinks of the brand in a given situation: "Which brands are suitable for use in situation X?" This is actually a more specific interpretation of brand awareness: it does not just include all brands of which the consumer knows the name, but only those brands that are relevant for the consumer in the target group.

Table 4.1 Sample questions for measuring brand awareness and brand salience

Brand recall	*Which pubs in Groningen do you know?......*		
Brand recognition	*Which of the following pubs in Groningen have you heard of?*		
		Yes	*No*
	The Three Sisters	O	O
	Warhol	O	O
	O'Malley's Irish Pub	O	O
	Pintelier	O	O
TOMA	*Which pub in Groningen comes to your mind first?..........*		
	TOMA can also be measured by taking the brand that is first mentioned in the brand recall question.		
Brand salience	*If you plan to go to a pub in Groningen, which of the following pubs would you consider?*		
		Yes	*No*
	The Three Sisters	O	O
	Warhol	O	O
	O'Malley's Irish Pub	O	O
	Pintelier	O	O

Table 4.1 summarizes the questions that can be asked in a survey to measure awareness and salience. Here we use the example of a survey about pubs in the city of Groningen, a student city in the North of the Netherlands. We return to this example in Section 4.5.1.

Awareness and salience together determine whether a brand is included in the evoked set. The next step is to establish the image of the brands included in the evoked set. In the following sections we describe the methods to do this.

4.4 Heartshare: measuring brand associations through qualitative research

The purpose of image research is to map the associations connected to a certain brand. This can be done with qualitative and quantitative research techniques.

Qualitative research aims to explore a certain situation or to gain deeper insight into that situation. Often, however, qualitative research does not receive a lot of attention. After all, managers are judged on measurable results and these should be expressed in numbers. And numbers are tracked with data analytics or with quantitative research. Quantitative research is usually carried out by means of questionnaires (surveys) that are presented online or by telephone to large groups of respondents.

However, before measuring certain values, benefits, or product attributes in image surveys, it must first be clear which aspects are relevant to the end user. And then qualitative research is often the most suitable. That is why we are now discussing a number of qualitative research methods to measure brand image. We first pay attention to laddering. Then a number of projective techniques are discussed. In Section 4.5 we discuss quantitative methods for measuring brand image.

4.4.1 Laddering

Laddering can be used to determine the means-end chain of a brand. **Laddering** zooms in on the brand in a series of interviews with respondents from the target group. During such an interview a number of aspects of the brand are discussed. The interviewer will want to go in-depth as much as possible by continuously asking questions such as: "Why is that important for you?." Incidentally, focus groups are used instead of in-depth interviews. In a focus group, a number of consumers discuss the brand under the guidance of a moderator. The advantage of a focus group is that people can respond to each other. In a successful focus group, participants stimulate each other to think creatively about the brand. This stimulating creative process is, however, highly dependent on the participants in the focus group and on the qualities of the moderator.

The easiest way to discover brand associations during an interview or group discussion is to simply ask respondents about their associations. With **free association** you are asked what you think about a particular brand or product category. Think of questions such as: "What do you think of Lipton tea?" or "What is the ideal tea moment for you?" The associations that one has with the brand or product can then be used to map out the associative network around the brand. For example, if you think of a steaming teapot in which a Lipton tea bag should be dipped, and then it takes some time to make the tea, then the interviewer can ask questions about the product characteristics and usage situation. The conversation could then be something like this:

INTERVIEWER: What do you like most about tea?
RESPONDENT: It creates a moment when we are together with the whole family and take time for each other. (Benefit: quality time with the whole family)
INTERVIEWER: And could you also use another brand of tea for this?
RESPONDENT: Lipton represents quality. I prefer to use a quality product for my quality time. (Distinction with the competition)
INTERVIEWER: Why is the tea moment important for you?
RESPONDENT: I think it is important that we take time together. My family is important to me. (The value of family life is therefore important)

Another approach is to use the "**five Ws and one H**." This is a way of questioning that is also used in journalism and in crime investigations. With regard to image research, this method results in the following questions:

- *Who* uses the brand?
- *What* do you do with the brand? What is the brand used for?
- *When* do you use the brand?
- *Where* do you use the brand?
- *Why* do you use the brand? What benefits does it give you?
- *How* do you use the brand?

Sometimes it is difficult for respondents to explain in words why they use a certain brand. An in-depth interview about Heineken among students, by using the five Ws and one H, for example, risks that the answers do not go much deeper than:

> *'I drink it with my friends (who) when we go out (When).*
> *We then drink it in the pub (Where)*
> *When we have fun together (Why)*
> *I drink it directly from the bottle (How)*

This is not really new information for Heineken. In some product categories (beer for instance) there is also the risk of socially desirable answers.

In the examples discussed so far, a direct questioning technique has been used. In **direct techniques**, the consumer is directly asked about elements of the brand image. When it is difficult for consumers to put their opinion into words, a more indirect technique could be considered. This can be done through projective techniques.

4.4.2 Projective techniques

With **projective techniques**, the respondent is not asked directly for a specific topic. The classic example of a projective technique is the **Rorschach test** or inkblot test (Keller, 2012). In this test, often used in psychological research in the sixties of the last century, respondents have to react to inkblots. By having respondents indicate what the inkblot makes them think about, the psychologist hopes to gain insight into the personality of the respondents. In his description of projective techniques, Keller also refers to a well-known example in marketing (see Example 4.1).

Example 4.1 Split-run test

In the forties, instant coffee was introduced in America. A major innovation: people no longer had to grind coffee beans. However, this time-saving innovation was barely sold at the start, and management wanted to know why. Two shopping lists were tested in a survey. These shopping lists were identical, but with one important difference. On one shopping list, between the other supermarket products, a pot of coffee beans was mentioned. On the other list this item was replaced by a pack of Nescafe instant coffee. A split-run test was used: one group of respondents received the first list, the second group the other list. Respondents had to assess the housewife who had made the shopping list. The investigation revealed the cause of the disappointing sales of the instant coffee. The housewife of the list with the instant coffee was judged as "lazy," "unable to plan the household," and even as "a bad wife."

The advantage of projective techniques is that they offer creative possibilities to make the respondent think. This creativity is also a disadvantage. Interpretation of results is sometimes very subjective. It is therefore important to clearly keep the research objective in mind during the research.

Examples of projective techniques that can be used for image research are word associations and sentence completions, interpretation of situations, or making comparisons. With **word associations**, respondents are presented with a word (Summer, coziness, fish and chips, etc.) and asked what they think when they hear that word. Sentence completion helps respondents to associate to a certain brand or situation: "I eat Snickers when…"

Respondents can also be asked to interpret or make associations on a certain situation. One can for example show a picture of a family around a table full of burgers and fries, after which the respondent is asked to give a description of this family. If necessary, a comparison can be made between brands, for example by presenting a different group of respondents either with the burgers and fries wrapped in McDonald's packaging or with Burger King packaging. This kind of **storytelling** can yield a wealth of information, under the condition that the situation is controlled and framed in the right way by the researcher.

Brands can also be compared with countries, activities, professions, animals, or famous people. An example of this is the **Photosort technique**. Respondents receive a number of photos of, for example, animals or famous persons, and then have to indicate which animal or person best fits the brand. This technique can be used well as an icebreaker at the beginning of an in-depth interview or focus group. For example, if the respondent indicates that the brand is most similar to a dolphin, the following question may be asked: "Why do you think this brand is like a dolphin? Which characteristics of a dolphin fit well with this brand?" A related method is that respondents are asked to find photos and text from online sources or, for example, a number of magazines that reflect their feelings about a brand and to put them together on a "**moodboard**." Also, with this method respondents are then asked why they chose certain photos or text. So, in effect the collection of material is a way of facilitating respondents to express their feelings about the brand.

4.5 Heartshare: measuring brand associations through quantitative research

There are many different methods to measure brand image. These methods are often based on a certain vision of what a brand image is, and often emphasize specific aspects of the meaning structure of a brand. In this section, we discuss the following methods:

1. measuring the evaluation of brand attributes with the multi-attribute attitude model
2. measuring brand values with the Value Compass
3. describing the character of a brand with Aaker's brand personality model
4. describing the brand on the basis of brand archetypes
5. creating a brand space by means of perceptual mapping
6. determining the brand strength with the Brand Asset Valuator (BAV)

4.5.1 Multi-attribute attitude model

The **multi-attribute attitude model** is an elegant model for analyzing and assessing brand image. Unfortunately, the name of the model is not very elegant, but don't let the complex name intimidate you.

The model essentially shows that the appreciation for a brand is determined by the importance attached to certain attributes or benefits, in combination with the extent to which the consumer believes that the brand can deliver these attributes or benefits. The model therefore establishes a link between the desires of the consumer and the associations that the consumer has with the brand. In order to do so, the model uses three indicators:

■ Attributes: these are the product properties, benefits, or brand values that play a role in a certain product category. These attributes can therefore relate to every level of the means-end chain.
■ Desires of the consumer: these are operationalized by looking at the importance weight that is attached to each attribute.
■ Beliefs: these are the associations consumers have with the brand; in other words the extent to which they "believe" that a brand performs well on an attribute.

We illustrate the application of this model with the example about nightlife in the Dutch city of Groningen (see Example 4.2).

Example 4.2 Assessment of nightlife in Groningen

The multi-attribute attitude model is used for the assessment of the following three entertainment venues in Groningen: grand café The Three Sisters, "night pub" Warhol (more a club than a pub), and Pintelier, a bar known for its variety of craft beers. The results are shown in Table 4.3. The questionnaire that can be used to get these results is shown in Table 4.2.

Table 4.2 Research questions for measuring importance weights and beliefs

Can you indicate, on a scale from 1 to 10, how important the following are when you go for a night out?

Good music	…
Variety of quality beer	…
Having a good time with friends	…
Dancing	…
Romantic evening with partner	…
Meet new people	…
Meet nice boy/girl	…

Can you evaluate The Three Sisters, Warhol, and Pintelier on the following properties? Again, you can indicate your judgement on a scale from 1 to 10

Good music	…
Variety of quality beer	…
Having a good time with friends	…
Dancing	…
Romantic evening with partner	…
Meet new people	…
Meet nice boy/girl	…

Table 4.3 Illustration of the multi-attribute model

Product attribute	Importance weight (desires)	Beliefs			Brand ratings		
		Three Sisters	Warhol	Pintelier	Three Sisters	Warhol	Pintelier
Good music	6	6	8	3	36	48	18
Variety of quality beer	4	7	1	10	28	4	40
Having a good time with friends	9	7	5	8	63	45	72
Dancing	7	6	8	1	42	56	7
Romantic evening with partner	1	3	2	4	3	2	4
Meet new people	6	5	8	4	30	48	24
Meet nice boy/girl	8	7	9	5	56	72	40
Total					258	275	205

The questionnaire in Table 4.2 lists a number of product attributes. These attributes could have been obtained, in a focus group or in interviews with consumers in the target group, i.e. from preliminary qualitative research. In this example, the list is a mix of attributes (variety of quality beer) and benefits (such as having a good time with friends). The attributes (or benefits) are then presented to respondents in the target group by means of quantitative research: the questionnaire in Table 4.1.

Respondents have to make a judgement about their own desires ("How important are...") and about their beliefs ("Evaluate the following brands on..."). Table 4.3 presents the result for one respondent. This is someone who likes to enjoy a nice time with friends, would like to dance as well, and also would like to meet a nice person.

Different respondents obviously have different importance weights: some people prefer dancing whereas others prefer to taste a variety of beers. As a result, different market segments can be found in such a study, for example a segment that is looking for a romantic evening, a segment that wants to have fun with friends, or a segment that wants to listen to good music. Wishes can also vary depending on the mood of the respondent. Depending on their mood or on the situation, people can be a part of different target groups.

When we look at the beliefs of this respondent, we see that he believes that the Pintelier has a great variety of good beer. However, this is less interesting for this respondent; he especially wants to have a nice evening with friends. This is possible in the Pintelier too, but according to this respondent the probability to meet a nice person here is small.

Not only importance weights but also beliefs can differ from respondent to respondent. For example, someone might believe that the music in Warhol (more alternative night club music) is terrible, while another person can find this music great. After all, we measure the opinions of respondents, not hard facts.

The brand ratings are calculated by multiplying beliefs and weights. For instance, the score for good music is $6 \times 6 = 36$ for The Three Sisters; for Warhol this is $6 \times 8 = 48$.

The overall brand rating is obtained by adding the ratings per attribute. For this respondent, Warhol scored highest, with a score of 275 points. According to the multi-attribute attitude model, this respondent gives the highest attitude score to this venue.

The multi-attribute attitude model thus illustrates that the brand image is a combination of the desires of the consumer and the beliefs of that consumer about this brand. Desires and beliefs relate to product attributes, benefits and/or values, and can be functional, symbolic, or experience-oriented in nature. This is an important point. This type of research often seems to limit itself to functional product characteristics. However, we want to emphasize here that a brand image is generally based on emotional benefits.

The power of the multi-attribute attitude model is not so much that you can "calculate" a preference. After all, making choices is usually more than a chilly calculation but merely a process of unconsciously weighting feelings. The main relevance of the model is that it makes explicit the needs, desires, and beliefs that influence choice behaviour. But this is also a drawback of this model. By emphasizing the complete dissecting of brands in specific attributes it implicitly assumes high involvement. However, as indicated in Chapter 1, many choices are taken under low involvement. Just consider for yourself how often you have decided for a night out as explicit and detailed as described in Example 4.2. And this point brings us back to our earlier discussion on the difference between Sharp's emphasis on availability and the traditional marketing approach.

4.5.2 Brand values

Chapter 3 indicates that people use values to guide them in their choices. But brands are also described in terms of their brand values. **Brand values** are a kind of promise, they indicate what the brand stands for. We refer to the most important values of a brand as the brand's core values. Companies and brands often profile their core values prominently. Unilever, for example, has as core value *vitality* (www.unilever.co.uk) and its major competitor Proctor & Gamble profiles itself with the values *integrity, leadership, ownership, passion for winning,* and *trust* (www.pg.com). Other examples are: *respect, enjoyment, and a passion for quality* (Heineken) and *respect, dignity, care for community, and environmental sustainability* (Starbucks). Example 4.3 presents the value statement of Coca Cola.

Example 4.3 Value statement of The Coca Cola Company

On their website, The Coca Cola Company highlights the following values that serve as a compass for all activities of The Coca Cola Company (explanations of the values taken directly from the company website):

- **Leadership**: *The courage to shape a better future.*
- **Collaboration**: *Leverage collective genius.*
- **Integrity**: *Be real.*
- **Accountability**: *If it is up to you, it's up to me.*
- **Passion**: *Committed in heart and mind.*

■ **Diversity**: *As inclusive as our brands.*
■ **Quality**: *What we do, we do well.*

Source: www.thecoca-colacompany.com

Actually, it is quite strange to talk about brand values or brand personality: people live, have a personality, and live their life according to their values, while brands obviously are not living organisms. But attributing human characteristics to brands does make sense. Brands are often judged as if they were living beings, with human characteristics: brands can be seen as cool, adventurous, sweet, attractive, or fun. Research has also confirmed that people attribute human emotions, personality structures, and goals to brands (Aggarwal & McGill, 2007). Just as some people think sustainability is important and other people find it especially important to have fun, we also feel that some brands represent sustainability, and other brands represent pleasure. Brand management can of course stimulate this kind of associations by explicitly profiling certain values.

The consequence of thinking in brand personality and brand values is that consumers (partly) determine their preferences and choices based on the personality or values that they perceive in the brand. But we can take the parallel between people and brands even one step further. Research has also shown that consumers interpret brand values in a comparable way to their own values (Kostelijk, 2016). In other words the Value Compass applies not only to consumers but also to brands! The website www.valuecompass.nl offers the possibility to create value profiles for brands.

The **value profile of a brand**, the totality of values with which a brand is associated, can thus be displayed with the help of the Value Compass. We demonstrate this here with a number of examples, taken from the study of Kostelijk (2016). In this study, brand values were presented to a sample of Dutch respondents. This sample consisted mainly of students and is therefore not representative of the Dutch population. Figure 4.3 illustrates the brand values of Disney. The darker

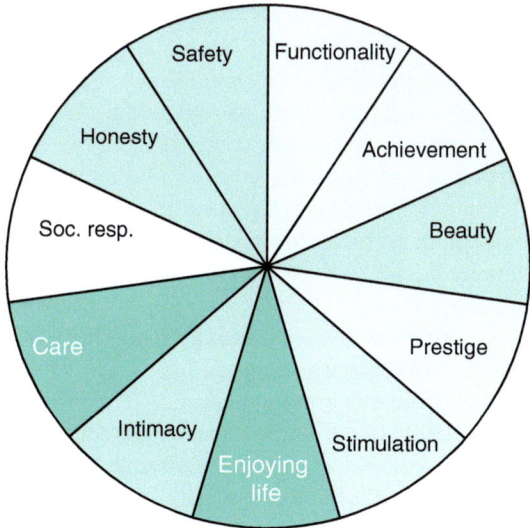

Figure 4.3 **Brand value profile of Disney**

Figure 4.4 **Brand value profile of Toyota**

coloured values are more strongly associated with the Disney brand. We can see that two brand values are perceived to be central to this brand: *care & affection* and *enjoying life*. Disney apparently offers the opportunity to spend a fun time together with friends and family. According to consumers, the brand represents to a far lesser extent values such as reliability, prestige or social responsibility.

In the second profile, Toyota is used as an example. This brand evokes a very different picture and seems to represent values such as safety and functionality, while according to the surveyed consumers the brand also stands for social responsibility. According to Figure 4.4, Toyota is not characterized as a brand that evokes a lot of fun, appearance or prestige.

When comparing the Value Compass of Toyota and Disney, it is striking that the profile of Disney is darker coloured. Overall, Disney apparently evokes stronger associations than Toyota and can therefore be regarded as a "stronger" brand. The question, however, is to what extent we can compare these two brands directly with each other. They operate in very different sectors and the respondents in this study (students) were perhaps more interested in visiting an amusement park than in buying a car. It is generally more useful to compare brand values of brands operating in the same sector. In Figure 4.5 we have made a comparison between three car brands: Audi, Toyota, and Volvo.

Figure 4.5 shows that Audi is a relatively strong brand: the brand scores higher on most values than the other two car brands. Audi distinguishes itself as a stimulating and prestigious brand with an attractive appearance. The brand also stands more for enjoying life than the other two brands. Volvo stands out as a brand that values safety, while the brand also associates with more prestige than Toyota. In comparison with the other two brands, Toyota distinguishes itself primarily as a brand that represents social responsibility.

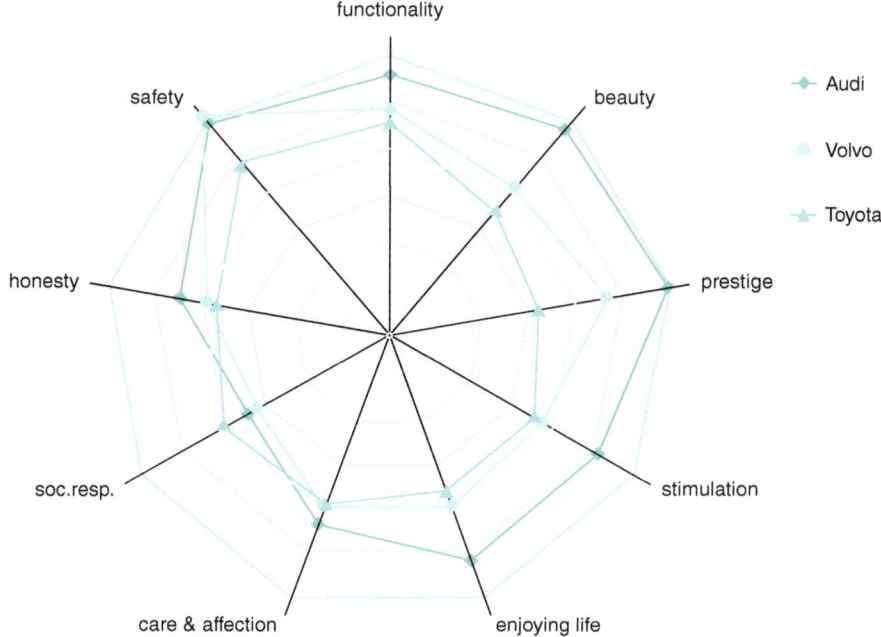

Figure 4.5 Comparison of three car brands

To determine perceived brand values, consumers can judge brands by using Likert-scaled propositions[2] such as:

[Brand X] represents [Value Y]

4.5.3 Brand personality

The brand personality is the description of a brand in terms of personality traits, as if this brand is a person. Sometimes a brand is (consciously or unconsciously) identified with a certain personality, so that this brand can be "characterized" as a certain character. Think for example of Nespresso's George Clooney.

The most well-known **brand personality** model was developed by Aaker (1997). In this model, five personality dimensions are defined, based on which a brand can be described. Aaker uses the following dimensions (see Figure 4.6):

- sincerity: characteristics as friendly, honest, original, or cheerful
- excitement: daring, young, imaginative, trendy
- competence: reliable, intelligent, successful
- sophistication: upper-class, feminine, charming
- ruggedness: masculine, tough, outdoorsy

---

2   The Likert scale is a 5-point scale, ranging from strongly disagree to strongly agree. Example: To the statement "Toyota is fun," the respondent can react with strongly disagree, disagree, agree nor disagree (neutral), agree, or strongly agree.

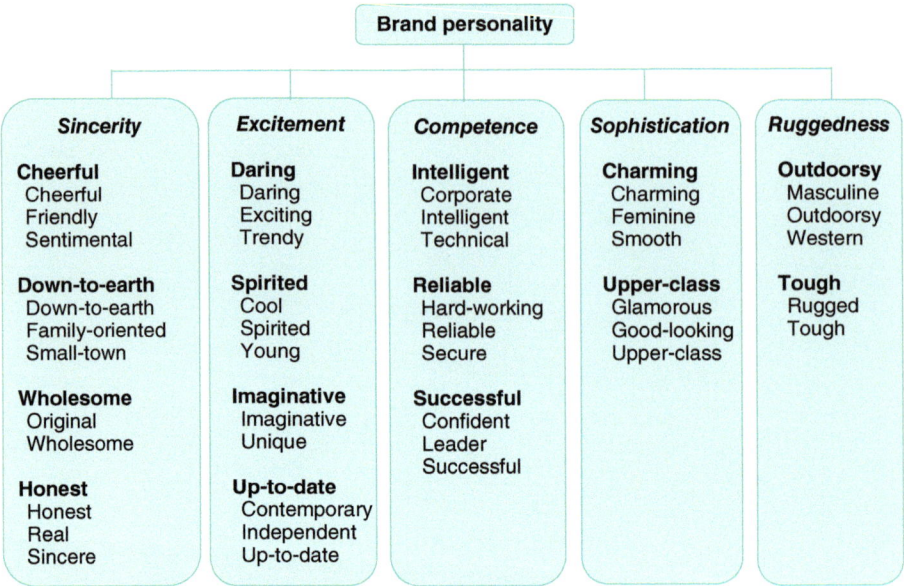

Figure 4.6 **Brand personality dimensions (Aaker, 1997)**

The example of Nike in Figure 4.7 illustrates that the brand personality dimensions can be used as a kind of thermometer for the personality of a brand. This figure, based on a US consumer survey, shows that Nike is seen primarily as an exciting and cool brand, but that the sincerity score lags somewhat behind. Interpretation of personality scores is of course even more interesting when scores can be compared with competing brands.

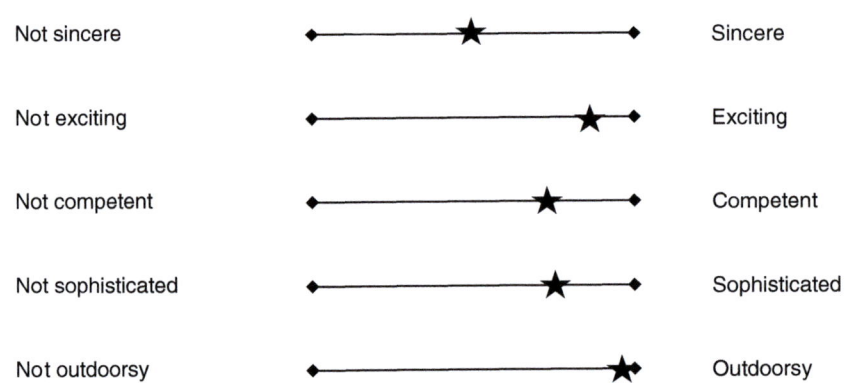

Figure 4.7 **Brand personality dimensions for the Nike brand (based on data from Keller (2012))**

Brand personality dimensions can be translated into personality traits that can be measured with a Likert scale, in a similar procedure as was used to measure brand values. This then leads to statements such as:

Nike is trendy

In her original research, Aaker designated a number of personality traits for measuring the personality dimensions (see Figure 4.6). We have to point out, however, that these original items were developed from American research and that they do not always fit in with other contexts. Concepts such as outdoorsy, tough, and small-town, for example, match with the American spirit in states like Texas and Arizona, but may not match well with the interpretation of brands in the European context. Further research by Aaker illustrated this: in a study with Spanish respondents, the following personality dimensions were found: excitement, sincerity, sophistication, peacefulness, and passion (Aaker, Benet-Martinez, & Garolera, 2001). For specific brand research it may therefore be preferable to first develop items that are specifically tailored to the context of the brand in question by means of focus groups, before quantitatively testing them.

Brand personality and brand values are related concepts. In both cases, human characteristics are attributed to brands. There is, however, an important difference between values and personality traits. Personality properties represent how someone is, while values are personal goals. We can best illustrate this difference with an example (Example 4.4).

Example 4.4 Why we prefer to describe brands in terms of brand values instead of brand personality traits

*Good-looking is both a value in the Value Compass and a personality trait in Aaker's brand personality framework. Good-looking as a trait leads to statements such as: "I am good-looking." Such a statement does say something about how someone is, but it does not necessarily say anything about how someone wants to be. **Being** good-looking (as trait) does not automatically mean that someone **wants to be** good-looking (as value). This is different with values. Values are goals that someone wants to achieve, and this gives a direct relationship with behaviour. Someone who values good looks will do and buy things that help him or her to look good, even if this person is not good-looking. Hence, good-looking as value results in statements such as "I think it is important to look good," and this directs behaviour, for example by putting make-up, wearing fancy clothes, or joining the fitness club.*

The example illustrates that brand values are the goals that the brand wants to achieve; they express what the brand stands for and what the brand would mean for the consumer. Brand values therefore tie in closely with the benefits that the consumer is looking for, something that is also expressed by the connection between benefits and values in the means-end chain (see Section 3.3.2). This relationship is less direct with brand personality (Kostelijk, 2015). This is why we prefer to describe brands in terms of brand values.

4.5.4 Brand archetypes

A variant of brand personality is the brand archetype. An **archetype** is a prototype, a kind of basic model that serves as a standard description for a certain type of personality: the loving mother, the wise elder, the macho Don Juan, and so on. Mark and Pearson (2001) used this concept to define 12 brand archetypes:

- the explorer: the independent explorer (for example Land Rover)
- the outlaw: the rebel; a brand that goes against the rules and the establishment (Harley-Davidson) or tries to compete with the market leader (easyJet versus Ryanair, Avis versus Hertz)
- the jester: the carefree brand that stands for pleasure (Pringles, Ben & Jerry's)
- the lover: seductive and irresistible (Magnum)
- the caregiver: the caring brand (Nivea)
- the everyman: reliable and functional (HEMA, Muji)
- the innocent: the brand that stands for youthful innocence and having a carefree time (Disney, Innocent Smoothies)
- the ruler: the successful leader (Hugo Boss)
- the sage: the wise brand (BBC, Weightwatchers)
- the magician: transforms lives, the brand that helps you to be different than you are (Axe/Lynx, Red Bull) or makes dreams come true (Disney)
- the hero (Nike)
- the creator (Apple)

A difficulty with archetypes is that the names are very subjective and that different people can have different associations with the chosen names.

Photo 4.2 **The carefree jester as archetype: Pringles. Photo released under Pexels license: free for commercial and non-commercial use**

4.5.5 Perceptual mapping

The previous models assume that the consumer consciously envisages which properties, values, or benefits play a role and how important these are. Especially in a situation of low involvement, however, consumers will not consciously consider all sorts of aspects. This does not mean that these aspects do not play a role. Of course, the consumer still buys because of the benefits that the brand delivers, but due to low involvement or routine, these benefits disappear in the background in decision-making and are no longer consciously experienced. But even in a situation of high involvement, not all desires are expressed. For example, it is quite possible that one of the reasons to buy a BMW is to impress the neighbours; but it is unlikely that this is mentioned in a questionnaire.

In the section on projective techniques (Subsection 4.4.2) we already discussed a number of methods to reveal subconscious or unconscious motives. However, there is also a quantitative technique that positions brands in relation to each other, without asking the consumer for a detailed comparison. This method is called **perceptual mapping**. In a perceptual map, brands are placed in a two-dimensional space. Such a perceptual map is also called a **joint space**. Figure 4.8 gives an example of a joint space for the car market.

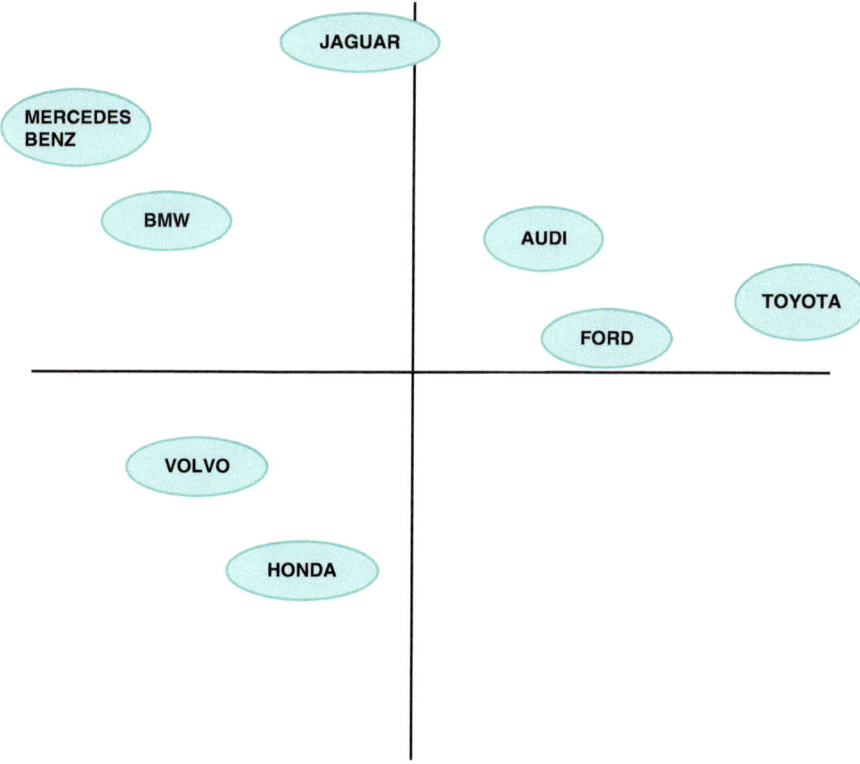

Figure 4.8 **Joint space for the car market**

Perceptual mapping is a technique that can be executed in a fairly simple way. To make the perceptual map in Figure 4.8, you only need to measure the attitude towards a brand on a Likert scale, with a question such as "I like BRAND X." Table 4.2 gives an example of the survey questions that can be used for this purpose.

The idea behind perceptual mapping is the following. If, on average, Mercedes enthusiasts also like BMW relatively more often, these brands will be relatively close to each other in the joint space. And if BMW enthusiasts have a little more appreciation for Audi than the people who like Mercedes, then BMW will also be slightly closer to Audi in the perceptual map. Perceptual mapping uses **multidimensional scaling (MDS)** (Borg & Groenen, 2005). This is the same technique that Schwartz (1992) and Kostelijk (2016) used to map their value systems. This analysis calculates the distances between the brands on the basis of the answers given and then places them in a perceptual space. MDS can easily be executed in a statistical program such as SPSS (Statistical Package for the Social Sciences; see the note in Table 4.4).

If you take a good look at the joint space in Figure 4.8, you will notice that the brands are placed here, but that the horizontal and vertical axes have no name. That makes sense: after all, we asked about the appreciation for a number of brands, not the reason why people appreciate it. Yet people, consciously or unconsciously, have certain motives why they value a brand. These reasons are the implicit reasons of why brands are positioned on a certain location in the perceptual map, but they have not yet been specified. If we do want to say something more specific about the brand image, it is therefore necessary to name the axes. The naming of the dimensions often takes place on the basis of the judgement of the responsible manager or the researcher. For example, in Figure 4.8 the horizontal axis could represent economy

Table 4.4 **Survey questions for perceptual mapping**

Below you can find a number of statements in which we ask your opinion about a number of car brands. Can you indicate for each statement to what extent you agree, on a scale from 1 (totally disagree) to 5 (totally agree)?[a]

	1	*2*	*3*	*4*	*5*
I like Audi	O	O	O	O	O
I like BMW	O	O	O	O	O
I like Dacia	O	O	O	O	O
I like Ford	O	O	O	O	O
I like Honda	O	O	O	O	O
I like Jaguar	O	O	O	O	O
I like Mercedes-Benz	O	O	O	O	O
I like Mitsubishi	O	O	O	O	O
I like Toyota	O	O	O	O	O
I like Volvo	O	O	O	O	O

a   *For the interested reader: enter the results of a survey as in this table in SPSS and then go to ANALYZE. Then in the pop-up menu click SCALE. Here you find three variants of the multidimensional scaling: PREFSCAL, PROXSCAL, and ALSCAL. The authors' favourite: PREFSCAL.*

in use and the vertical axis for the perceived prestige of the brand. A perceptual map can also be presented to a focus group, as input for a group discussion about the positioning of the presented brands.

Finally, we would like to point out an extra possibility of perceptual mapping: showing the preferences of the respondents. Based on the pattern of the answers, it is possible to determine the preference of a respondent. This works in the following way. Suppose that someone appreciates Audi, Honda, and Toyota; then his ideal car would be a combination of these three brands. This ideal car would then be placed somewhere between these three cars in the joint space. MDS is able to determine for each respondent where his or her ideal brand would be. This preference is then indicated by means of a point in the perceptual map. A survey of let's say 300 consumers then leads to a joint space with 300 points, with each point representing the ideal of a consumer. Figure 4.9 shows the brand space with the car brands again, but now including the ideal points as well.

In reality, ideal points often appear in clusters. Such a cloud of nearby points is actually a segment of consumers. For example, Figure 4.9 shows a segment that is interested in a car such as an Audi or a Ford, while there is also a cluster of consumers in the upper right-hand corner of the figure, of whom the ideal car is apparently not yet on the market. This might seduce Toyota to reposition itself by

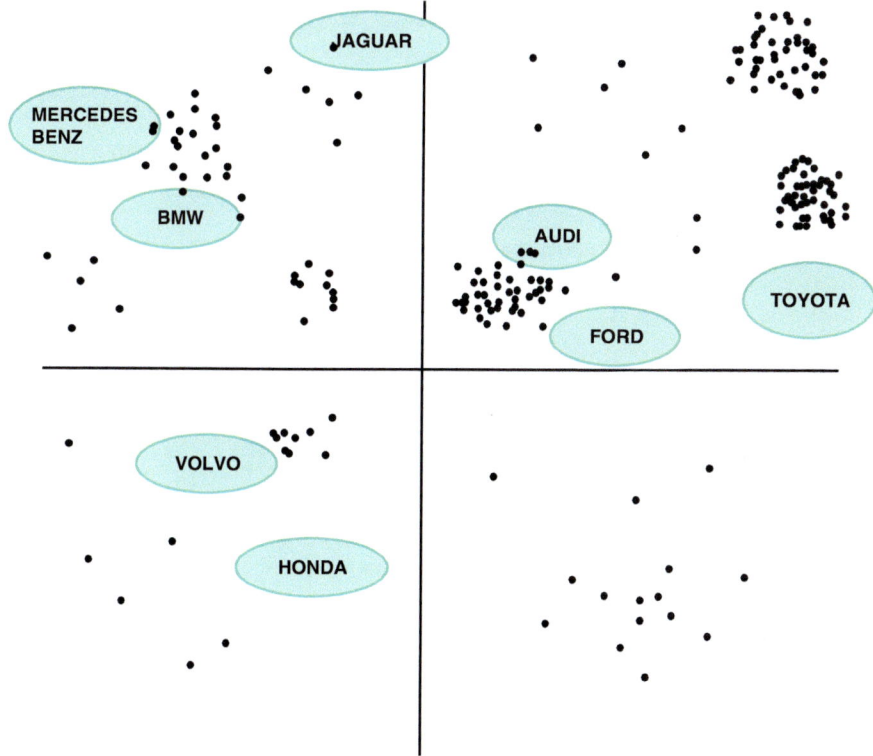

Figure 4.9 **Perceptual map with ideal points**

slightly strengthening the prestige of the brand (if the vertical axis indeed represents prestige).

The combination of consumer ideals and the position of the competing brands implies that perceptual mapping provides insight into the brand image of the competitors as well as in the existence of potential target groups. This makes perceptual mapping not only easy to apply but also a powerful tool for positioning research.

4.5.6 Brand Asset Valuator

The BAV is an instrument developed by Young & Rubicam in 2013. The BAV is not directly an instrument that measures brand image; it is more an indicator for the consequences that a certain image has on brand equity. In the model two dimensions are used to measure brand equity: brand vitality (growth potential) and brand stature (the current power of the brand). For **brand vitality** two indicators are used in this model:

1. Differentiation: this concerns the extent to which the brand differs from other brands.
2. Relevance: this concerns the extent to which the brand meets the needs of the consumer. This is in line with the interpretation of the concept of brand salience in this chapter.

Brand stature also consists of two indicators:

1. The esteem for the brand: this concerns the degree to which brands are valued and create good feelings. Esteem is related to the degree of loyalty for a brand.
2. Brand knowledge: this concerns the extent to which the consumer is familiar with the brand and the extent to which the brand is part of that consumer's life.

Based on global consumer research, in which so far around 800,000 consumers from more than 50 countries have participated, the image of a large number of brands has been monitored. In this research, the four dimensions were converted into a large number of questions about image and user aspects of these brands.

The BAV model assumes that the strength of a brand consists of the combination of brand vitality and brand stature. These two dimensions can be represented visually as the two axes of what Young and Rubicam describes as the **PowerGrid** (see Figure 4.10).

Four types of brands are distinguished in the PowerGrid. The *new and unfocused brands* are brands that are new in the market, and therefore have not yet gained any fame and appreciation. According to the logic of the model, these brands must put their energy into strengthening their relevance and differentiating themselves. The upper left quadrant consists of *niche players and unrealized*

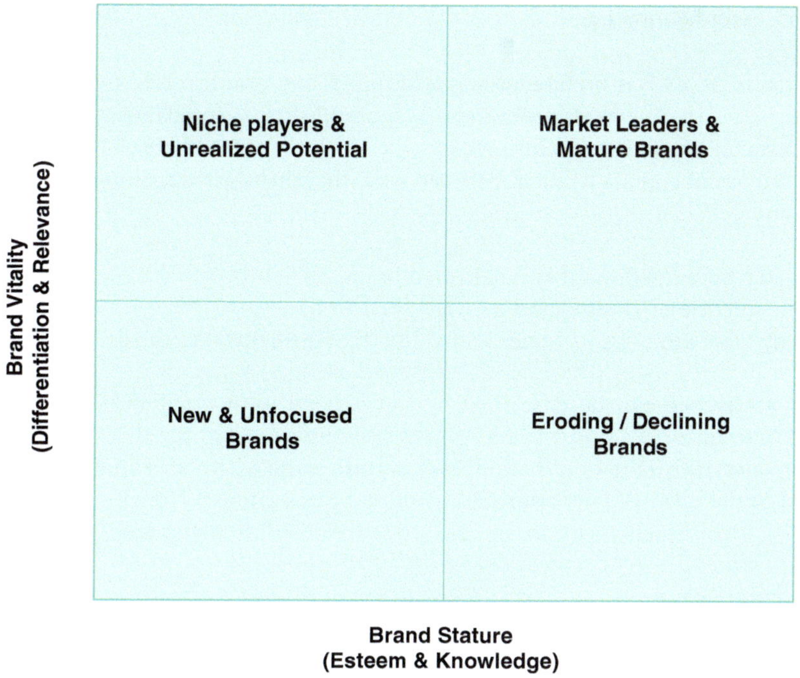

Figure 4.10 **Brand Asset Valuator**

potential: brands that are already relevant and distinctive, and are therefore vital, but have not yet translated this into a dominant position in the market. Think for example brands such as Instagram or Snapchat. If brands, because of their vitality, become known to growing number of people, and if they are also increasingly appreciated by everyone, they shift to the upper right quadrant: *market leaders and mature brands*. It contains brands such as Heinz, Pampers, or IKEA, but also a number of brands that have grown online. For example, a brand like Facebook has in recent years made the switch from emerging to established brand. Until a few years ago, only students and people who described themselves as "trendy" had a Facebook account, while nowadays everyone can be found on Facebook. Sometimes it is argued that Facebook is facing decreasing vitality partly due to competition with Instagram (also owned by Facebook). Finally, if the vitality of a brand decreases, the brand ends up in the lower right quadrant: *eroding and declining brands*. Today, we see decreasing vitality in many retail brands that struggle to keep their position against the fierce competition from Amazon, Alibaba, or other online giants. These retail brands have in many countries a successful heritage of decades, and are appreciated by a large audience, but due to the rise of the internet their relevance has decreased. This has translated into decreasing numbers of visitors and decreasing sales, and a strategic struggle for deciding about the future of the brand.

4.6 Brand preference

Consumers develop a preference for a brand if this brand meets their needs and desires better than competing brands. The brand then succeeds in delivering what the consumer is looking for. This means that at one or more levels of the means-end chain the brand realizes a match between what the consumer is looking for and what the brand delivers:

- match between desired and delivered brand attributes
- match between desired and delivered benefits
- match between brand values and values that are central to the consumer

Brand preference can be described in comparison with other brands ("I prefer brand X to brand Y"). But brand preference might also imply that the consumer feels involved with the brand and feels a certain bond with the brand, a certain degree of **brand loyalty**. This bond can be more or less intense. Here we describe four levels of involvement, with an increasing sense of relationship with the brand:

1. brand affect
2. brand love
3. brand community
4. brand engagement

Brand preference is a result of the favourable associations that the brand realizes with the consumer. We already indicated in Section 4.2.3 that the development of a preference generally not takes place in situations of low involvement. These are the situations in which the consumer buys a brand because he knows it, without further thought or comparisons with other brands. In such situations there will hardly be any feeling of brand affect, brand love, or brand engagement. Marketers who have to deal with such buying behaviour (and that is according to Sharp widespread) can actually skip the rest of this section. For the rest of our readership we now discuss the four forms of brand preference.

4.6.1 Brand affect

Marketers like to see consumers having a good feeling about their brand. This is **brand affect**. Brand affect can be measured with Likert-scaled statements such as:

- *I like brand X.*
- *I am satisfied with brand X.*
- *Brand X is nice (or sympathetic, attractive, or something similar).*

An explicit form of affect is created by Facebook. Consumers can communicate their appreciation for a brand (or a person or an event) by clicking on the "like" button.

Someone who likes a brand is not yet a fan of that brand or a brand ambassador. Just think of yourself: not every time you click on the "like" button on Facebook; there is a deep emotional relationship. It is just a first step.

Photo 4.3 Facebook uses the "thumbs up" symbol to express "likes". Public domain, with permission of Facebook, Inc.

4.6.2 Brand love

Brand love concerns the degree of passion (love) that consumers feel for a certain brand. This goes a level deeper than mere satisfaction or a "good feeling" about that brand. After all, satisfaction in itself does not mean passion or love, but you need this passion to make a customer a true ambassador of the brand. You can hardly expect WOM advertising without a passion for the brand. True brand love means passion, a consumer who declares his unconditional love for a certain brand. Brand love can be measured with statements such as:

- *I love this brand.*
- *I am passionate about this brand.*
- *This brand makes me completely happy.*
- *This brand is great.*

Photo 4.4 An expression of brand love for Starbucks. © Erik Kostelijk

Research has indeed shown that brand love leads to a greater degree of brand loyalty, and more positive WOM advertising (Carroll & Ahuvia, 2006). Love or passion for a brand was used by advertising agency Saatchi & Saatchi to describe brands as "Lovemarks." Lovemarks are brands that receive both love and respect from customers and know how to touch customers in their hearts (Roberts, 2005). On the website of Saatchi & Saatchi this is explained as: "Lovemarks reach your heart as well as your mind, creating an intimate, emotional connection that you cannot live without. Ever." In the chapter on brand values (Chapter 3) we had already seen that a Lovemark exhibits at least the following three brand values:

- *Mystery.* A Lovemark has its own story, connects with the dreams of its customers, and offers them inspiration.
- *Sensuality.* A Lovemark stimulates the five senses (feeling, seeing, smelling, hearing, and tasting).
- *Intimacy.* Consumers feel commitment, sympathy, and love for a Lovemark.

The following citation illustrates the love that someone can feel for his Lovemark, in this case Skechers shoes:

> *This is the highest quality brand I've ever used! With Skechers I feel more confident, more fashionable, and more stylish than before. I'm always wearing them and they're a perfect match for every event. Love you so much, Skechers!.*
>
> (Source: www.lovemarks.com)

According to the Lovemarks' website, important Lovemarks are for instance Apple, Guinness, Lego, and IKEA.

4.6.3 Brand community

Creating a **brand community** is nowadays a hot topic for many companies and brands. The importance of social media for marketing is strongly increasing; many companies use Facebook or similar media to showcase their brands. After all, companies and brands want to be present on social media and use these media to strengthen the relationship with the customer. For this purpose, brand communities are created via for example Facebook and forums. In such a brand community, a group of users or fans of a brand share their commitment or passion for this brand. But brand communities are obviously not reserved for social media only. A brand community is therefore a group of brand enthusiasts who use the community as a platform to share their love for the brand. The extent to which someone sees himself as a member of a certain brand community can be measured with statements such as:

- *I feel a bond with other users of this brand.*
- *Through this brand I get in touch with nice people.*
- *I would like to share my experiences with this brand with others.*

Members of a brand community therefore not only feel an important relationship with the brand but also a strong bond with the other users of the brand (Muniz & O'Guinn, 2001). Brand community goes a step further than brand love: you are not only admirer of a certain brand, but you also want to share this with others.

A classic example of a brand community relates to the Harley-Davidson brand (see Example 4.5).

Example 4.5 Brand community of Harley-Davidson

Already in 1983 the Harley Owners Group (HOG) was founded, a worldwide motorcycle club owned by the Harley-Davidson company. The club (approximately one million members worldwide, mainly in the United States but also many members in Europe) allows Harley-Davidson to maintain direct contact with its customers. The club is divided into different regional chapters; about 1,400 of them exist worldwide. For Harley-Davidson "Hog" (pig) is more or less a honorary title: they call their own product Hog and the factory "Hog Heaven." The buyer of a new Harley-Davidson motorcycle receives a free one-year membership with the HOG motorcycle club and benefits from offers that are specifically tailored to the Harley-Davidson driver.

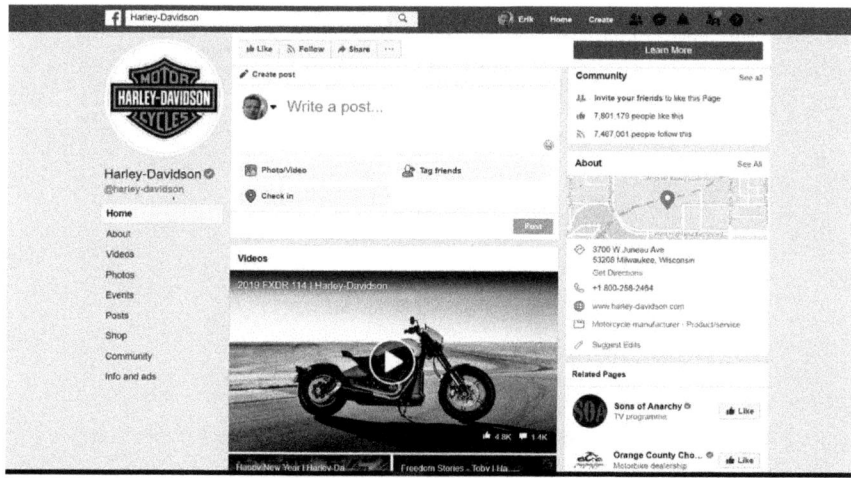

Photo 4.5 The Facebook community of Harley-Davidson has almost eight million likes. Screenshot provided with permission of Harley-Davidson, Inc.

It is important to repeat here one of our earlier comments. The brand preference phase will often be largely skipped in situations of low involvement. In such a situation, the effectiveness of a brand community is also limited. This is a warning for brands that put a lot of energy in their social media presence while they are active in a market with predominantly low involvement. In Chapter 7 we further discuss the use of social media.

4.6.4 Brand engagement

Brands can do more than create a relationship with others. They even have the opportunity to become an integral part of someone's identity (Edson Escalas & Bettman, 2005). For example, consumers can show others who they are or what they stand for, by buying or using certain brands. This is clearly visible in brands that function as status symbols. For example, there is a clear difference in the image between the typical BMW driver ("handsome sportive guy") and the typical Jaguar driver ("stylish old money"). But a brand can also become an extension of yourself in other ways, and, as it were, become part of your own identity. For example, joining or donating to an organization such as the World Wildlife Fund or Human Rights Watch can occupy a very central place in someone's life, which could eventually lead you to sacrifice your free weekend to organize a fundraiser to raise money for these organizations. The photo shows another example: a brand like Hello Kitty can become so strongly part of your own identity that you want to dress or behave completely in the style of this brand.

Photo 4.6 **"Hello Kitty" stimulates brand engagement. Source: istockphoto.com.**

The extent to which a brand is part of someone's identity is called **brand engagement**. It can be measured by using statements such as:

- I have a special personal relationship with this brand.
- I feel a personal bond with this brand.

A high level of brand engagement ensures a far-reaching form of brand loyalty. To create this ultimate form of commitment, it is very important to create a match between the identity of the brand and the identity of the users of that brand. After all, you have to touch the user in his heart.

4.7 Brand behaviour

The ultimate goal of successful positioning is that customers start and keep on buying the brand. In most cases, however, we want to achieve more than just a one-off purchase. Preferably customers continue to buy and distribute positive mouth-to-mouth in the meantime: the marketer prefers to see that every customer becomes an ambassador for the brand.

4.7.1 Purchase intention

Marketing literature often refers to **purchase intention**: the extent to which a consumer intends to buy a brand. This is measured in research with statements such as:

- *The next time I buy chocolate, I buy Milka.*

It makes sense to ask for purchase intention in market research. After all, it is easier to measure in a questionnaire than the purchase itself: the actual purchase takes place in a later stage and to keep track of consumer purchases, often more complex tracking methods are required such as asking consumers to keep a diary of their purchases, or in case of online purchases, the use of analytics. However, asking for purchase intentions has an important disadvantage. Intentions do not always lead to an actual purchase. By asking intentions, consumers are going to rationalize what they will do the next time. And then well-known brands will generally surface: few people will indicate in a survey that next time they will buy a private label chocolate. But once you arrive in the supermarket you might notice that the private label is on sale and also looks good. Consequently, intention measures overestimate brands such as Milka or Nestlé (in case of chocolate) and sometimes can be seen more as an indicator of awareness than as a purchase indicator.

In addition, actual purchase also depends on a number of preconditions. Not only the availability of the product but also the availability of the required budget is very important: "I would like to buy that great apartment, but my bank thinks otherwise." Research has shown that purchase intention gives a good prediction of behaviour in only about half of the cases (Sheeran, 2002).

Based on the principle that past behaviour is often the best predictor of the future, there is an alternative. You can also ask consumers what they did last time: "What brand of chocolate did you buy last time?"

Brand loyalty implies that the consumer repeatedly buys the same brand: every time the consumer buys chocolate, he buys Milka chocolate. In the ideal world, a loyal customer will not only always buy the same brand, but he will also want to tell others about it. In that case the loyal customer becomes an ambassador for your brand.

4.7.2 Ambassadors stimulate word-of-mouth

WOM is an important consequence of a good relationship between customer and brand. Brand preference and brand loyalty are important conditions before customers proceed to positive WOM.

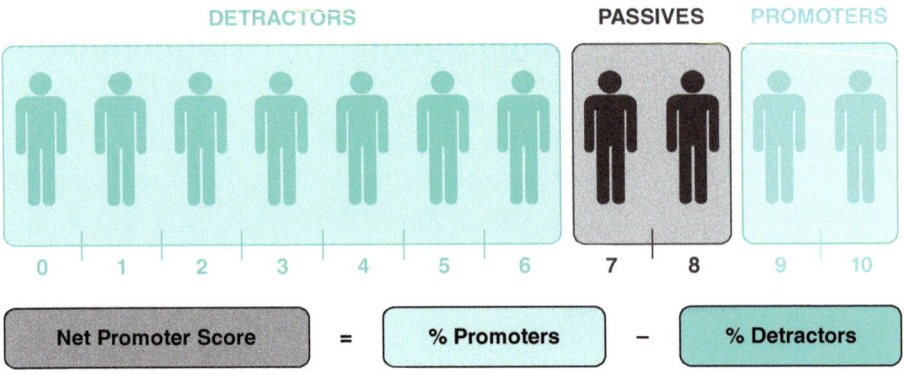

Figure 4.11 Net Promoter Score

WOM is an indicator of the extent to which someone wants to act as an ambassador for a certain brand. This makes positive WOM an important indicator for the success of brand positioning. With the rise of social media, the importance of WOM has increased enormously. People can influence a large number of others through blogs, Facebook, or Instagram with the positive or negative comments they make about a certain brand. We also need to realize that people are often much more likely to express their dissatisfaction than to tell others that everything went as planned. A complaint comes quicker than an ambassador. This emphasizes the importance of continuously monitoring what people say about your brand, and it also emphasizes the importance of continuing to strive for excellent customer experiences.

Creating positive WOM has become an important objective for many marketing and communication activities. After all, a negative remark is extremely harmful for a brand. And a recommendation by friends or acquaintances is much more effective than any commercial message. The importance of WOM has received a lot of attention since the publication of the article *The one number you need to grow* (Reichheld, 2003). Central to this article is the **Net Promoter Score (NPS)**. The NPS measures customer ambassadorship by asking customers to indicate on a ten-point scale how likely they are to recommend the brand or organization to friends and family. Subsequently, the respondents are divided into Promoters (scores of 9–10), Passives (scores of 7–8), and Detractors (6 and lower) (see Figure 4.11). The NPS is then calculated by subtracting the percentage of detractors from the percentage of promoters.

The NPS is a popular benchmark and is currently used by many companies, including Apple and Philips. Reichheld even states that the NPS is the most important indicator that a manager needs in order to measure the loyalty of his customers.

Table 4.5 gives averages of the NPS score by industry. For individual companies, the score may be higher or lower than this average.

Because of the cultural sensitivity of the instrument, it is not wise to compare NPS scores between countries. We have to keep in mind, for instance, that the average

Table 4.5 Net Promoter Score: industry averages

Industry	NPS rating (October 3, 2018)
Apparel & fashion	43
Electronics	52
Fast food	33
Supermarkets	29
Car manufacturers	44
Entertainment	22

Source: www.npsbenchmarks.com.

NPS score varies from country to country: compared to the United States, consumers in Europe tend to give lower scores for the same level of satisfaction.

Although there is no academic evidence that NPS is a better indicator than other criteria, measuring the level of recommendation is an interesting thought that approaches expected behaviour. The interesting aspect is that customers who rate your brand with a 7 or even an 8 will not recommend you! This only happens with a 9 or higher. This explains why Veldhoen and Van Slooten (2010) propagate that 9+ experiences should be created.

Summary

The focus of this chapter is brand image. Brand image relates to the associations that consumers have with the brand. We made a distinction between mindshare and heartshare. Mindshare is the degree to which the brand is "top of mind," i.e. the degree to which consumers think about the brand at the moment that they feel a certain need. Brand positioning focused on creating mindshare implies that the purpose is to include the brand in the evoked set of the consumer.

Heartshare relates to the extent to which the brand image matches wishes and preferences of consumers. Heartshare is developed if the brand manages to evoke favourable and unique associations. The purpose of creating heartshare is to establish strong, positive, and distinctive brand associations.

A favourable brand image is important for a brand. After all, a good image leads to brand preference, and if consumers prefer a brand, then it is more likely that they buy the brand or talk positively about it with others. We have also seen in this chapter that, certainly in a situation of low involvement, mindshare alone can be enough to realize brand behaviour. After all, with low involvement, you buy the brand that comes to mind first, without taking a close look at brand associations of competing brands.

The problem with such things as brand awareness, brand image, or brand preference is that they are not simply known. They have to be measured first. That is why we have given extensive attention in this chapter to measuring these concepts. Table 4.6 summarizes this point. The nightlife venue "The Three Sisters" in the Dutch city of Groningen was taken as an example.

Table 4.6 Measurement of brand image, brand preference, and brand behaviour

Positioning dimension	Indicator	Example question/statement
Mindshare (evoked set)	*Brand recognition* *Brand recall* *TOMA* *Brand salience*	*Have you heard of "The Three sisters"?* *Which pubs in Groningen do you know?* *The brand that is mentioned first in the question "Which pubs in Groningen do you know?"* *If you plan to go to a pub in Groningen, which of the following pubs would you consider?*
Heartshare (associations)	*Brand attributes:* *- beliefs* *- importance* *Benefits:* *- beliefs* *- importance* *Values:* *- beliefs (brand values)* *- importance (consumer values)*	*"The Three Sisters" has good music* *Good music is important to me when I go for a night out* *"The Three Sisters" is a good place to dance* *Dancing is important to me when I go for a night out* *"The Three Sisters" represents sustainability/romance/coziness* *Sustainability/romance/coziness is important to me when I go for a night out*
Brand preference	*Brand affect* *Brand love* *Brand community* *Brand engagement*	*I like "The Three Sisters"* *I love "The Three Sisters"* *A night out in "The Three Sisters" makes me completely happy* *"The Three Sisters" is great* *I feel a bond with other visitors of "The Three Sisters"* *I would like to share my experiences in "The Three Sisters" with others* *I have a special personal relationship with "The Three Sisters"* *I feel a personal bond with "The Three Sisters"*
Brand behaviour	*Word-of-mouth (NPS)* *Purchase intention*	*On a scale from 0 to 10, how likely is it that you would recommend "The Three Sisters" to a friend or colleague?* *The next time I will go for a night out in Groningen, I will come to "The Three Sisters"*

Chapter 5

Brand identity

5.1 An introduction to brand identity

Positioning activities aim to bring the brand perception of the target group in line with the brand experience desired by brand management. Brand image (as experienced by the target group) must therefore correspond as much as possible with the identity of the brand. Before the brand can be positioned towards the target group, it is important to have the identity of the brand clearly in mind. That is why we now pay extensive attention to brand identity.

The identity of a brand is reflected in the core values of that brand. In Chapter 3 we formulated **six conditions** with respect to **brand values**:

1. The core values of a brand reflect the conviction that something is important for that brand.
2. Brand values motivate to action.
3. Brand values are choice criteria; they determine in what the brand should invest.
4. Brand values transcend specific situations. That is why brand values are relevant for all stakeholders.
5. Brand values can be prioritized: some values are more important for a brand than other values.
6. The combination of brand values determines the identity of a brand, and consequently, the positioning of that brand. Because the relevance of values differs from brand to brand, different brands also have different priorities and thus make different choices for their positioning.

In this chapter, brand identity is discussed on the basis of these six conditions. Every condition is discussed in a separate section: what does this mean for the brand? What are the consequences? Before we proceed, however, Section 5.2 first elaborates on what brand identity really is and how it can be measured.

5.2 Identity and image

In Chapter 2 brand identity was defined as the core of what the brand actually is, the brand's own personality. The core values of the brand are reflected in the **brand identity**. This sounds very nice, but where does that brand identity come from? Is it sufficient for the marketing manager to define a list of good-sounding core values and title them "The identity of our brand"? To start with the latter: that's of course not how it works. Cees van Riel, an authority in the field of corporate communication, describes identity as the set of characteristics that the members of the organization see as typical for their own organization (Van Riel, 2010). According to Van Riel, it is therefore not only the opinion of management, but identity concerns everyone in the organization that has to do with the brand: identity is "inside" the people and culture of an organization.

In this section we discuss the concept of identity according to the model of Birkigt and Stadler (1986). Then we discuss the types of identity as distinguished by Balmer and Grayser (2002). Finally, we take a closer look at the measurement of brand identity.

5.2.1 The identity model of Birkigt and Stadler

According to Birkigt and Stadler (1986), identity consists of four components (Figure 5.1):

1. personality
2. behaviour
3. communication
4. symbols

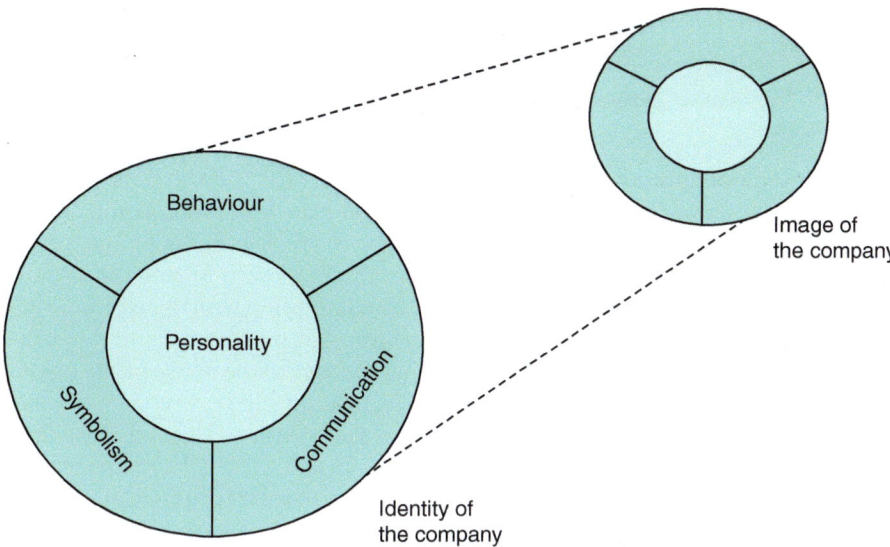

Figure 5.1 **Adapted from the model of Birkigt and Stadler (1986)**

Personality is the core of identity according to this model. Birkigt and Stadler describe this as: *"das manifestierte Selbstverständnis des Unternehmens"* (the manifestation of the company's self-perception). Symbols are things like logos and visual design of a brand, but also George Clooney can be considered more or less a symbol for Nespresso. Behaviour can be described as the way in which a brand actually presents itself to the outside world, for example in products or activities. Communication is the way in which the brand claims to present itself. There is a difference between words and actions. For example, a service provider can say that people are very customer-oriented (communication), but long waiting times and not very knowledgeable employees at the customer service department (behaviour) can give a completely different impression.

It makes sense that personality is the core of identity. In the **Birkigt and Stadler model**, the other three aspects are seen as *components* of the identity. But it is also conceivable to consider these three aspects as the *consequences* of a certain identity. Then the logic is: a brand or organization has a certain personality. And because of that personality, the organization exhibits a certain behaviour (in which communication can also be considered a form of behaviour) and chooses a certain symbolism. Communication, symbolism, and behaviour thus in fact constitute the external appearance of identity. Van Riel (2010) states that behaviour (the way in which a brand presents itself to the outside world) has a much greater influence on the image than symbolism and communication. He states that about 90% of reputation and image is a consequence of behaviour, and communication and symbolism only affect the remaining 10%.

The concept of identity is – certainly in communication literature – often used for the entire organization. This also happens in the model of Birkigt and Stadler. It is then referred to as **corporate identity**. The addition of the word "corporate" suggests that the concept of identity is limited to organizations as a whole. According

Figure 5.2 **The relation between identity and image**

to us, however, not only companies such as Unilever but also individual brands (e.g. Dove, Magnum) have an identity. In our description below the word identity refers to both corporate brands and individual brands.

The model of Birkigt and Stadler establishes a link between identity on the one hand and brand image on the other. However, the relationship with image is not very clear in the model. The most important distinction that we can make between the two terms is that identity is internal whereas image relates to the image of the organization among target groups (i.e. externally). The relationship between identity and image becomes more obvious when we talk about **shared vision**. The shared vision is specific to an organization and can be seen as the guidelines for all communication of that organization. The identity counts as one of the elements of this shared vision (Van Riel, 2010): the brand identity serves as the (shared) point of departure for positioning the brand towards its target group(s). After all, the identity of the brand forms the basis for the brand image that one wishes to create in the target groups. In Figure 5.2 (which is a replication of Figure 2.3) we graphically represented the relationship between identity and image.

It makes sense to use the brand identity as the point of departure for the brand positioning, but there are two reasons why it is less easy than it seems:

1.   There is not one single brand identity.
2.   It is difficult to measure identity unequivocally.

With respect to the first issue it can be said that "the" identity does not exist. Identity is trapped in the people and culture of the organization, but different people within the organization will have different ideas about it. Management usually has specific ideas about the desired appearance of the brand, but the question is whether communication, symbolism, and behaviour of the brand actually match management's perception. There can be a lot of noise between the ideas of the management and the actual execution. Balmer and Grayser (2002) distinguish five different types of identity, which we discuss in the next section.

5.2.2 Types of identity according to Balmer and Grayser

Balmer and Grayser (2002) distinguish the following types of identity:

1.   The *ideal identity*: this is the optimal position that an organization can occupy in a certain market, given the capabilities of the organization and the context in which it operates. This ideal identity cannot be determined objectively, but can be deduced from a thorough internal and external analysis.
2.   The *desired identity*: this is the identity that top management hopes and wishes to achieve. One would expect this to correspond with the ideal identity, but that

does not have to be the case. This is because top management develops a certain vision for the brand, formed by a combination of rational but sometimes also more emotional elements.

3. The **communicated identity**: this is the way in which an organization or brand presents itself to the outside world through communication and symbols.
4. The **actual identity** relates to behaviour: the activities and performances of the brand in the market. The difference between communicated and actual identity becomes clear when the brand promises certain things in communication, but does not deliver them.

Balmer and Geyser also distinguish a fifth type, namely the **perceived identity**. Perceived identity can be considered imagery, the way in which the brand is perceived by the stakeholders. The perceived identity of the brand is what we describe in this book as the **brand image**, the sum of all impressions and feelings that customers and other stakeholders have about the brand. We define **brand positioning** as all activities of the organization to bring the brand image in line with the desired identity.

Differences between actual and desired identity can be caused by a difference in perception between top management and other employees about what the identity is and what it should be. This discrepancy is particularly important in service organizations. Service is after all people's work. In service marketing, extensive measurement methods have been developed in which the quality of service is related to differences between desired and actual service. A well-known example is the **SERVQUAL model**. For a more detailed explanation, we refer to more specialized literature on service marketing.

This brings us to the second complication in the use of brand identity as a starting point for positioning: the unambiguous measurement of the brand identity.

5.2.3 Measuring brand identity

Identity is more difficult to measure than image, also given the differences in types of identity as described in the previous section. When researching the identity of a brand, it is therefore foremost important to carefully define which type of identity is being measured.

When measuring identity, interviews can be done with management and other employees in an organization. In an interview, they can be asked what the brand stands for. Such a direct question is probably useful for management but may be too abstract for other employees. Moreover, there is a risk that employees will discuss the formal line of management. An alternative is to use **laddering** techniques (the same technique as discussed in the chapter about brand image) (Van Rekom, 1997). When using laddering for measuring brand identity, the following questions can be used as a first start:

- What is your job?
- What exactly do you do in your daily work?
- Why do you do that that way?
- Why is this important for [brand X]?

A laddering interview aimed at uncovering identity starts with tangible aspects such as the position and activities of the employee. Then the interview zooms in through further questions. This makes brand identity more tangible during the conversation and establishes a relationship between the core of the employee's own activities and the core values of the brand. By engaging in conversations with several employees, differences between management's opinion and the opinions of other groups of employees also emerge.

Further understanding of the brand identity can be obtained by applying the multi-attribute attitude model as described in Section 4.5.1. If exactly the same questions are used in identity measurement as in image measurement, this also offers a good opportunity to compare identity and image and to identify possible gaps. If an important gap emerges, this might motivate a new direction for marketing or communication activities.

We argued that the core values of the brand are embedded in the brand identity. This makes brand identity the expression of these core values. Brand values, and therefore brand identity, have to meet a number of conditions, as indicated in Section 5.1. We now go deeper into each of these conditions.

1. Brand values are a conviction: Section 5.3.
2. Brand values motivate action: Section 5.4.
3. Brand values force choice: Section 5.5.
4. Brand values – relevant to all stakeholders: Section 5.6.
5. Brand values prioritize: Section 5.7.
6. Brand values guide brand positioning: Section 5.8.

5.3 Brand identity is a conviction

Brand values, and consequently the brand identity, have to reflect what is important for the brand. As such, **brand values are the conviction** that these matters are important for the brand. This conviction can often be traced back to the vision for the brand, as formulated by management. This formulation is sometimes explicit, for example in the form of a **mission statement**. The mission statement of Starbucks in Example 5.1 illustrates this. A distinction can be made between mission and vision (Alsem, 2019). A mission is what the company is and does; a **vision or ambition** is what the company wants to achieve in the future (see also Chapter 2).

Example 5.1 The mission of Starbucks (www.starbucks.com)

The mission of Starbucks is: "to inspire and nurture the soul - one person, one cup and one neighbourhood at a time." To this end, Starbucks lists a number of principles, which are defined around the company's main stakeholders (growers, employees, customers, shareholders, and the community in a more general sense).

Our coffee
It has always been, and will always be, about quality. We're passionate about ethically sourcing the finest coffee beans, roasting them with great care, and improving the lives of people who grow them. We care deeply about all of this; our work is never done.

Our partners
We're called partners, because it's not just a job, it's our passion. Together, we embrace diversity to create a place where each of us can be ourselves. We always treat each other with respect and dignity. And we hold each other to that standard.

Our customers
When we are fully engaged, we connect with, laugh with, and uplift the lives of our customers – even if just for a few moments. Sure, it starts with the promise of a perfectly made beverage, but our work goes far beyond that. It's really about human connection.

Our stores
When our customers feel this sense of belonging, our stores become a haven, a break from the worries outside, a place where you can meet with friends. It's about enjoyment at the speed of life – sometimes slow and savored, sometimes faster. Always full of humanity.

Our neighbourhood
Every store is part of a community, and we take our responsibility to be good neighbours seriously. We want to be invited in wherever we do business. We can be a force for positive action – bringing together our partners, customers, and the community to contribute every day. Now we see that our responsibility – and our potential for good – is even larger. The world is looking to Starbucks to set the new standard, yet again. We will lead.

Our shareholders
We know that as we deliver in each of these areas, we enjoy the kind of success that rewards our shareholders. We are fully accountable to get each of these elements right so that Starbucks – and everyone it touches – can endure and thrive.

The conviction that something is important for the identity of an organization or a brand must be reflected in everything that the organization does and must be a conviction for everyone who works there. In that context, we should refer to the **DNA** of the brand (Alsem, 2019): the values embedded in a brand are the blueprint for how the brand behaves and what is important for that brand just as human DNA encodes someone's personality and identity.

What is this belief based on? In the previous section we already indicated that identity is more than a marketing manager who writes a few lines with buzzwords. A well-defined brand identity should be related to the strengths of that brand. In that context, the resource-based view was introduced in Chapter 2: the view that a strategy is based on the core competences of an organization. In Chapter 2 we then arrived at the core of marketing: connecting the wishes of the target groups with the identity of the brand. A successful brand positioning ensures that this connection is established.

Brand values and brand identity in themselves do not yet create a distinctive position. Here we arrive at the third C in the **positioning triangle**: besides the company's resources and identity (the first C) and the customer's needs and desires (the second C), differentiation from competition (the third C) is also important. This distinction can be achieved through so-called **points of difference** (PODs). PODs are those brand attributes or benefits that make the difference with competing brands.

PODs must be based on unique (combinations of) resources. PODs thus form the basis for creating a **sustainable competitive advantage (SCA)**. This concept has been central to literature on competitive analysis and competitive strategies since the eighties of the last century (Porter, 1980, 1985). A competitive advantage – a relative strength of the brand or organization that is relevant to the customer – is considered sustainable if the competitor is not able to imitate. An SCA, provided that this is also experienced as such within the organization, forms the start of the positioning process. Figure 5.3 gives a schematic representation of the SCA.

Consequently, the identity of a brand can be considered to contribute to an SCA under the following conditions:

■ The brand identity is relevant to the customer: there is a match with the benefits looked after by the target groups.
■ The brand identity is based on resources that the competitor does not have or only to a lesser extent: the resources form a relative strength and create a POD.

Marketers are often strongly focused on customer needs and creating a difference with competition. In itself this is a correct setting. However, the internal element should not be overlooked: activities are only successful if they are based on a belief

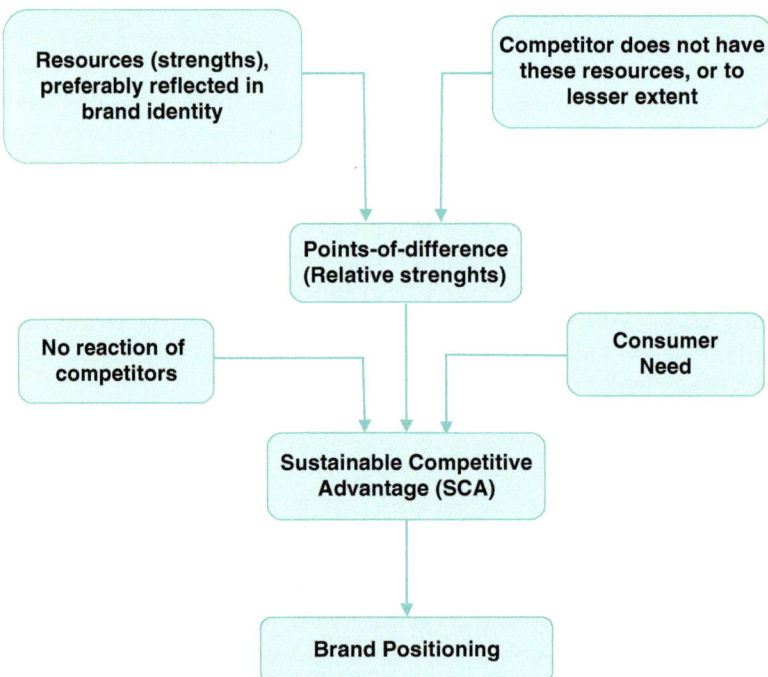

Figure 5.3 Sustainable competitive advantage

that is embedded in the core assets of the organization. This conviction must then also be translated into the brand: targeted investments are continuously needed to strengthen these resources and build the brand, and a targeted use of the marketing mix is necessary to position the brand. The conviction that certain values are important for the brand thus encourages action. And this conclusion leads us to the second requirement for brand values.

5.4 Brand identity motivates action

Brand (or corporate) identity, and the brand (or corporate) values on which the identity is based, creates the shared vision that guides communication (Section 5.2.1). However, identity is more than communication. Birkigt and Stadler state that only 10% of the reputation of an organization is determined by communication and symbolism. 90% of the reputation results from behaviour: everyone working with the brand or representing the brand should recognize themselves in the identity and then act accordingly.

Aligning the behaviour of an organization to the identity, thus aligning the behaviour of the people within that organization, requires that the identity is anchored in the culture of that organization, and anchored in all aspects of business management. If sustainability is a core value for a certain brand, then sustainability should be translated into all details in the production process. After all, the consumer has to buy a brand that not only radiates 100% sustainability but also is made of 100% sustainable. Of course, this applies not only to more societal brand values such as sustainability but also to all other values with which the brand profiles itself.

To create some more understanding on how this works, we now look at the organization from the perspective of the **value chain** concept. The value chain concept was developed by Porter (1985). According to this model, an organization can be seen as a collection of activities, each of them contributing to the design, the procurement, the production, the marketing, the sales or the (after-sales) service of the products or brands of that organization. If sustainability is a relevant brand value, then sustainability should be integrated in every value-added activity. Sustainable purchasing implies a choice for suppliers that use sustainable processes or resources. Sustainability in production implies a production process with little environmental impact. Sustainability as a starting point for research and development (R&D) implies a continuous push to develop product designs having a lower ecological footprint, and so on.

The **brand identity therefore guides the activities** of each department in the company. Fully integrating brand identity and brand values in each organizational activity requires a complete screening of the entire value chain, so that these values can be operationalized for each activity in this value chain.

The example of sustainability also illustrates that managing brand identity does not limit itself to just the company. Consumers (or other stakeholders) associate the brand with the complete **supply chain** in which the brand operates: from the moment the raw material is obtained up to and including the moment in which the brand is used in the customer's home. The brand will be held responsible for everything that happens in that supply chain. For more societal brand values, this seems obvious: if suppliers do not produce sustainably or ethically, this reflects directly on the brand. Increased transparency through digital media will only reinforce this trend (see Example 5.2). But it also applies to all other brand values. For example, a fashion brand that stands for elegance and style has to work with high-quality raw materials that enable elegant design. The identity of a brand must therefore be reflected in the entire value chain of the company, but at the same time it directs supply chain management (anything related to planning and execution of activities in the supply chain) for the entire supply chain in which the brand operates.

Example 5.2 The chocolate industry should be more serious with its CSR policy

Chocolate producers invest more than one billion dollars in programs aimed at a more sustainable supply chain. However, the companies provide only limited insight into the results of their investments. "Companies have to do more than indicating that they only use sustainable palm oil," according to the report "A taste of the future" of KPMG Sustainability. This report discusses developments and trends in the global chocolate industry. According to this report, the consumer is becoming increasingly sensitive when it comes to sustainable business practices and he increasingly uses the social media to express his concerns. This pressures the sector to show what progress it is making in the sustainable use of resources (like land, labour, and water).

KPMG notes that access to information about products will become increasingly easier in the future. Apps will give consumers insight into the ecological footprint of products. Moreover, a digital revolution has taken place at the beginning of the chain. 70% of the inhabitants of West Africa have a mobile phone. Companies are responding to this development by collecting data on the harvest through programs such as CocoaLink. This increasing transparency will drastically change the supply chain of cocoa.

Summarized: brand values motivate action. They force the company to organize the entire production process in such a way that the brand identity is expressed as powerfully as possible. The value chain approach emphasizes the internal business processes, as well as the business processes that take place at suppliers and other companies in the supply chain. In each stage, optimal integration of the brand's core values should be pursued. Optimalization implies that the brand strives to excel – there can only be a competitive advantage if the brand identity is not only consistently applied but also to a higher extent than competition does. Obviously, investments cannot be maximized everywhere. And this brings us to the next requirement that can be set to brand values: brand values force choices.

5.5 Brand identity forces choice

Consumers choose a certain brand because they believe that this brand can meet their needs or because they feel connected to the identity or the values for which the brand stands. This has consequences for the marketing and communication of the brand: it must be made clear what the brand stands for. But as we have seen in the previous section, this also has consequences for internal operations: a brand identity requires targeted investments to support this identity. This forces to make choices: a brand cannot invest maximally in everything and a brand cannot communicate that it excels in all aspects. The core values of the brand determine in what the brand should invest, and therefore also where the brand should invest less: **brand values force choice**. We will discuss these choices in more detail in this section, and in particular the importance of a consistent choice. We discuss a number of value strategies that help making that choice. Finally, we emphasize the importance of making and consistently implementing choices.

5.5.1 Importance of a consistent choice

From the market's perspective, a combination of core values should preferably be profiled in such a way that they match the needs of the customer and that they are distinctive compared to competing brands. But from the brand's perspective, these values should involve assets and capabilities in which the brand is really "good": the communicated brand identity should match the core competences of the company. But these values only amount to a strong brand image when they are mutually reinforcing brand values. According to the Value Compass, values of adjacent value types reinforce each other, while opposite values represent opposing motivations that conflict with each other rather than strengthening each other. This means that the brand should be connected to values that belong to the same value type or to value types that are located close to each other in the Value Compass. Hence, we see that, in addition to connecting with the needs of the customer, evolving from the brand's core competencies, and creating a distinction with the competition (the three Cs), a fourth benchmark arises: consistency. The importance of selecting a **consistent value profile** is illustrated in Example 5.3.

Example 5.3 Core values of two healthcare institutions (Alsem & Kostelijk, 2013)

Hospital A uses the slogan: "You can trust our professional health care providers." In this slogan, two core values come to mind: trust and professionalism. These two values can be placed in the Value Compass. The brand value professionalism matches the value type of functionality: the healthcare provider has excellent staff with full medical expertise and is therefore well equipped to do what the care provider should do – providing good care. The brand value trust creates an image of a safe environment where the client does not have to worry, where he can safely put his life in the hands of the professionals. This is in line with the value type safety. These values reinforce each other and create the image of an organization, where the client is safe and treated by professionals: Figure 5.4.

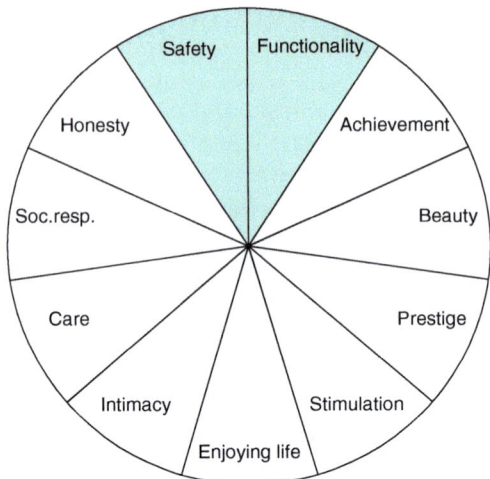

Figure 5.4 **The Value Compass of hospital A**

Hospital B profiles the following core values: "Reliable, leading in healthcare and close to you." Reliability suggests, as with institution A, a safe, professionally operating organization. Leading in healthcare refers to leadership: an organization with a certain professional status. However, close to you is a more intimate value; this creates an image of an organization where the client is treated with attention, a care institution that creates a certain homely feeling: Figure 5.5. These values seem to cover the entire Value Compass. The final picture, however, is diffuse: what does this organization really stand for?

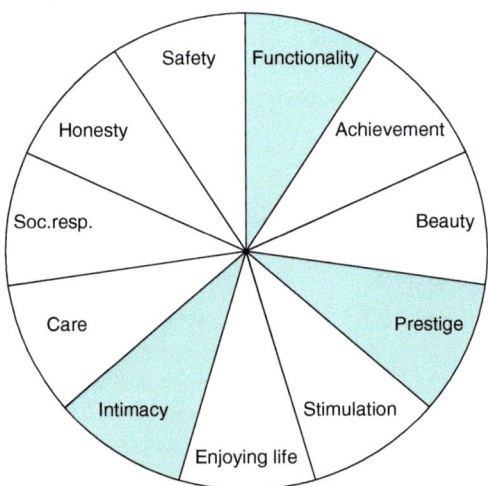

Figure 5.5 **The Value Compass of hospital B**

Example 5.3 illustrates that a strong value profile can only be realized when the organization chooses to profile itself with mutually reinforcing values.

5.5.2 Value strategies

The importance of consistent choices is also emphasized in some other models. In the much-cited article "Customer intimacy and other value disciplines," Treacy and Wiersema (1993) emphasize that every company must make a fundamental choice for a particular value strategy: where does the company want to excel? They distinguish three value strategies. Porter (1980) uses a format that is similar to the value strategies of Treacy and Wiersema. He distinguishes three generic competitive strategies. We first discuss the three strategies of Treacy and Wiersema, and then those of Porter.

Value strategies of Treacy and Wiersema

Treacy and Wiersema distinguish three value strategies or **value disciplines**:

1. product leadership
2. operational excellence
3. customer intimacy

PRODUCT LEADERSHIP

Product leadership is a corporate strategy where the company wants to excel in a certain product category by means of offering the highest quality. Meeting the needs of the customer translates in this strategy into developing innovative products

Photo 5.1 Samsung is a good example of a product leader. Photo © Hans Olav Lien (cc-by-sa/2.0), with permission of Samsung. This Samsung store is in the shopping mall "SM Aura Premier" in Bonifacio Global City, Metro Manila, The Philippines

or services. The consequence of this strategy is a well-developed **R&D** department: excelling in innovative products implies continuous investment in product **innovation**. In service-oriented companies, a strategy of product leadership also strongly focuses on human resources: recruiting and continuously training the best people. After all, the quality of a service provider is in the quality of the people that provide the services. Examples of product leaders are companies such as Apple, Tesla, or (in the fast moving consumer goods) Procter & Gamble.

OPERATIONAL EXCELLENCE

Operational excellence literally means excellence in the efficient execution of all business processes. An operational excellence strategy is aimed at delivering products at the lowest possible cost to the customer. "Low costs" is often translated into "low price," but this is not necessary; an operational excellence strategy is aimed at removing as many of the thresholds as possible that could prevent the customer from buying the product. This may include a low price, but no delays, delivery on time, standardization of the product so that the customer knows exactly what he can expect, or maximum convenience. Examples are companies such as Ryanair, IKEA, and McDonald's. McDonald's makes a standard menu available as quickly and as cheap as possible. The concept of **convenience** has been implemented to such an extent that the customer does not have to leave his car to get his Big Mac. Efficiency is created by **standardization**: a limited number of business processes that are perfectionated in all detail and that fit together seamlessly. For the customer, the consequence is clarity (for example, the McDonald's menu is largely the same throughout the world), but often also a limited choice. Operational excellence implies continuous managerial attention for efficiency and rationalization (cutting costs) in the internal processes.

Photo 5.2 **McDonald's is a good example of operational excellence. Source: McDonald's Multimedia Library.**

Customer intimacy emphasizes the individual customer: the company excels by being the best in customization to the customer's needs. Key concepts are relationship marketing, customer relationship management (CRM), and customer loyalty. Customer intimacy means that knowledge of the needs of the individual customer is translated into a perfectly customized offer. On a small scale this could be the village hairdresser who knows all his customers personally and knows exactly what style they want. On a larger scale, a good customer database and a customer tracking system are of vital importance. An internet environment offers plenty of opportunities for this, which is why customer intimacy companies are often found online. Examples are companies such as Amazon that create personalized offers based on continuous analysis of the behaviour of its customers. Also for many service providers, individual customer contact is very important. With customer intimacy, like in the other value disciplines, the company must strive to excel. After all, individual contact is important to every service provider, but excelling means that your customer approach is more personal and better customized than the services of competing organizations.

Photo 5.3 **Amazon.com uses individual preferences to create personalized offers**

Porter's generic competitive strategies

Porter (1980) distinguishes three generic competitive strategies:

1. **Product differentiation**: creating a distinction with respect to the competition.
2. **Cost leadership**: aiming for the lowest cost level in the industry.
3. **Focus strategy**: an approach in which one specific market segment is served as well as possible.

Product differentiation and cost leadership resemble the product leadership and operational excellence strategies of Treacy and Wiersema. However, Treacy and Wiersema start with the customer's point of view, while Porter puts more emphasis on the internal business processes. Cost leadership, for instance, is a strategy in which the entire value chain of the company must be analyzed, and then costs for each activity in this value chain should be minimized. This, as we saw in the previous section, applies to the whole supply chain. Notorious are the examples in which companies such as US retailer Walmart pushes suppliers to deliver at lower costs, or Ryanair that squeezes every penny out of the salaries of its employees.

Porter emphasizes the importance of choice. If a company chooses cost leadership, then this has to be implemented in every element of the business process: every aspect of the business should be designed so efficiently that it operates with the lowest costs possible. If the company fails here, it remains stuck in the middle. Just imagine those electricity companies or internet providers that promise you plenty of flexibility and choice, until you have a problem and you try to get in touch with customer service: difficult to reach by telephone and once you have them on the line they are unable to solve your problem. The marketing and communication departments are apparently aiming for product differentiation, but the other business processes have not (yet) managed to make this move. Porter shows that making choices and consistently implementing them throughout the organization lead to significantly higher profitability. The alternative, not a 100% choice, means that the company remains "**stuck in the middle.**"

5.5.3 Implications of choice

We emphasize the importance of consistently implementing the chosen strategy. The aforementioned strategies of Porter and Treacy and Wiersema are choices at corporate level, i.e. with implications for the entire business. The choice for a brand identity is a brand level choice: choosing (and fulfilling!) a brand promise. A consistent brand identity implies choosing brand values that reinforce each other, so they are logically connected with each other. The Value Compass is a tool that can support this choice: a real **compass** tells you from which direction the wind blows; the Value Compass shows you from which direction your values "blow."

The fulfilment of the brand promise implies that brand values must be operationalized in every activity related to the brand. Porter's wise lesson is that the entire value chain must fit the chosen strategy. Hospital A of Example 5.3 therefore has to ensure that trust (safety) and professionalism (i.e. functionality) must be visible in every aspect of the care provided to its patients – and thus the service provision. And hospital B should make a choice. This might be strengthening "close to you" (i.e. intimacy) into every detail, for example by investing in a cozy environment such as a pleasant walkway in the hospital with a café where patients and family can spend quality time together, and many opportunities to be in touch with the doctor or the nursing staff in a "warmer" environment than a sterile room where the surgeon in his white coat can be consulted after a quarter of an hour anxiously waiting in a cold hospital waiting room. An alternative for hospital B is a focus on leadership (perhaps specializing in new and innovative treatments for particular diseases). Creating a brand identity therefore means making choices, not only in marketing and communication but also in the entire business.

5.6 Brand identity: relevant to all stakeholders

The **brand identity is relevant to all stakeholders**. We discuss this in more detail in Section 5.6.1. In Section 5.6.2, we describe methods to gain insight into the importance of stakeholders and their interests.

5.6.1 The stakeholder concept

Communication to each stakeholder group starts with the same set of brand values. It is not possible to profile one identity towards one stakeholder and another identity towards the other. On the other hand, it is possible to emphasize certain aspects of the brand identity, depending on the objectives you wish to achieve. We purposely talk about stakeholders (plural): communicating the brand identity deserves a broader perspective than just communication with the commercial target groups of the brand.

In marketing, the focus is traditionally on one of these commercial target groups, namely the customer. The marketing concept dictates that an organization has to meet the needs of its customers in order to remain profitable in the longer term. This idea puts the customer first. When we use this logic to discuss brand identity, the main idea is that a favourable image is created towards the customer in the target group, in such a way that this customer is convinced that the brand meets his needs.

With the emergence of more socially and strategically oriented visions on marketing, however, the importance of other stakeholders is increasingly emphasized. This obviously happens when it comes to communicating corporate aspects with social relevance such as the social responsibility of an organization or the sustainability of the production process. Values such as social responsibility are important for the customer, but they also support the organization's reputation for a broader audience and for relevant interest groups or government organizations. The importance of a favourable image towards stakeholders with a large influence on a company is evident. A stakeholder approach is therefore frequently used in (marketing and corporate) communications (Hillebrand, Driessen & Koll, 2015).

But the importance of a stakeholder approach is not exclusively relevant at corporate level, nor is it limited solely to communicating social values. A broad commitment is also important at the level of the individual brand, when it comes to communicating the brand identity. After all, the customer does not decide in isolation, but he is continuously influenced by reference groups, news in the media, or news updates that appear daily on his Facebook page. An image is therefore not only shaped by the brand itself but also by the word-of-mouth of all other stakeholders involved. And this makes stakeholder management important at the brand level.

A **stakeholder** is any group or individual who can affect or is affected by the achievement of the organization's objectives (Freeman, 1984). With a more strategic vision on brand identity, it is therefore important to include all relevant stakeholders, not just the end user. These stakeholders can be found in the supply chain: customers, but also suppliers and distributors are important stakeholders from a marketing perspective. Stakeholders can also be found outside the company's supply chain; consider employees, the local community (e.g. neighbourhood residents near a supermarket or a chemical plant), consumer organizations, environmental groups, journalists, bloggers, or authorities on local, national, or European level. All these groups or organizations influence the brand image, positively or negatively.

5.6.2 Categorizing stakeholders and their interests

An intuitive method to identify stakeholders and their interests is described by Bryson (2004). This method consists of the following stages:

1. a brainstorming session in which a list of possible stakeholders is created
2. listing, for each stakeholder, the criteria used by the stakeholder to assess the brand or organization
3. a quick scan of each stakeholder's opinion about the brand; in its most basic form, colour schemes can be used such as green (positive), yellow (neutral), or red (negative)
4. for each stakeholder, describe what can be done in the short term to satisfy the stakeholder
5. identify the deeper issues that affect the relationship between the brand and the stakeholder or between the brand and a group of stakeholders

This technique provides a good insight for each stakeholder in important issues, both for the short term and in the long run. The risk, however, is an unstructured list of stakeholders. Not every stakeholder is equally important. That is why a number of techniques have been developed in management literature, aimed at classifying the stakeholders. A much-used method is **the power versus interest grid** (Eden & Ackermann, 1998). This method divides stakeholders by using two criteria:

- the extent to which the stakeholder is interested in the brand, or the brand's activities (interest)
- the potential influence of the stakeholder on the brand (power)

Combining these criteria creates a matrix with two dimensions (see Figure 5.6).

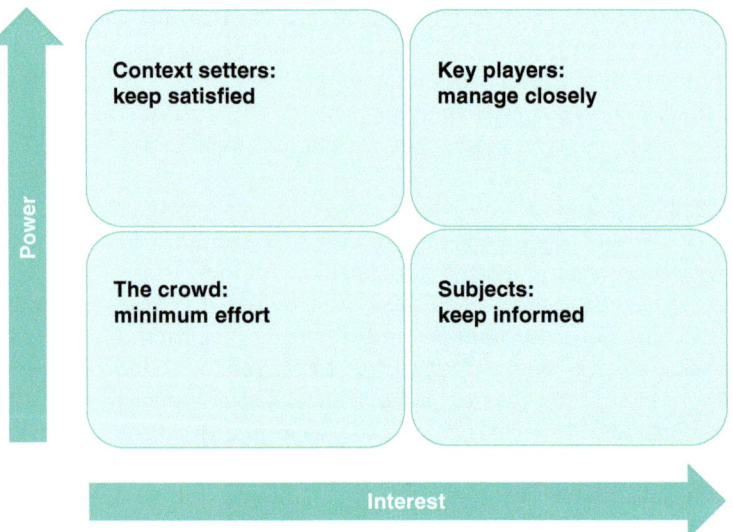

Figure 5.6 **Power versus interest grid**

Four types of stakeholders are distinguished in the power-interest grid:

1. *Key players* have a lot of interest in the brand or organization that markets this brand and can also exert a large influence on this brand. Opinion leaders can be important key players through the power of word-of-mouth. Just think of the influence that famous fashion bloggers can have on brands like Hugo Boss, Diesel, or ZARA. Journalists also often play a key role in supporting or damaging a favourable brand image. And in a completely different context, organizations have to take account of certain government agencies. Example 5.4 illustrates this.
2. *Subjects* have a lot of interest in the brand, but only have limited power and can therefore exercise only little influence. The individual consumer in the target group usually belongs to this group.
3. *Context setters* have little direct interest in the brand, but potentially exert a lot of influence. Many governmental organizations or other regulatory organizations belong to this group. An example is the Volkswagen emissions scandal in 2015. The United States Environmental Protection Agency (EPA) discovered that Volkswagen had fiddled with environmental tests: they had found that Volkswagen had intentionally programmed turbocharged direct injection (TDI) diesel engines to activate their emissions controls only during laboratory emissions testing which caused the vehicles' emissions to meet US standards during regulatory testing, but emit up to 40 times more polluting substance in real-world driving. The resulting publicity had a huge negative impact on the Volkswagen brand.
4. Finally, there is *the crowd*: they have no direct interest in the brand, and generally only limited possibilities to exercise influence. This could be the general public: people outside the direct target group of the brand. This group is less important for communication, although account must be taken that the crowd can be mobilized if the brand is associated with important social issues. Brands can be confronted with this when sourcing in unethical ways from less-developed countries or when they outsource part of their production process to third parties (or to low-income countries) that do not respect good working conditions of employees. Due to the rise of social media, the influence of the crowd has increased in recent years, and this is increasingly becoming a factor to take into account.

Example 5.4 The European Commission is a key player for Google

The European Commission officially accused Google of abuse of power, and issued a fine of €1.49 billion for breaching EU antitrust rules. This fine was issued in March 2019, after Google was already fined €4.34 billion in July 2018. The Commission accused Google of giving priority to its own services over those of competitors. For example, Google shows prices of products through price comparison Google Shopping. These appear above the search results, reducing the supply of, for example, Amazon and other comparisons and webshops. "The Commission fears that users will not necessarily see the most relevant search results," according to the European Commission in a statement.

According to the Commission, the same misuse of power can be seen when searching for hotels or tourist attractions where Google already displays its own assessments before it shows the results of, for example, Yelp and Tripadvisor. Google's practices would have had a negative impact on consumers and innovation. The Commission requires that Google adjusts the way the search engine works, and that it will treat its own service the same as competing services. The total fine is close to 5% of Google's annual turnover.

Google says in a comment that it is perhaps the most used search engine, but that there are many other services that people find information nowadays. The company mentions competitors such as Bing and Yahoo, but also services such as Amazon, Expedia, and eBay. Google states that the companies complain that they are negatively influenced by Google, but that their figures show otherwise. For example, in a blog Google compares its own Google Shopping with traffic on Amazon and eBay.

Each stakeholder can be approached specifically, depending on the power and interests of the stakeholder. Different communication strategies are possible. Bryson (2004) distinguishes the following possibilities:

- to inform
- to consult ("we engage the conversation with you")
- to involve the stakeholder in the process
- to collaborate

In real life, also a strategy aimed at persuading the stakeholder will often be used. The most far-reaching form of interaction is empowerment: making the stakeholder part of your activities and providing him with the means to influence the outcomes. As a general rule, a stakeholder deserves more attention when it exerts more power, or is affected more by the brand's activities. The stakeholder approach can be linked to the position of the stakeholder in the power versus interest grid:

- Key players should be closely monitored and, wherever possible, direct interaction with them should take place.
- Subjects should be kept satisfied.
- Context setters should be permanently informed.
- Finally, the crowd receives only limited attention but negative imagery must be prevented, because otherwise the crowd could be mobilized via social media. If this happens, often little more can be done than trying to limit the damage through crisis communication.

5.7 Brand identity prioritizes

The identity of a brand can be operationalized by using the brand values that are central to that brand. This results in a specific combination of brand values for each brand. Take, for example, the car market. A brand like BMW emphasizes sportivity, strength, and design, for Toyota sustainability and efficiency are more prominent, for Peugeot comfort, and Volvo emphasizes safety and reliability. Of course, emphasizing certain values does not mean that the other brand values are not present. In every car you have to be able to sit comfortably, every car brand invests in sustainability, and safety is important for every car brand. But a certain (desired) brand identity reflects a priority. This prioritization puts certain values "in the heart of the brand": in the communication about the brand, in the production of the brand, but also in the requirements imposed on suppliers.

This implies that the **brand identity creates priorities**: some values are more important for a brand than other values. This emphasizes the importance of an integrated approach, where clarification of these priorities is important. The interdependence of important brand values should be considered in this integrated approach. As indicated in Section 5.5, the choice for a brand identity implies a focus: maximum synergy can be achieved by choosing mutually reinforcing brand values.

In the previous sections, we emphasized the importance of a carefully chosen brand identity. We found **four essentials** that are of key importance when prioritizing brand values:

- *Relevance*: the brand must be embedded with brand values that are relevant for the target group (and for other stakeholders).
- *Distinctiveness*: there must be a brand identity that is distinctive from competition.
- *Based on strength*: the brand's identity and the associated brand values must come from the competences (core resources and capabilities) of the organization.
- *Consistency*: the underlying brand values must reinforce each other.

Labelling the brand identity – for example by naming the values that the brand stands for – is a creative process that takes place within the playing field created by these four essentials (see Figure 5.7). This creative process can be done during brainstorming sessions of the management team, but it can also be (partly) outsourced to specialized agencies. In both cases, it is important that the playing field is clearly described, for example by making each of the four essentials explicit.

By defining brand identity and/or brand values, the priorities for the brand are made explicit. This sounds logical, but applying a focus is often a big problem in the "real" world. Many organizations think that they are good at everything; many managers want to be able to mean "everything" for "everyone." The moral of our story is that brands do have to choose certain core values. After all, positioning is the art of omission.

Example 5.5 illustrates how brand values can be tested against the four essentials.

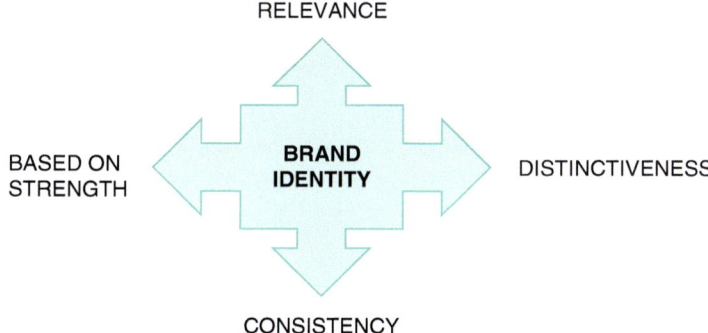

Figure 5.7 **The four essentials of brand identity**

Example 5.5 Use of the four essentials to define brand identity

The marketing manager of a cookie brand, known for its different types of cookies, wanted to gain more insight into the brand identity. His first step was to map out possible brand values through management interviews with employees based on the laddering technique (as described in Section 4.4.1) and brainstorming sessions with management. In the interviews and brainstorming sessions a fairly large number of brand values were mentioned: nutrition, coziness, family tradition, honest and familiar, part of warm family life, sustainability, respect, care for people, passion for quality, knowledge of food technology, efficiency, craftsmanship, originality, creativity, unique taste experience, and innovation.

A quick look at the Value Compass shows that with these brand values almost every quadrant of the compass is covered. All these brand values together therefore do not give a clear direction to the brand identity. Moreover, these are far too many brand values for clear and unambiguous communication towards the stakeholders. The marketing manager therefore decided to test these brand values against the four essential benchmarks.

The relation with the company's core competences and the extent of differentiation from the competition were assessed by a hired consultant, while the relevance for the target group was tested in a number of customer panels and a panel with other stakeholders (mainly suppliers). The results were summarized for each brand value in the form of a rating on a scale from 1 to 10. The result is shown in Table 5.1.

Table 5.1 Rating of brand values

Brand values	Rating		
	Based on competences	Relevance for the target group	Distinctive from competition
Nutrition	8	3	5
Coziness	7	8	7
Family tradition	9	6	8
Honest and familiar	9	7	6
Part of warm family life	7	8	6
Sustainability	5	8	3
Respect	5	6	3
Care for people	6	7	3
Passion for quality	9	8	6
Knowledge of food technology	8	4	4
Efficiency	8	2	6
Craftsmanship	7	6	8
Originality	7	6	8
Creativity	3	8	5
Unique taste experience	5	9	5
Innovation	6	6	4

Table 5.1 demonstrates that not every brand value is just as important for the brand. The manager allows for a minimum score of 6 for each benchmark. As a result, the brand values printed in bold remain.

A test of the remaining benchmark (consistency) by using the Value Compass shows that there are two clusters of brand values: a cluster around the value types care for each other and honesty (family tradition, honest and familiar, part of warm family life) and a group around functionality and performance (passion for quality, craftsmanship, and originality). These two types of values can possibly be communicated in combination, using two-sided positioning, but management could also decide to prioritize brand values. In the latter case, either the more "social" brand values are emphasized or the more functional brand values. It is important that management recognizes that brand values have an effect on one another, and that not every combination of brand values produces the desired synergy.

5.8 Brand identity guides brand positioning

In the previous section we showed the importance of prioritizing brand values. Because of this prioritization, certain brand values become central to the brand. For example, the biscuit brand from Example 5.5 could opt for the value statement "honest biscuits grounded in a warm family tradition." This statement can be displayed graphically with the Value Compass (see Figure 5.8). Freely translated, this figure tells that the brand represents honesty and care & affection, with a touch of security and intimacy.

Brand identity results from the combination of values that are central to the brand. Figure 5.8 is thus a representation of the (desired) brand identity. The management decision to emphasize tradition, warmth, honesty, and trust makes these values the essence of symbolism, communication, and behaviour with regard to the brand, as indicated in the model of Birkigt and Stadler (Section 5.2.1). The desired

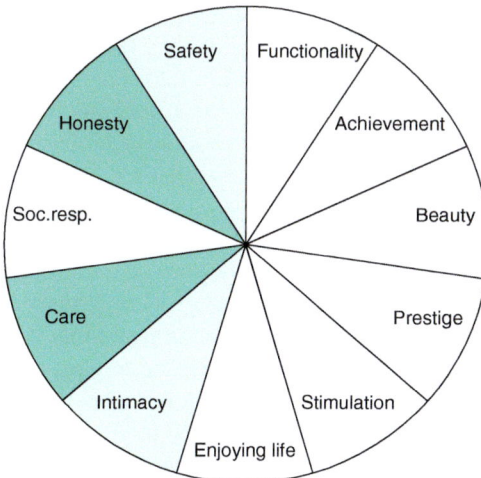

Figure 5.8 **Example of a value profile**

brand identity, based on these brand values, forms the start for decisions with respect to the brand positioning, which is the more concrete promise of the brand to stakeholders, and all matters and activities expressing this: the **brand identity guides brand positioning**. You can think of things like logo design, the packaging of the biscuits, communication campaigns for the brand, and so on.

But, as we have indicated in this chapter, a brand identity is not an empty shell. The cookie brand derived its identity from an extensive internal audit, but the brand now also has the task to implement the identity in all details and where possible to reinforce it. Choosing a certain identity sets priority, and therefore has consequences not only for the positioning of the brand but also for investments in the brand.

Summary

The identity of a brand is the core of what the brand actually is, the brand's own personality. The brand identity reflects the core values of the brand. A distinction can be made between the actual identity of the brand (as perceived by the stakeholders) and the identity desired by management. This desired identity is certainly of great importance for the development of a positioning strategy: positioning is aimed at bringing the image of the brand with the target group in line with the desired identity of the brand. Obviously, the desired identity cannot differ too much from what the brand actually has to offer. You cannot promise the consumer something you cannot deliver.

A condition for success of a brand is that the activities of that brand are based on an SCA. This is the case if the brand meets a consumer need and if the strengths of the brand are based on resources that the competitor does not have or has to a lesser degree. A well-chosen identity succeeds in communicating this. With a well-chosen identity, the brand can therefore distinguish itself from the competition. In this chapter we have set four essentials for a carefully chosen brand identity:

- *Relevance*: the brand must be embedded with brand values that are relevant for the target group (and for other stakeholders).
- *Distinction*: there must be a brand identity that is distinctive from competition.
- *Based on strength*: the brand's identity and the associated brand values must come from the competences (core resources and capabilities) of the organization.
- *Consistency*: the underlying brand values must reinforce each other.

Expressing an identity is more than just communication. The identity of the brand is a conviction that must be expressed in all activities of that brand. You cannot promise anything if you cannot deliver it. This has as a consequence that the identity of the brand must be deeply rooted in the organization, and that it has to be experienced as such by all employees of the company. This also implies that an identity cannot really be "chosen," but will have to be deduced from what the company is doing and have to be formulated in distinctive, relevant, and focused terms.

Finally, we need to emphasize that marketers are naturally inclined to focus their attention on the consumer. But the identity is not only of interest to the consumer in the target group. We emphasized in this chapter that the brand identity must be communicated to all stakeholders relevant to the brand.

Chapter 6

Brand positioning: mindshare and heartshare

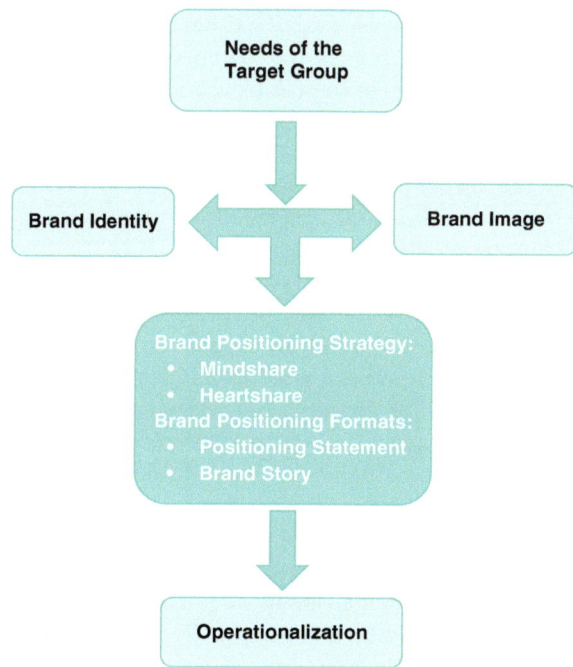

Needs of the Target Group

Brand Identity

Brand Image

Brand Positioning Strategy:
- **Mindshare**
- **Heartshare**

Brand Positioning Formats:
- **Positioning Statement**
- **Brand Story**

Operationalization

6.1 An introduction to brand positioning strategy

The development of a brand positioning strategy takes place in a number of stages. These stages are shown schematically at the beginning of each chapter:

1. Needs assessment and target group choice: "Who do we want to serve with our brand?"
2. Determine the current brand image: "How does the target group perceive our brand and the competing brands?"

3. The brand identity: "What does our brand stand for?"
4. The brand positioning itself: the choice of the positioning strategy and the concrete description of this strategy in images and wording.
5. Operationalization of the positioning strategy: the translation of the positioning in marketing and communication activities.

The first three stages of the positioning process have been described in the previous chapters. In this chapter we discuss the choice of a positioning strategy and the actual expression of this strategy. Subsequently, in Part III, a number of important consequences of brand positioning are highlighted.

In brand positioning, specific aspects of the brand are emphasized. Literature often makes a division into four types of positioning:

- **Informational positioning** emphasizes the distinguishing advantages of using the brand: "New Tide (laundry detergent) gets your clothes white, even at 30 degrees." The emphasis is on functional benefits. These benefits are often linked to physical product attributes, the so-called reason why: "Why does Tide give a pure white result? Because there is bleach in it."
- **Transformational positioning** uses symbolic or experience-oriented benefits. A link is made with the core values of the target group: if a beer commercial shows how the beer is drunk with a group of smiling friends in a cozy pub, this is in line with important values for the target group such as friendship and good fun.
- **Two-sided positioning** connects benefits both with functional product attributes and with consumer values. In this way the entire means-end chain is covered. Just think of a possible commercial for spaghetti sauce. With such a sauce it is very easy and quick to prepare a delicious meal (benefits), because there are all fresh ingredients in it and only hot water needs to be added (product attributes), and then the camera moves to a cheerful family at the dining table: tasty and quick means more quality time with your family (good family life as important value).
- A fourth alternative is to position the brand by using elements from the **execution** of the campaign. In that case no direct relationship with the brand itself is made, although certain elements may have an indirect relationship. A good example is the way Nespresso is using George Clooney to position the brand. Clooney is not a product feature or a benefit of Nespresso, but he is an actor who evokes a certain image and perhaps represents values that are also important to the average Nespresso drinker.

In this chapter, we discuss the development of a brand positioning strategy. We first look at the objectives for brand positioning: Section 6.2. In Section 6.3 positioning is related to mindshare and heartshare. Mindshare and heartshare are then used as the basis for creating a positioning strategy in Section 6.4.

The implementation of the positioning strategy depends on a number of factors. In Section 6.5 three of these factors are discussed:

- the decision-making process and the involvement of the consumer in the target group
- the type of product
- the stage in the product life cycle

Finally, the last section of this chapter details the actual expression of the brand positioning, in the form of a positioning statement, a Brand Key or a brand story.

6.2 Attitude formation and objectives for brand positioning

Positioning is aimed at giving the brand certain associations. By means of these associations, the company tries to create an optimal match between the brand experience and the needs of the consumer in the target group. This match should ultimately lead the consumer to take action: he should buy and use the brand.

Brand associations create a specific image about the brand. This brand image consists of two aspects:

- mindshare: the degree to which the consumer feels that the brand is relevant to him
- heartshare: the extent to which the consumer has positive associations with the brand

Mindshare and heartshare together lead to a certain **attitude** about the brand. Attitude is a concept from psychology and refers to a state of mind: the attitude of a consumer about a brand is the evaluation of this brand which can be positive or negative. Attitudes consist of three components:

- a **cognitive component**: the knowledge the consumer has about the brand. This can be influenced by for instance providing information about the product.
- an **affective** component: the feelings or emotions about the brand. An affective evaluation of a brand concerns matters such as: I like the brand, the brand is sympathetic, sensational, sweet, warm, and so on.
- a **behavioural** component: the behavioural intention of the consumer. This relates to the tendency to take action or not, for example by buying the brand.

The success of positioning activities can be measured by the extent to which the positioning contributes to realizing the **marketing objectives**. These are the objectives for which the marketing executive can be held primarily responsible. Marketing

Photo 6.1 **Cheers with Maallust beer: an appeal to the affective component. Photo provided with permission of Maallust beer**

objectives are often expressed in terms of sales or market share, but other criteria can also be used (Alsem, 2019):

- variables that are an indicator of the relationship with the customer such as the degree of customer loyalty or customer ambassadorship
- more brand-oriented indicators such as brand awareness or the extent to which target groups have certain associations with the brand

We see a distinction between "hard," measurable marketing objectives (sales, market share) and "softer" objectives that express the relationship with the customer or the strength of the brand. These types of objectives should normally be in line with each other. More favourable brand associations strengthen the relationship with the brand, which means that the customer will buy more of the brand, which, in turn, leads to higher sales or a larger market share.

The success of positioning activities can be measured by means of brand-oriented and relationship-oriented criteria. **Positioning objectives** can be linked to the way in which consumers form an attitude about a brand.

It is often assumed that an attitude develops in a certain order. First a consumer learns information about the brand; this knowledge creates a certain feeling, and on the basis of this feeling a purchase decision is made. A number of models have been developed that use attitudes to describe the decision-making process of consumers. The best known of these models is the **AIDA model**. This model expresses four stages in attitude development:

1. Attention (for the product)
2. Interest (in the product)
3. Desire (to have the product)
4. Action (to purchase)

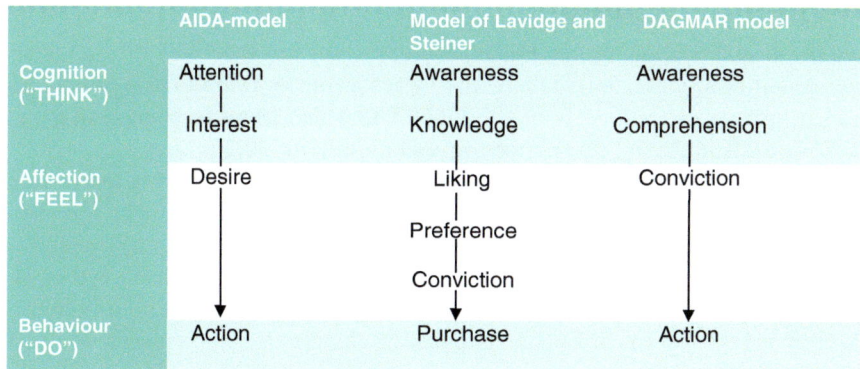

Figure 6.1 **Classical hierarchy of effects**

Similar models are the Lavidge and Steiner model, and the DAGMAR model (Defining Advertising Goals for Measuring Advertising Results). These models and their relationship with the three attitude components are shown schematically in Figure 6.1.

These models are mainly used as tools to identify "bottlenecks" in the decision-making process. We explain this by using an example of a hypothetical holiday park (Example 6.1).

Example 6.1 Holiday Park PleasureStay

A survey among the target group of PleasureStay (families with young children) was used to collect data about the attitude of the target group towards this holiday destination: see Figure 6.2.

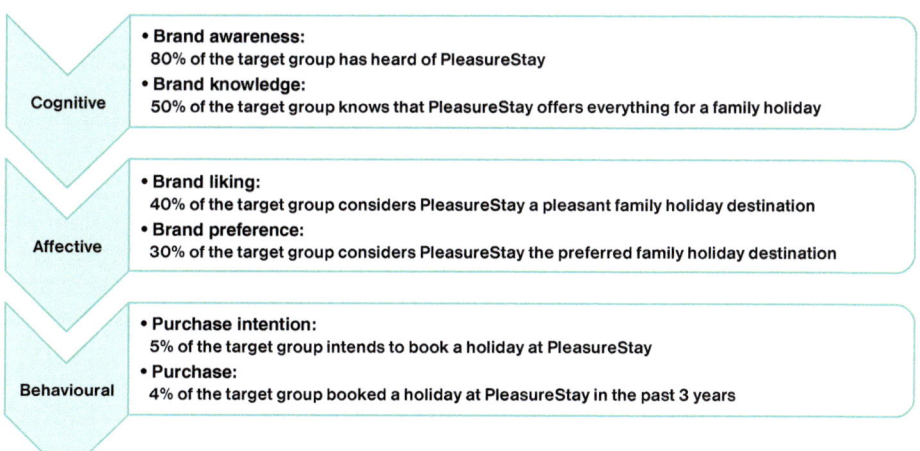

Figure 6.2 **Attitudes towards the fictional holiday park PleasureStay**

In developing a positioning strategy, emphasis is often placed on those stages where the largest decline occurs. For PleasureStay, for instance, we see that, despite a high brand awareness, only half of the target group is aware of the possibilities that PleasureStay offers for a family holiday. There also seems to be a lot to gain in the transition from brand preference to purchase intent: 30% prefers PleasureStay, but nonetheless only 5% of the target group wants to spend a holiday there. These figures can be used to define goals related to increasing brand knowledge (for example "at the end of the campaign 70% of the target group knows that PleasureStay offers all the facilities for a perfect family vacation") or purchase intent (for example "after the campaign, 20% of the target group wants to spend a holiday in PleasureStay"). This type of objectives gives direction to the implementation of the positioning strategy.

Models such as the AIDA model are also called classical **hierarchy of effects** models. They assume a fixed sequence of attitude development: a consumer develops a feeling for a certain brand only after having knowledge or collecting information, and only then action will be taken: knowledge – feeling – action.

However, this sequence does not always seem to be so fixed. Especially with important choices (purchase of a house or choice for a holiday destination) extensive decision-making takes place. But in many other buying situations, decision-making is much less extensive, or sometimes even impulsive. This can vary from buying an ice cream on a hot summer day to purchasing a new pair of shoes "because they look so beautiful in the shop window." The Sharp studies described in Chapter 1 showed that many choices are taken under low involvement. According to Sharp, brand awareness is the crucial factor when there is low involvement.

The way in which brand attitudes are formed therefore differs from brand to brand, given the situation in which the brand is used, the involvement of the target group, and so on. What is essential, however, is to gain a good insight into the way in which brand attitude is formed in the specific context, and thus how the brand image is created. This is decisive for the optimal design of positioning activities. Regardless of the attitude model that is used, positioning has to focus on those stages in the decision-making process where the brand loses many customers.

6.3 Brand positioning: heartshare or mindshare?

Positioning can focus on strengthening mindshare or on strengthening heartshare. Mindshare mainly relates to the knowledge about the brand, while heartshare is more in line with the feeling that the brand evokes. Mindshare emphasizes the cognitive attitude component, while heartshare emphasizes the affective component. Issues such as the current attitude or involvement of the target group, differences in type of product, or the personal taste of the marketer influence this emphasis. Informational positioning seems to fit more with the creation of mindshare, while transformational positioning seems more effective for realizing heartshare.

Ries and Trout (1986) described positioning as *the battle for your mind*. Essential here was the creation of a mental position: the desired image of the brand in the mind of the consumer, in comparison with the competitor. Consumers should initially know a couple of things about the brand: if you do not know that a Magnum is a certain type of ice cream, you won't buy it either. "Battle for your mind," however, is not synonymous with mindshare. Influenced by the theories of Keller and Kotler, and also by the emergence of forms of marketing that emphasize the importance of the relationship with the customer (such as Customer Relationship Management), the feelings aspect became increasingly important: positioning not only conveys certain associations, but these associations must also create a good feeling for the consumer, so that this consumer feels connected to the brand and becomes a loyal customer. This made heartshare central in positioning: positioning conveys a feeling that creates brand preference. Defining brand values also fits with this thought.

The ideas of Sharp bring us back to mindshare. In line with this, Floor, Van Raaij, and Bouwman (2015) emphasize that people more or less automatically have to connect a brand to a certain need. They state that the brand must be available mentally and physically at the moment the need arises. This is mindshare: the brand pops up in your mind on a moment when the brand is relevant. Floor, Van Raaij, and Bouwman developed a model derived from the ideas of Sharp. This model emphasizes two things: relevance and dominance. **Relevance** refers to the extent to which the brand is connected to the needs of the target group. Positioning is then aimed at inextricably linking the brand to the need: when a certain need arises you immediately think of the brand. So: you are at the swimming pool, it's summer and warm, and then immediately you think of Magnum. In this context, positioning is aimed at incorporating the brand into the evoked set by building powerful associations between brand and need.

Dominance implies that the brand must be present everywhere or at least in those places and moments where the need arises. Presence is both physical and mental. Floor, Van Raaij, and Bouwman emphasize the importance of translating the brand identity into a (limited) number of personality traits or brand values. These traits or values ensure consistency in everything the brand does. This line of thought corresponds to the use of the brand values as key element in the shared vision that guides all brand communication, as discussed in the previous chapter. Continuous repetition of the same message reinforces itself and creates dominance. Another aspect that influences the dominance of the brand is the use of brand elements. Brand elements can be colours, music, smells, or symbols. Examples are Nike's Swoosh and the yellow M used by McDonald's. These markings should be consistently communicated in all brand communication. Another important aspect of **dominance** concerns the physical availability of the brand: the touchpoints. Touchpoints are moments when consumers are in touch with the brand (shop, website, commercial, moments when the product is used), see Figure 6.3. Touchpoints ensure that the brand is dominantly present at important purchase locations (online and offline), and immediately available when desired.

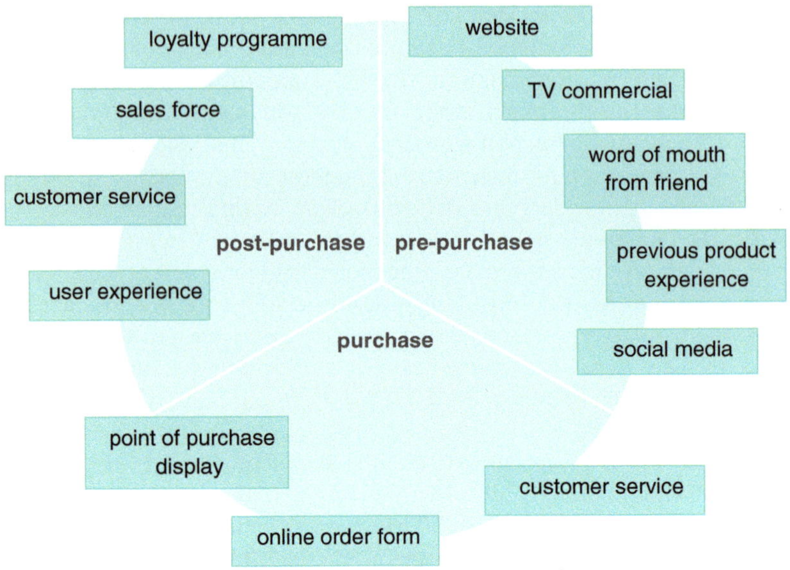

loyalty programme

website

TV commercial

sales force

word of mouth
from friend

customer service

post-purchase   pre-purchase

previous product
experience

user experience

purchase

social media

point of purchase
display

customer service

online order form

Figure 6.3 **Touchpoints**

6.4 The development of a successful brand positioning strategy

Positioning leads to strengthening the "brain position" of the brand, and thus to increased brand strength. But how can you position your brand successfully?

In the previous chapters we provided the building blocks that are important in the preparation of a positioning strategy:

1. Identification of the target group and insight in what the brand means for that target group: this involves the means-end chain: relevant product attributes, the benefits that the target group is looking for, and the values to which these benefits are linked.
2. Insight in the current brand awareness and brand image; this includes knowledge about the brand associations in the target group (attitude formation).
3. Definition of the desired brand identity; we referred to the four brand identity essentials: based on strength, relevance, consistency, and distinction.

With these three building blocks prepared, we can start defining the desired positioning. Broadly speaking, this desired positioning can focus on two levels:

■ mindshare: strengthening brand relevance
■ heartshare: strengthening brand associations

The choices to be made here depend, among other things, on the current brand attitude among the target group. For example, if brand awareness is low or if brand awareness is enough to trigger purchase (like in a low involvement context), mind-share is more obvious. If, on the other hand, the target group knows the brand, but only arouses limited positive feelings, or the wrong feelings, a positioning based on heartshare makes more sense. And heartshare also works well in a high involvement context.

In this section we pay attention to realizing the desired brand image through brand relevance (mindshare) and brand associations (heartshare). We end this section with some guidelines for defining the positioning strategy.

6.4.1 Positioning strategy focused on mindshare: strengthening brand relevance

In mindshare, a distinction can be made between brand awareness and brand knowledge on the one hand, and brand relevance on the other. **Brand awareness** is the extent to which the target group knows the brand name; brand knowledge is the extent to which the target group knows that the brand has certain properties.

Brand relevance is a level deeper than brand knowledge. It implies that the knowledge about the brand is so strongly developed that the consumer thinks of the brand whenever he feels a certain need. With brand relevance the brand is included in the evoked set of the consumer. In the case of a holiday park like PleasureStay, for example this means that as soon as the target group thinks about vacation or wants to plan a holiday, PleasureStay is automatically top of mind. Dominant presence of the brand when the target group feels a need is essential for creating brand relevance. As indicated in Section 6.3, it is important to know the touchpoints and to ensure that the brand is very present and visible in these touchpoints at times when the consumer feels a certain need. An informational positioning seems to be most appropriate for creating brand relevance: the consumer needs to know what the brand stands for and is constantly reminded of this.

6.4.2 Positioning strategy focused on heartshare: strengthening desired brand associations

A strong brand is a brand that manages to create strong, relevant, unique, and consistent brand associations. Brand associations can relate to functional aspects of the brand, to the feelings that the brand evokes in the target group, or to previous experiences with the brand, but associations can also be based on the opinion that friends or family have about the brand.

Positioning focused on the heartshare relates to one or more of the three levels of the means-end chain of a brand:

- brand attributes
- benefits
- brand values

To realize this, both informational and transformational positioning can be used. Two-sided positioning is preferable to completely cover the means-end chain: benefits are then linked with both product attributes and values. We discuss the different possibilities by using an example of the Center Parcs, a company exploiting holiday villages for the "short break market" – family holidays for a couple of days or a weekend. Example 6.2 presents (an adapted version of) a press release of Center Parcs.

Example 6.2 "Really together" new slogan for Center Parcs (source: www.centerparcs.nl, February 25, 2015)

More and more people are longing to escape from the hustle and bustle of daily life and spend more time together. At Center Parcs there is something for everyone at any time of the day and the whole family can participate in an activity of your choice thanks to our extensive range of activities. That is why Center Parcs launches the new slogan: "Really together." In this new profile, our four core values are summarized: emotion, share, care, and joy.

Really together
"Center Parcs is more than a simple holiday or weekend destination. It is a unique concept that meets everyone's needs. A moment of peace, where beautiful moments can be experienced together. Whether one comes to relax or just to get an adrenalin kick, everyone will experience the time of his life," emphasizes Vanessa Diriart, Vice President Center Parcs Europe – Groupe Pierre & Vacances Center Parcs.

New activities
Because every family is unique, Center Parcs has developed new activities to experience and share together. Center Parcs focuses on different target groups in all its parks across Europe. Some examples of these new activities are:

- *Building rafts and treehouses. In the middle of nature, in the forest or on the edge of the lake, build a raft or treehouse together with other children. Who has a good plan? Who can teach others to make knots?*
- *Family workshops. Working together on a painting or some other creative project creates a bond between parent and child. Enjoying the end result together does that too.*
- *Family paintball. Follow the instructions of your captain – or are you the captain? Children and parents enter the Cool Factor Arena and face a tough paintball battle. Do you dare?*
- *The Eden cottage. For a wonderful holiday with a group of friends, with the family, or for a reunion, you can go to the spacious XXL cottages, with space for 12–16 people. The new generation of cottages, the Eden cottages, are spacious, light and fully inspired by nature. They do not only fit in completely with their green environment but the materials used also provide a luxurious and natural atmosphere.*

***Photo 6.2* Family time at Center Parcs. Photo used with permission of Center Parcs**

Now we analyze the relation between the brand positioning strategy and the means-end chain. The example of Center Parcs is used here as example.

Positioning based on brand attributes

According to the multi-attribute attitude model discussed in Section 4.5.1, a distinction must be made between **the importance** of an attribute (the degree to which the consumer desires the attribute), and **the beliefs**: the extent to which the consumer "believes" that the brand possesses the attribute. In terms of positioning strategy, this offers two possibilities:

1. Influencing the needs of the target group by reinforcing the importance of certain attributes. Center Parcs can, for example, emphasize that holidays and activities together with your family are inextricably linked, and that a holiday park must be equipped with such activities.
2. Strengthening brand beliefs: the extent to which the target group associates the brand with certain attributes. Center Parcs could position itself as the holiday park with fantastic activities such as paintball and building huts.

Influencing consumers' needs (importance) and strengthening the beliefs can very well go together in one campaign. It does not have to include only existing product attributes. A creative positioning strategy could also highlight features that have not yet been associated with the product category: adding new attributes. The origins of the Center Parcs company provide a good example. In a time when holidays consisted of going to a campground or renting a house, Center Parcs decided to enrich the holiday experience with new concepts such as a subtropical swimming paradise.

Positioning based on benefits

The second level of the means-end chain relates to benefits. Benefits can be functional, social, or aimed at a certain experience. In a holiday park this includes benefits such as to relax, to re-energize, to have fun with the family, to meet nice people, or to experience new things. As with product attributes, also with benefits a distinction can be made between importance and beliefs:

3.   Influencing the needs of the target group by reinforcing the importance of certain benefits. Center Parcs emphasizes, for instance, that a relaxed time together with your family is the most important of a holiday.
4.   Strengthening brand beliefs: the extent to which the target group associates the brand with certain benefits. Center Parcs positions itself as *the* place where you can enjoy together with your family or partner: "Really together."

Positioning based on brand values

The values are at the highest level of the means-end chain. Positioning based on brand values means that the brand puts its brand values first.

5.   Profiling the core values that reflect what the brand really stands for, and demonstrating that they are in line with the values that the target group considers important.

Hypothetically, a positioning strategy based on brand values could also make the distinction between beliefs on the one hand and the importance of values on the other hand. However, the difficulty here is that the importance that the target group attaches to certain values is largely related to the consumer's personality, and therefore can hardly be influenced. In many cases, the importance of certain values should therefore be seen as a given. Therefore, a brand positioning strategy based on brand values is mainly focused on beliefs: the extent to which the target group should associate the brand with certain brand values.

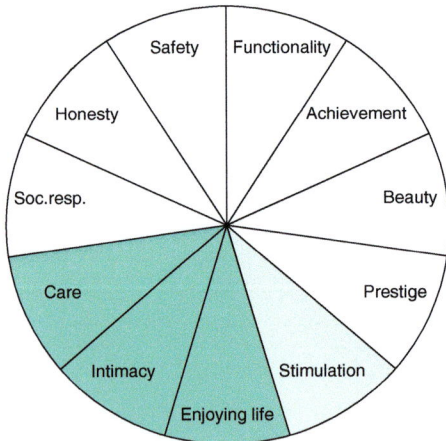

Figure 6.4 **Value profile of Center Parcs**

The communicated brand values must comply with the four brand identity essentials mentioned in the previous chapter: based on strength, relevance, consistency, and distinction. The Value Compass can be used to define brand values. Figure 6.4 displays the brand values of Center Parcs (emotion, share, care, and joy) in the Value Compass.

The Center Parcs example also highlights the importance of two-sided positioning: connecting brand values, benefits, and attributes with each other. The brand values (emotion, share, care, and joy) are carefully tailored to the most important benefits in the park's positioning: to relax and to experience quality time together with your family. Subsequently, the park has developed new activities (brand attributes) that fit in with this: family paintball, family workshops, and even a new type of holiday home to optimally share time with family and friends. For brand positioning, we advise to use as much as possible an integrated approach by linking product attributes with benefits and brand values.

6.4.3 The four laws of branding

Alsem and Klein Koerkamp (2012) distinguish four **laws of branding**. These laws largely correspond to the four essentials of brand identity (Chapter 5.7), and provide guidelines for a successful brand positioning strategy (Figure 6.5)

1. *Focus*: base your positioning on your own strength, with a focus on those core values and competences that lie in "the heart of the brand."
2. *Distinction:* make a difference with the competition.
3. *Relevance*: matches the wishes of the customer.
4. *Consistency*: positioning elements must reinforce each other, be implemented consistently over time, and be consistent for the various products that "hang" under the brand.

1 Focus on strength

Positioning is the art of omission. Telling too much leads to ambiguity. People will not remember too many details at the same time and a story has more impact when there is a clear message. Consequently, make choices, **focus**, and use the **KISS principle**: Keep It Simple, Stupid. Sometimes "and Repeat" is added to this. And "Less is More" also shows it well.

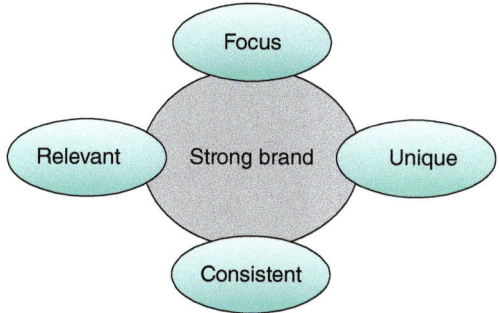

Figure 6.5 **The four laws of branding**

Brands must therefore define their core values as clearly as possible: Volvo is safety. Miele is durability and Germany efficiency. The Value Compass can be used to define these values. Of course, the focus is on those core values that tie in with the core competences of the brand.

As already indicated in Section 5.7, creating focus is often a big problem: many organizations feel that they are good at everything; many managers want to be able to mean "everything" for "everyone." A further complication is that a positioning is often the sum of multiple opinions within the management. So even if, for instance, the marketing manager wants to focus on local involvement, if the management believes that the international character must also be communicated, there will be no clear briefing to the advertising agency and no sharp campaign either.

2 Distinction: make the difference

It's difficult to make choices. And in addition, often generic promises are made: "We deliver quality." "Customer first." It sounds great, but everybody repeats each other. Uniqueness is needed to make the difference. Therefore, the brand has to search for its DNA: the resources that make the brand unique and that create **distinction** with competition. When translating the uniqueness of the brand into a campaign, a concept must be chosen in which this uniqueness is presented simply and clearly, in a way that distinguishes the brand from the competitor.

3 Be relevant to the customer

A brand positioning should have **relevance** for the customer. If, in the course of time, the customers' needs change or other important developments take place in the environment, brands may shift accents in the positioning. Once a positioning has been chosen, it does not have to be 100% set in stone. But the underlying identity is, and this determines the extent to which changes in positioning are possible.

Brand elements as well should be relevant and at the same time linked to the brand identity. Brand name and visual design should always be derived from the overall brand positioning. In reality it often happens that a new visual design is created, without being connected to the identity. The push for a "cool and trendy" corporate identity should always depend on the target group and positioning.

Relevant communication is also essential in the implementation. This relates to content and form. Especially in terms of form, sometimes big mistakes are made. The biggest mistake is an overload in creativity. With this we mean the use of a creative concept that has nothing to do with the brand or with the target group, for example the use of humoristic elements without a substantial link with the brand. Communication then might excel in creativity, but if it does not fit the brand, it is useless. Creativity must always be at the service of the brand and suit the customer's desire for experience.

4 Be consistent

Consistency relates to consistency between brand values, but also consistency in the brand portfolio and consistency over time. Building a strong brand takes time. Customers have to be reminded again and again of what the brand stands for so that they feel more and more connected with it, which means continuous repetition of aspects of the brand that reinforce each other. This requires a long-term vision.

Consistency also applies to the content of the communication. A brand cannot have a different personality from one day to the next. That is not credible and is confusing. It does not make sense either; a personality only changes little over time. In brands, however, it often happens that brands suddenly want to be "someone else." With all the loss of credibility that results.

Consistency of the products under the brand umbrella is also important: which products can be labelled with the brand? Extensions that have little or no fit with the parent brand can detract from the strength or credibility of the brand image. In Chapter 8 we further discuss brand extensions.

6.5 Brand positioning and the decision-making process

As indicated in the previous section, positioning is aimed at strengthening brand awareness and brand relevance, or at establishing or strengthening a particular brand image. The effectiveness of positioning depends in part on the strength and quality of the positioning activities themselves: a creative, well-developed campaign has more impact than a less successful campaign. However, effectiveness also depends on the consumer and on the extent to which the product is important for the consumer.

This section discusses three aspects that influence the consumer decision-making process:

- the degree of involvement of the consumer
- the type of product
- the stage in the product life cycle

6.5.1 Impact of involvement on the decision-making process

Not every decision is equally important. You might know from your own experience that you spend more time and energy on choosing a holiday destination than buying a bottle of cola. The importance of a specific purchase decision is indicated by the term involvement. **Involvement** is defined as the relevance that a particular brand or message has for someone, depending on his needs, values, or interests (Zaichkowsky, 1985).

Involvement can vary from low to high. The level of involvement influences the amount of energy that is put into the consumer decision process. In its most extensive form, with an extremely involved consumer, this leads to **extensive problem solving**. The **decision-making process** then consists of five phases (Figure 6.6):

1. *Need recognition*: the consumer experiences a need. Needs can be triggered in many ways: it is warm and you seek refreshment; the weekend is coming and you want to do something fun; your laptop broke down and you need a new one, and so on.
2. *Information search*: the consumer looks for possible solutions for his "problem." The need for refreshment can be solved in the swimming pool or

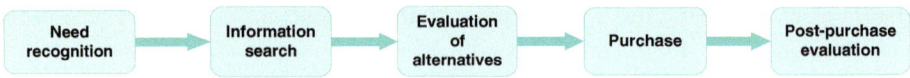

Figure 6.6 **The consumer decision-making process**

in ice cream. The solution for spending a good weekend can be found in a weekend trip with friends or a gaming marathon on the couch. Information about laptops can be found online or in the store. Mindshare is important at this stage: choices can only be considered if they are included in the consumer's evoked set.

3. *Evaluation of alternatives*: before making a choice, the brands or choice alternatives must be compared. Comparison is made on the basis of the functional, symbolic, or social benefits of the choice alternative. In this stage, brand image plays an important role: the consumer forms an opinion about the brands he considers. The multi-attribute attitude model described in Section 4.5.1 is a formalized method for comparing alternatives.

4. *Purchase*: do we take our kids to Disneyland or to Legoland? Will it be a Samsung or an Apple? Ultimately, the consumer takes a choice based on the results of the comparison in the previous phase. Heartshare can give preference to a certain brand and thus determine the choice.

5. *Post-purchase evaluation*: after the consumer has bought and used the chosen alternative, an assessment takes place; does the choice meet the expectations? **Satisfaction** can be seen as a combination of experience and expectations: if the experience is better than the expectations, then the consumer is satisfied. However, if the experience is worse than the expectations, dissatisfaction is the result. In brand positioning, too high expectations should be prevented.

Brand positioning is connected with every stage of the decision-making process. In problem recognition and information search, the creation of mindshare is emphasized: the brand must be relevant to the problem that needs to be solved and the brand must be dominantly present ("available") in the evoked set of the consumer. When assessing and choosing brands, the consumer develops a preference for a specific brand. Preference may arise because the consumer believes that the brand is best able to fulfil his needs or because he has the "feeling" that a particular brand is the right choice. Preferences relate to heartshare: the brand evokes positive associations, which means that the consumer prefers this brand to another brand.

The decision-making process described here is in line with the attitude-formation process discussed in Section 6.2. Knowledge is gathered during the information search (cognitive), after which a feeling develops during the evaluation of alternatives (affective), after which action can be taken (conative). In the development of attitudes, it was already noted that this process does not have a fixed order and can vary from situation to situation. When positioning a brand, it is important to take into account that decision-making is not always an extensive process and that often stages are skipped. In addition to extensive problem solving, two other forms of buying behaviour are distinguished: **limited problem solving** and **routinized response behaviour**.

With limited problem solving, the consumer is involved with the buying process, but he already formed a certain image through previous experiences with the brand or the product category. Consider, for example, a family that has visited theme parks before: the choice for a future visit is mainly nourished by previous experiences and by brand image that has already been formed in the past. Then the information search stage and the evaluation of alternatives can be done fairly quickly. Positioning activities then can aim at reinforcing or confirming existing images or existing patterns, or – and that is much more difficult – to change existing images and patterns. Finally, low involvement leads to routinized response behaviour. Choices are then taken out of habit or impulsively and the decision-making process is very limited. This applies, for example, to many products that are bought in the supermarket. In Chapter 1, we already indicated that most decision-making processes now take place under low involvement.

The level of involvement has consequences for the effectiveness of positioning activities. A committed consumer pays more attention to communication about products or brands, or commercial messages, and he will also look at other aspects than someone with low involvement. The **Elaboration Likelihood Model (ELM)** (Petty & Cacioppo, 1986) examines the consequences of low and high involvement (Figure 6.7).

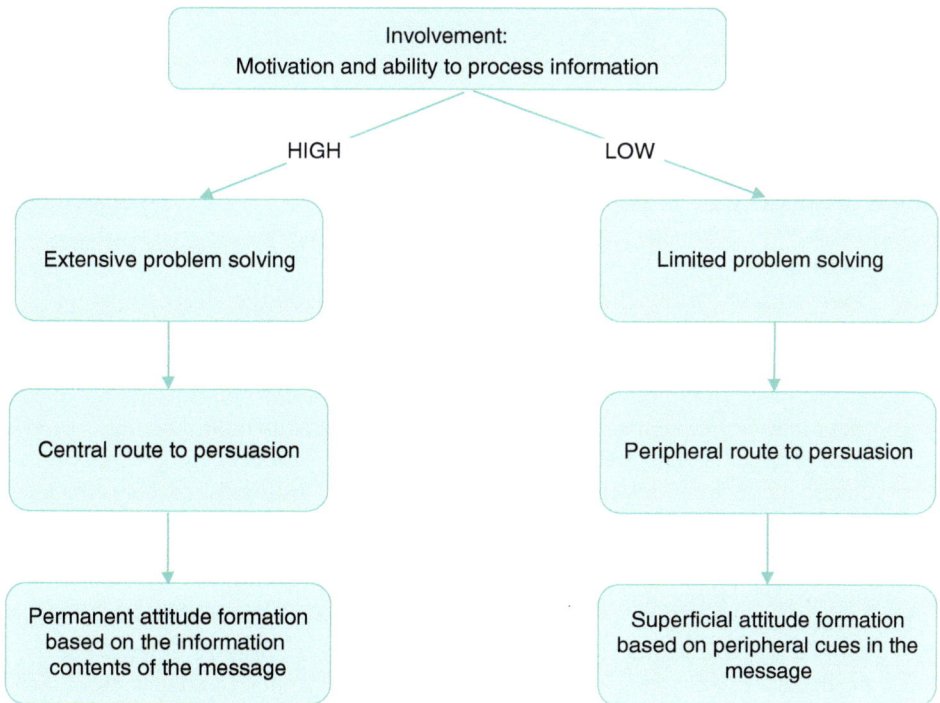

Figure 6.7 **The Elaboration Likelihood Model**

Extensive problem solving takes place under high involvement. The consumer then has the motivation and the ability to process information. The consumer follows **the central route to persuasion**: he takes the time to listen to information and will form his opinion on the basis of substantive arguments. Low involvement leads to the **peripheral route to persuasion**. The consumer puts little effort into listening to information; substantive arguments do not or hardly touch him. Consumers can only be persuaded up to a limited extent; opinions are based on "peripheral issues" such as the colour, tone, or shape of the message. Attitude formation via the peripheral route is more superficial; created associations are often only temporary and must be confirmed by continuous repetition.

This theory has consequences for positioning: a message for involved consumers must be different than a message that is processed under low involvement. Positioning under low involvement can focus more on mindshare, for example, through continuous repetition or prominent presence of the brand. Another strategy for low involvement is to create feelings: to have the consumer experience symbolic or social benefits or to present an atmosphere that is related to the core values of the brand. After all, the non-involved consumer pays little or no attention to content, and is mainly influenced by form: music, attractive images, or a likeable person who recommends the brand. The involved customer, on the other hand, listens to facts and buying reasons and is less influenced by the form of the message. In that case, a positioning strategy can focus more on instrumental brand properties.

6.5.2 Influence of the type of product on the decision-making process

Based on involvement and the amount of effort that the consumer wants to do, three types of products can be distinguished:

- **Convenience goods**. These are products ("categories") for which the consumer wants to make little effort to purchase them, so also little effort to gather information (and therefore little attention to communication about the product or brand). Routinized response behaviour is often the norm for these products. This applies to almost all **fast moving consumer goods**: non-durable products that are used frequently in almost every family. Think of food, body care products, detergents, light bulbs, or batteries. All these products are generally purchased under low involvement. Two variants are distinguished here. On the one hand there is buying out of habit: *I buy new Colgate because we are out of toothpaste*. On the other hand variation can be an important motive (so-called variety seeking behaviour): *Let me try this new taste of crisps*.
- **Shopping goods**. These are products for which the consumer is prepared to make some effort. He wants to be able to compare and try brands. Often these are products for which people go shopping. Think of clothing, holiday trips, or new furniture. Information is collected quite extensively. Compared to convenience goods, brand communication receives more attention.
- **Speciality goods** are of central importance to the consumer; a lot of effort will be made to purchase them. Often it is a brand that you specifically want to have: an

exclusive car, a Mont Blanc fountain pen, or a bottle of Chablis. A speciality brand does not have to be extremely expensive; the point is that the brand and/ or the category is so special for the consumer that he only wants that one and nothing else.

This classification says something about involvement and the amount of energy that the consumer wants to invest in the buying process and information search. For shopping goods and particularly speciality goods, consumers pay more attention to brand communication, making it easier for the brand to find a "listening ear." This again has consequences for the effectiveness of a particular positioning, but this connection is not always clear. We illustrate this for shopping goods in the following example.

Example 6.3 Positioning strategy for shopping goods

Some shopping goods, such as clothing, furniture, or cosmetics, have a major impact on someone's life and are sometimes even seen by people as an extension of their own personality. Transformational positioning that emphasizes symbolic or social benefits or that connects with important values of the target group then makes sense. The following figure illustrates.

Photo 6.3 **Perfume and make-up: shopping goods with high symbolic value. Photo CC0 public domain**

By contrast, shopping goods such as travel insurances or laundry machines seem to invite for choices based on instrumental benefits, making informational positioning more appropriate (see the next image).

Photo 6.4 Laundry machines: a shopping good with mainly instrumental benefits. Photo CC0 public domain

A distinction like the one in Example 6.3 can also be made for speciality goods and convenience goods: sometimes the consumer is looking for information and sometimes for a feeling. For some product categories, therefore, informational positioning based on instrumental benefits seems more appropriate, while in other product categories a transformational positioning seems to be preferable. There are also product categories in which both aspects are important; cars form a good example.

Informational positioning is also associated with products that solve consumer problems: washing machines clean dirty clothes, painkillers kill pain, education makes you smart, health care improves your health, and so on. This type of products change a negative, unpleasant, or risky state in a neutral situation. This is in contrast to products that add value: these products change a neutral situation into a positive situation: holidays, candy, or designer clothes. For these products, a transformational positioning often seems more appropriate. But there are many exceptions to this distinction. For example, perfume but also shower gel or deodorant are generally transformationally positioned: they are often profiled as making the man attractive to the woman (or the woman for the man, depending on the target group). In essence, however, deodorant and perfume are problem solvers: they prevent unpleasant body odour.

Based on the distinction between degree of involvement on the one hand and the "emotional value" of the product (informational or transformational) on the other, Rossiter and Percy developed a matrix in which four types of products are distinguished (Rossiter, Percy & Donovan, 1991). Table 6.1 shows this **Rossiter-Percy grid**.

An approach such as the Rossiter-Percy grid suggests that a detailed classification can be made in the most appropriate positioning strategy for a certain

Table 6.1 **Rossiter-Percy grid**

	Informational (solving problems)	Transformational (adding value)
Low involvement	Matches Laundry detergent Many fast moving consumer goods	Beer Snacks Shower gel
High involvement	Washing machines Travel insurance Refrigerators	Clothes Cosmetics Holiday travel

product category: a kind of cookbook recipe for choosing the right brand position-ing strategy. But nothing could be less true. Such an approach leaves little room for the creative aspect of brand positioning. And more importantly, we have to keep in mind that the consumer is not rigid. Brands can fulfil a very different function depending on the consumer, the situation, and the moment: when a guy invites his new girlfriend for a romantic Italian dinner at his place, for instance, wine and pasta sauce become shopping goods with a high emotional value, while these products in a lot of other contexts are convenience goods. Therefore, it is often better to refer to situation-specific involvement than to involvement in a product category in general.

6.5.3 Influence of the product life cycle on brand positioning

The **product life cycle** describes the stages that a product goes through from the mo-ment it arrives on the market. The life cycle of a product is usually visualized by means of a graph that shows the sales over time. It is usually assumed that this curve is S-shaped and that four stages can be distinguished (see Figure 6.8).

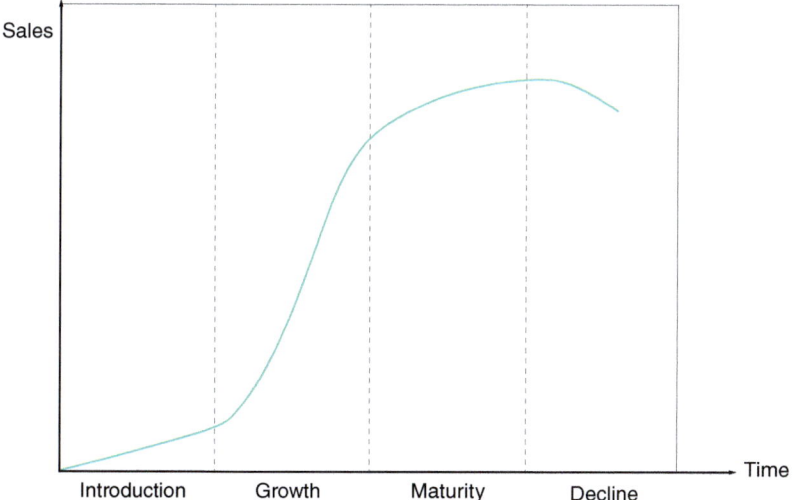

Figure 6.8 **The product life cycle**

In the **introduction stage** the product is new to the market. There is a slowly growing sales: there are few consumers who know or use the product and distribution is limited. When brands come up with a new product, the positioning must be aimed at communicating the essence of the product: its attributes and the benefits for the consumer. Consumers have to learn what the new product can do for them. When, for example, the first non-alcoholic beer arrived on the market, the consumer had to be explained what that is. An informational positioning makes sense in the introduction stage; positioning is aimed at familiarity and relevance of the new product.

The **growth stage** shows an increasing growth in sales: the product is catching on, distribution is increasing, and more and more consumers are buying it. At the same time, more and more competitors are entering the market. In the growth stage, the emphasis is on creating brand preference: emphasizing the unique benefits or brand values of your brand. A distinction must therefore be created, functional or transformational. When major beer brands such as Heineken and Budweiser came up with a non-alcoholic variant, they tried to "conquer" customers by means of the strength and the appearance of their own brand name. The growing market in the growth stage prevents a fierce battle for market share: if a brand knows positions well, and if this matches the benefits or values that consumers are looking for, there will usually be place for that brand in the market. As a result, in addition to establishing brand relevance, creating a strong brand image is also important in the growth stage.

The following phases are characterized by saturation. In the **maturity stage,** sales are initially still growing, but this growth is getting smaller. Eventually, the growth levels off and then changes into a slow decline in sales. In mature markets, most consumers already have the product at home. Increasing competition implies that every percent in market share is contested heavily. Brands can only grow at the expense of others. In the maturity stage, distinctions between brands are often small. Mature markets are typically the markets that Sharp (2012) envisages when he talks about low involvement. Positioning should then be focused on brand relevance: a very strong association between the brand and the need for it. If the consumer feels a certain need (for ice cream, a new detergent, or a pasta sauce), then he must first think of your brand. Other strategies that are commonly used in this stage:

- The emphasis on Unique Selling Points (USPs), sometimes compared directly with competition: the detergent that washes even better, the toothpaste that prevents cavities even more, and so on.
- An informational positioning demonstrating product improvement. Lay's potato chips (Walkers in the United Kingdom) is a good example. That brand profiles itself as market leader by constantly introducing new flavours on the market.
- A transformational positioning that emphasizes the core values of the brand: Coca-Cola (happiness), Heineken (enjoy responsibly), and Disney (inspiring joy and enchantment for the whole family) are good examples.

Finally, sales levels of a product in the **decline stage** begin to fall sharply: in this stage the product loses ground to alternative products. This market seems less interesting, but precisely because many brands leave the market, it is possible to build up a special niche position. For example, a number of record shops (offline and online) have built a strong position in vinyl records and are now reaping the benefits: a specific and currently again increasing segment of buyers continues to listen to long play vinyl records. A positioning strategy emphasizing a speciality status often fits well with this specific segment of enthusiasts that remain faithful to a certain product. However, brand associations with products in the decline stage do have risks: Nokia, for example, was never really taken seriously as a smartphone brand due to its association with the "old-fashioned" mobile phone.

6.6 Defining the brand positioning strategy

If the direction of the positioning strategy is determined, the next challenge is to put it into words. Loose phrases, management views, and flowcharts, but also brand values, must be converted into an engaging story. We give four possibilities to do this:

1. the positioning statement
2. the Brand Key
3. the brand story
4. the Golden Circle model

After discussing these possibilities, we will discuss the choice of the right words or images to describe the brand positioning.

6.6.1 Positioning statement

The positioning can be described concisely in a positioning statement. A **positioning statement** is a summary of the main ingredients of the brand positioning, and basically has the following form:

> *Our brand [BRAND NAME A] is for [TARGET GROUP B] better than [COMPETITOR C] because of [BENEFIT D]. We can make this happen because of [REASON WHY E], and it is a consequence of [BRAND VALUE F].*

The format for the positioning statement obviously does not always have to be the same; variations may occur depending on the emphasis that one wants to make. For example, the reason why will be of particular importance in informational positioning, and will be less prominent in transformational positioning. A possible positioning statement for Center Parcs could be:

> *Center Parcs is better for families with young children than other holiday destinations because of the unique family experience. We can offer this because we have many entertaining and innovative family activities. Our drive to provide a wonderful family experience results from our brand values emotion, share, care, and joy.*

6.6.2 Brand Key model

The **Brand Key** model is another format to define a brand positioning. The Brand Key consists of eight components (see Figure 6.9).

In the lower part of the Brand Key, essential market and target group information needs to be collected:

1. Target group: what is or are the most important target group(s) of the brand? The target group is not only defined by socio-demographic characteristics, but also in terms of attitudes and values.
2. Competitive environment: who are the main competitors and with what do they distinguish themselves? These can be direct competitors of the brand, but also brands that meet the same need but belong to a different product category. For a cinema chain such as Pathé cinemas, other cinemas are competitors, but also Netflix, or restaurants, or other entertainment venues.
3. Insight: a **customer insight** is a deeper purchase motivation that is important for both the brand and the target group. The insight answers questions such as: "Which motives are decisive in the selection process?" Sometimes insights are referred to as Unique Buying Reasons (**UBRs**), a concept that is used as a counterpart to the **USP**: USPs emphasize the unique aspects of the product, whereas UBRs shift attention to the unique reasons why consumers want the brand.

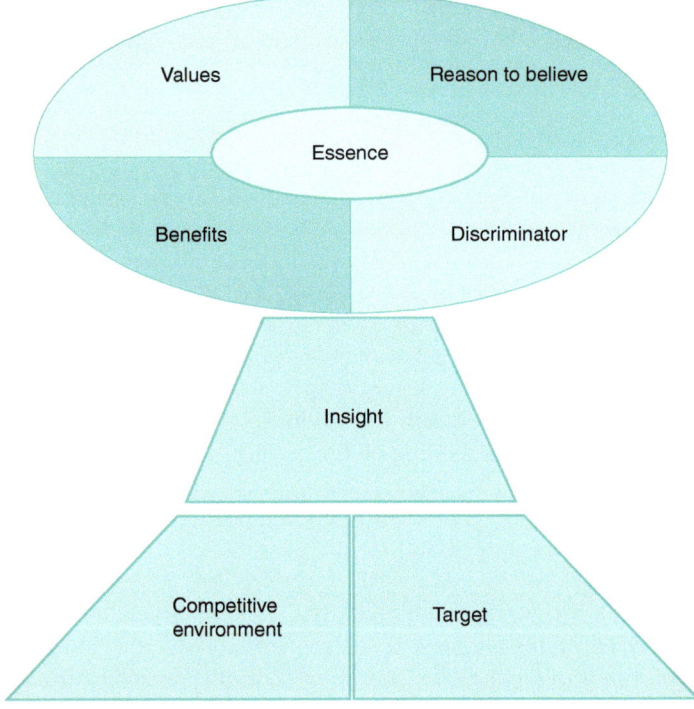

Figure 6.9 **The Brand Key model**

The upper part of the Brand Key relates to the brand itself:

4. Values, beliefs, and personality: what are the brand values (e.g. defined by using the Value Compass) and what is the brand personality?
5. Benefits: what are the functional, social, and/or experience-focused benefits of the brand?
6. Reasons to believe: this relates to supportive evidence; why would anyone believe that our brand has the advantages mentioned earlier?
7. Discriminator: what makes our brand different from all other brands?

Finally, the "heart" of the key contains the **brand essence**. The brand essence is the core promise of the brand, expressed in a short but powerful sense: "Head & Shoulders: dandruff care for great looking hair." The brand essence can also be used as the starting point for creating a slogan.

The Brand Key was developed by Unilever, but is also used by other organizations, either like this or in a slightly modified form. Consumer insights, i.e. the search for the most important purchasing motives for the brand, have an important role in these models.

6.6.3 Brand story

When articulating the brand positioning, a manager can also choose to convert the positioning into a story. **Storytelling** is a powerful tool to engage your audience. Stories are used to inspire, to convince, or to touch your audience through metaphors or other style elements. The power of a story is enhanced by the correct application of these style elements: a powerful positioning only becomes a powerful story if this story is also told in the right way.

The **brand story** is a description of the key elements of the brand positioning in the form of a story of not more than one page and preferably much shorter, approximately 400– 600 words. In literature, the term corporate story is often used (see, among others, Van Riel, 2010). This creates the suggestion that a story can only be told at corporate level, i.e. for the entire company. In our view, the essence of each brand can be represented in a story; that is why we prefer the term brand story. Example 6.4 shows the brand story of HEMA, a Dutch department store that expanded since the 1990s into a number of other countries.

Example 6.4 The HEMA story (www.hema.nl)

HEMA's dream: how did we start?
We go back in time, to the 1920s. Two Jewish entrepreneurs, Arthur Isaac and Leo Meyer, experience the Great Depression from close by. They see countless people who are struggling to make ends meet. Both men wondered: "Can we make the everyday life of these people a little easier?". This is how their dream started. Wouldn't it be a great idea to open a store especially for people that have to live on a small budget? A store

with simple articles for daily use, low-priced but good quality? Alfred Goudsmit, the director of a Dutch department store, reacts enthusiastically to the idea and incorporates the idea. The dream of the two men gets a name: the "Hollandsche Eenheidsprijzen Maatschappij Amsterdam" (Dutch standard prices company Amsterdam). On November 4, 1926, the first HEMA opens its doors in Amsterdam.

Shoppers in Amsterdam react with surprise: perfume and chocolate, women's and men's fashion and household items for only 25 or 50 cents. Quality at a low price is the message of the HEMA. And that message hits during the crisis of the thirties. Not only with the poor. The rich are also happy with HEMA. However, they send their servants, because in such a shop you don't want to be spotted as a lady or a gentleman.

After World War II, the economy is booming and people have more and more money to spend. HEMA is growing and is the first Dutch company to set up a franchise organization in 1958. We noticed that the consumer is becoming increasingly demanding and starts asking for quality. That is why we distinguish ourselves with unbeatable products: user-friendly, low-priced, and with a unique HEMA signature. HEMA can no longer be ignored in large and smaller cities. The brand is cool and trendy, for young and old, for men and women. Does this mean that we can lay back and relax? No, never. The consumer is changing and we are moving with it. We surprise him with new food departments and innovative fashion and hospitality concepts. The engine is our drive to excel, in making the simple special.

Photo 6.5 HEMA, since 1926. Photo © Jordy Schaap (cc-by-sa/4.0), with permission of HEMA

HEMA's identity: what do we stand for?

HEMA has proved it since 1926: a nice and easy life does not have to be expensive. Enter our stores and you'll notice immediately. Shelf for shelf you will find the best articles for every day: stylishly designed, original, of good quality, and with a surprisingly low priced. HEMA has Products that make you happy, whatever your budget, because they are special and yet so ordinary, a unique combination that you will not find in any other store. That makes HEMA really HEMA: a shop for everyone, in the Netherlands, but also in Belgium, Germany, France, and many other countries. HEMA can be summarized in a few words: the simple made special. Long before the term "private label" existed, we developed our articles ourselves, from towels to lamps and from underwear to bicycle lights – most everyday things, but 100% HEMA: accessible to everyone. Making ordinary things special is not just the design. It also includes our distribution, or bakery, our corporate office, and the interior of our shops.

A brand story must be experienced. It must be translated into everything the brand expresses. Often the brand story is also written down in, for example, internal publications or on the website. Heineken even published the Heineken story as a book.

A brand story is the brand positioning wrapped up in a story. A brand story combines management's ambitions and the wishes and feelings of the target group realistically but convincingly with the strengths of the brand. The story therefore communicates the brand identity and core values of the brand, and allows the target group to feel all the functional and emotional benefits that the brand represents. Van Riel (2010) mentions four requirements that a good story must meet:

1. Relevant: the added value for the target group must be clear.
2. Realistic: the message must convince, but it must be a realistic reflection of what the brand can deliver: no empty promises.
3. Sustainable: all stakeholders must agree with the brand story. A story with which certain interest groups disagree will quickly lead to harmful word-of-mouth via social media.
4. Open dialogue: the story must have been created in an open dialogue with all relevant stakeholders. For example, the opinion of the target group can be taken into account by presenting a concept brand story in a number of focus group sessions with people from the target group.

"A picture is worth a thousand words." It is tempting to think of a text in a story. But visual storytelling by using photography, video, or illustrations is becoming more and more important, especially in the current social media era. Research shows that a story with visuals leaves a stronger impression than a story in words (Omondi, 2013).

YouTube provides many corporate examples:

- Google makes an emotional appeal by showing that accessible information improves our lives in many special ways: www.youtube.com/watch?v=gHGDN9-oFJE&list=PL-kIBfSqQg3uMx9Z1fOpc7WPw2wDvbhFu
- Dawn Liquid Detergent tells you that the brand cares for more than just your dishes: www.youtube.com/watch?v=WpXx1C-0X0w
- The Guinness empty chair commercial tells us that "The choices we make reveal the true nature of our character." And obviously this not just reflects our choices, but also the brand's choices: www.youtube.com/watch?v=WnYgRJ2Z6IQ

Example 6.5 illustrates that a brand story, like the more "traditional" positioning statement, can serve as a starting point for the development of communication tools: in this case the New Zealand website.

Example 6.5 The New Zealand Story

New Zealand provides an excellent example of positioning based on brand values. On the country's website, www.newzealand.com, you are greeted with "Kia ora – welcome to New Zealand." There are four buttons representing the country's four target

Photo 6.6 Illustration of the New Zealand Story including the three core values. Photo provided with permission of New Zealand Story Group

groups: "Visit," "Invest," "Study," and "Live & Work." Each button of course gives access to specific information about its theme.

Interestingly, the entire website is linked to the New Zealand Story. In this story three core values underpin the country reputation programme:

- Kaitiaki: care for people and place
- Ingenuity: our fresh, outward-looking way of thinking
- Integrity: trust, honesty, humility, and reciprocal interest

The content behind "holiday with us" or the content behind the other three buttons is based on these brand values. The New Zealand Story is supported by a website (www. nzstory.govt.nz/), and can also be found (in a couple of variants) on YouTube: www. youtube.com/watch?v=DU7ZGTfpETk

6.6.4 The Golden Circle

In 2010, Simon Sinek introduced an interesting idea about how companies should position themselves. He stated that positioning is not just about what you sell or "how" you are different, but especially "why" you are different (Figure 6.10).

Sinek uses the example of Apple: the essence of the why of this brand is "think different." Apple does this by making products with a beautiful design that, at the same time, stimulates ease of use ("how").

Sinek's line of thinking stimulates the importance of having a vision for the brand. A vision often contains the opinion of the founder of a company. A good vision is very inspiring for employees and possibly also for customers.

This book focuses mainly on the "how" component of Sinek's **Golden Circle**: identifying the distinctive aspects of the brand. However, we do make a link with the "why" question because we emphasize the importance of values as the basis for positioning. Values highlight what brands (or consumers) consider important and that is close to Sinek's "why."

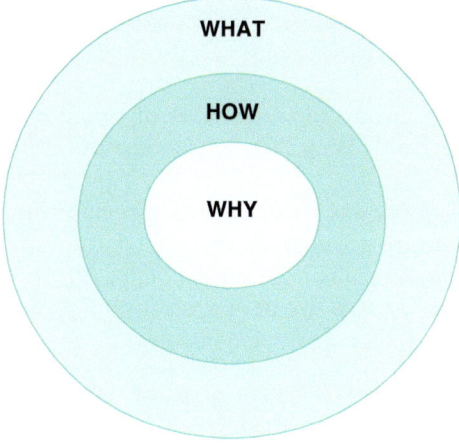

Figure 6.10 The Golden Circle

6.6.5 Positioning: finding the right words and images

Whether it is in the form of a statement or in the form of a story, ultimately the right words or images have to be chosen for positioning. How do you arrive at the final wording of the positioning of your brand?

The preliminary work, in the form of determining brand image and brand identity as discussed in the previous chapters, has been carried out. Armed with this knowledge, the responsible manager must determine a positioning strategy. This **positioning strategy** describes the way in which the brand image as desired by management must be achieved; further details of this positioning strategy also depend on the aspects discussed in this chapter:

- the decision-making process of the consumer in the target group
- the process through which the target group forms an attitude about the brand
- the degree of involvement of consumers in the target group
- the type of product to which the brand relates
- the product life cycle stage of the brand

The positioning strategy involves a number of choices:

- Is there a more informational or a more transformational approach?
- Does the positioning focus on mindshare or on heartshare, or on both?
- In the case of mindshare: is the focus on getting a reputation or brand relevance?
- In case of heartshare: which product characteristics, benefits, and/or brand values are put central?

These choices should be made by the manager responsible for the brand. It is, obviously, recommended to first create internal support, for instance with internal brainstorming sessions. Often the positioning strategy will be the result of a number of discussion rounds. These discussions can take place internally together with the management or with representatives of other (internal or external) stakeholders. A project team can also be composed, consisting of people involved in the brand positioning. If necessary, external support can also be used; consultants can be hired for this.

It is advisable to also involve representatives of brand-relevant stakeholders in this process, in order to avoid losing sight of customers or other stakeholders in the internal discussions.

The outcome of this process is the choice for a specific positioning strategy. This must then be converted into a beautiful piece of text or a collection of appropriate images. For this one can collaborate with a copywriter or a specialized agency. Preferably, two or three variants are developed in this phase. These concepts are presented to a number of focus groups consisting of consumers from the target group or from other relevant stakeholders. The precise definition of the positioning strategy will then be the result of these focus groups.

Summary

Positioning can be informational or transformational. An informational positioning focuses on the concrete benefits of using the brand, while a transformational positioning is focused on brand image or brand experience. We speak of two-sided positioning when these things are combined. Finally, positioning can be focused on execution elements, when the brand is positioned on the basis of certain elements from the campaign itself.

Positioning activities are aimed at influencing the image of the brand: you want to change or even strengthen the brand image. This brand image consists of all the associations evoked by the brand. These associations can be schematically represented in the form of the means-end chain. Product attributes, benefits, and customer values are linked to each other in such a means-end chain.

Brand positioning can be directed at each of those three levels. In the positioning, values can thus be emphasized, or product attributes, or benefits of the brand. In an informational positioning the functional benefits are emphasized, while in a transformational positioning the focus is on symbolic or experience-oriented benefits. At the highest level of the means-end chain, the positioning focuses on profiling brand values, and the aim is to connect with the central values of the target group. The Value Compass can be used here as an instrument. Finally, a positioning can also emphasize relationships between the three levels:

> We know that honey is healthy, but did you know that it is also very suitable as a sugar replacement in the tea? In that case, you are not only healthy, but you also surprise your family with something special.

In our view, an integrated approach is preferable.

The choice for a specific positioning depends on the desired attitude of the target group towards the brand. This attitude is the opinion of that target group about the brand, and consists of three aspects: knowledge, feeling, and behaviour. If a brand does not evoke the right emotions to the target group, then brand associations have to be emphasized in the brand positioning. In that case the means-end chain can be used as an instrument. This is what we have described as heartshare: creating positive and distinctive brand associations that meet the needs and desires of consumers. But we have also seen that a lot of decision-making takes place under low involvement, and that the consumer simply chooses the brand that pops up first. In that case, awareness is essential: the consumer must think of the brand when he feels a certain need. Positioning on the basis of mindshare aims at realizing brand awareness and brand relevance. Regardless of the positioning strategy, it is important to take into account the four laws of branding:

1. Focus: base your positioning on your strengths, with a focus on those core values and competences that lie in "the heart of the brand."
2. Distinction: make a difference with the competition.
3. Relevance: match the needs of the target audience.

4. Consistency: positioning elements must reinforce each other, be implemented consistently over time, and be consistent for the various products under the brand's umbrella.

The choice of a positioning strategy therefore depends on the brand image that should be realized in the target group, and it also depends on the degree of involvement of the target group. In this chapter we have also seen that the positioning strategy depends on:

■   the type of product (problem solving or value-added)
■   the stage in the product life cycle

This can be summarized as: creating a brand positioning is a creative process, but the responsible manager has to define clear criteria with which the positioning must comply.

The positioning strategy indicates a direction: in which direction should the image of the brand develop? This direction becomes tangible on the moment that the positioning is written down. Guidelines are focus, consistency, distinction, and relevance.

For the actual description of the positioning we indicated four possibilities:

■   the positioning statement
■   the Brand Key
■   the brand story
■   the Golden Circle model

Finally, although we are talking about "writing down the positioning," in the current digital age, a visual story is preferred: "A picture says more than a thousand words." And with a bit of luck, your brand story will then go viral on YouTube!

Case material
for Part II

Case 1. Adidas: Sports or hip-hop fashion?

Adolf "Adi" Dassler, a shoemaker, started the Adidas brand in his hometown of Herzogenaurach in 1949. Before that time, Adolf had a shoe factory together with his older brother Rudolf. One of their models had spikes; these shoes were worn by the legendary Jesse Owens during the 1936 Olympic Games in Berlin. In 1948 the brothers split up, and brother Rudolf founded the rival brand Puma. In 1954, the West German team won the world championships soccer on Adidas shoes. This was the debut of Adidas on the world market.

Currently, the Adidas company, also the owner of the Reebok brand, has problems with its share in the world market. Competitor Nike, Inc., with the brands Nike, Air Jordans and Converse, has acquired a share of almost 50% in the American market for sports shoes. The share of Adidas is only 9%, and has been declining since 2011. Of course, Adidas still dominates the most important sport on earth: the worldwide market share in the market for football shoes is around 39%. But here too, Nike is rapidly approaching. The warning is clear: in Western Europe, the home market of Adidas, Nike has been growing faster than Adidas.

However, the most important battlefield is in the United States. 40% of all athletic shoes in the world are sold there. And that is the market where now nine of the ten best-selling models are from Nike. That one other model is not even from Adidas, but from Under Armor, a brand that is now number 2 in the sports market in the United States due to its enormous growth. As a result, Adidas is now in third place in this market, while this brand once dominated the market. Much has been said about the rivalry between Adidas and Nike, but the rise of Under Armor really scared the managers at Adidas' headquarters in Herzogenaurach. The third place in market share in the sports market made the alarm bells ring. "That's how niche players often do," said Mark King, CEO of Adidas North America. "Two percent here, three percent there, and suddenly those small wins becomes a freaking 30%."

The iconic Adidas brand has lost much of its share in the American market. The problem is not a difference in walking comfort or quality of the shoe.

In the sports shoe market, brand image is king. The Adidas CEO points to the difference between American and European sports culture. Adidas' strategy was aimed at dominating football; it was assumed that success in football would stimulate the brand in other sports. This strategy worked for a long time in other countries, but not in the United States. After all, football is hardly a relevant sport there.

It seems clear that Adidas has not been present enough in American sports. To be successful in the United States, consumers must be reminded that Adidas is a "running-shooting-scoring" brand.

RUNNING THE WRONG WAY

In the critical U.S. market, Adidas footwear sales have struggled in the face of heated competition from the Swoosh and others.

GLOBAL FOOTWEAR SALES 2010– 14

$25 BILLION

U.S. FOOTWEAR MARKET SHARE, 2014

48.0%	Nike Inc. (Nike, Jordan Brand, Converse)
9.2%	VF Corp. (Timberland, Vans, Reef)
8.7%	Adidas Group (Adidas, Reebok)

Source: Sporting Goods Intelligence

Liedtke, Adidas' global brand manager, is even more explicit. He says that Adidas must "reset" everywhere, not just in the United States. He points out that young athletes no longer look at the three stripes as they did about 20 years ago. "Often we are not even in the evoked set," he says about the buyers of sports shoes. "That breaks my heart."

And yet, instead of sport, Adidas is associated with hip-hop culture by many American consumers. This dates back to 1986, when the rap trio

Run-DMC launched the song "My Adidas." Due to the increasing popularity of this segment, it was decided in 2000 to make a split into two business units: Sport Performance (sport shoes) and Sport Style (fashion and lifestyle shoes). Under this latter theme, Adidas collaborated with designers such as Jeremy Scott and Yohji Yamamoto, pop artists such as Katy Perry, Kanye West, and Pharrel Williams, and the brand even designed signature shoes with lesser-known rappers like Big Sean and Pusha T.

"Sport mixes more and more with fashion, with lifestyle, with streetwear," according to Adidas CEO Herbert Hainer. "I estimate that 80% of all basketball shoes sold will never see a gym. They are worn for status and to be cool. Sport has a connection with lifestyle, and I think that's good. At Adidas, we want to take advantage of that."

On a Thursday night in February 2015, Jay Z, Beyoncé, Rihanna, Sean ("Puff Daddy") Combs, Vogue editor Anna Wintour – "and no fewer than six Kardashians," – squeezed elbow to elbow into a SoHo event space to see Kanye West debut his "Kanye West x Adidas Originals Yeezy Season 1" collection. (Justin Bieber was there too, but apparently couldn't get a seat in front.) As a lone trumpet solemnly blared, 45 models marched out in a mélange of blousy sweatshirts, bomber jackets, and flesh-toned bodysuits. The buzz wasn't about the clothes, though. Hardly. It was about the sneakers.

The rapper followed his models on the catwalk sporting a pair: grey suede high-tops that fell somewhere on the fashion spectrum between mukluks and moon boots. These were the new Yeezy Boost, rumours (and sightings) of which had swirled around the web for months.

That night, not far from Madison Square Garden, West switched effortlessly from fashion designer to megawatt rap star, kicking off the NBA's All-Star Weekend – the world's most high-profile sneaker showcase – with a free concert, co-hosted by last season's league most valuable player (MVP), Kevin Durant. West praised Adidas from the stage and told the crowd to shun arch competitor Nike: "We ain't wearing that other company no more, right?" The very next night he was busting onstage at a Drake concert, handing the fellow superstar his signature sneaks. (Drake set them atop a speaker, where they remained for the rest of the set.) The next morning West was delivering pairs of the shoes to surprise fans at an Adidas store in SoHo.

The show, said the *Los Angeles Times*, drew "possibly one of the highest-wattage front rows in New York Fashion Week history." The *New York Times* said it "certainly had the front row of the year." *Glamour* said, "It was like, seriously packed."

The collaboration with Kanye West gave Adidas a lot of buzz. But whether it is going to give sales of sports shoes a new boost remains doubtful. Even with icons such as Kanye West, this strategy could be risky. Some analysts wonder whether the movement towards hip-hop fashion could ever make Adidas win over Nike again. An analyst makes the following comparison: "Think like it's a glass of beer. The fashion business should be your foam. The sports world is your beer. Adidas now creates a lot of foam but they don't have enough beer."

Hainer admits that Adidas has not performed well on the sports front. However, he emphasizes that this is not due to the attention for street fashion. "It's not because we did too much hip hop and celebrities. We just didn't do enough sport." He adds that Adidas will always remain true to its identity: "If you look at our new campaigns in the US, then they scream sports, sports, sports!"

Perhaps. But what to think of the $500 Yeezy duck boots. Nobody is going to play street ball with them.

Source: Fortune Magazine, June 1, 2015

Questions

1. Brand values and consumer values play an important role in creating a brand positioning strategy.
    a) On the basis of the Value Compass, assess with which values top sports is associated.
    b) Use the Value Compass to assess the values associated with fashion and hip-hop culture.
    c) Describe – based on your answers to the two previous questions – the positioning problem that Adidas is confronted with when it wants to profile itself as both a sports brand and a fashion brand.
    d) Give your own opinion: how should Adidas solve this dilemma? Motivate your answer.

2. Global brand manager Liedtke refers to the evoked set.
    a) What does the term evoked set mean?
    b) Which two conditions must be met before a brand is included in the evoked set?
    c) Which of these two conditions do you think is the most problematic for Adidas as a sports brand? Explain your answer.

3. The book distinguishes four indicators to measure mindshare.
    a) Which four indicators are these?
    b) Create research questions for measuring the mindshare of the sports brands Adidas, Nike, Puma, and Under Armor, for each of these four indicators.
    c) Investigate the mindshare of these four brands with a sample of at least 25 respondents. Analyze the results and then draw your conclusions.

4. The multi-attribute attitude model can be used to compare the image of Nike and Adidas brands.
    a) Define attributes (properties) that you would like to use to compare these brands. Use attributes that relate to both sports and lifestyle.
    b) Make the questionnaire with which you can compare Nike and Adidas according to the multi-attribute attitude model. Make sure

that you can measure both desires (importance weights) and beliefs, and use the attributes that you mentioned in the previous question.

c) Compare – by using the questionnaire you developed in the previous subquestion – the brand image of Adidas and Nike with a sample of at least 25 respondents. Analyze the results and then draw your conclusions.

5. At the end of the case, CEO Hainer refers to the identity of Adidas. What do you think is the identity of Adidas?

6. Use the four laws of branding to assess whether Adidas is currently a strong brand in the United States.

Case 2. The power of a brand story: "Meet me at Starbucks"

Starbucks can be found everywhere. The brand has become a real status symbol. For example, in many places you can see that people, after emptying their Starbucks cup, continue to hold on their cups for a long time. The most important thing for Starbucks is that customers do not feel like a customer, but more like part of the family. When you place your order, you will first be asked your name. Then the barista calls something like "one café latte for Peter." And then "Peter, your latte is ready." And when you leave, they say "Bye bye Peter." It gives the feeling of "they know me here, they like me." The homely feeling is enhanced by the relaxed chairs, and the tables dotted with newspapers, comic books, and magazines. The free WiFi makes the store the perfect place to work or meet your friends in a homely atmosphere.

In September 2014, Starbucks rolled out its first global campaign, under the theme "Meet me at Starbucks." This campaign mainly uses YouTube. For this global campaign, the focus is not on the products, as the company normally does through its advertisements. On the contrary, it is focused on brand experience by creating a brand story. In this story "real life stories" of people who meet at Starbucks are connected. This "story" was created in Starbucks stores in 28 countries, in just 24 hours. It became a powerful story of encounters, where shared experiences, memories, new ideas, business meetings, and romantic moments are interwoven with Starbucks as a common meeting place. The stories strengthened the campaign slogan "Inspiring and nurturing the human spirit – one person, one cup, and one at a time." This is not the first campaign of its kind for Starbucks, but it is the first time that the company did it on such a global scale.

The story starts with the text: "Every day around the world, millions of people gather at Starbucks, but it's never been just about the coffee." Then several people enter the story, and we get to see what they do when they go to Starbucks. The brand story of Starbucks is thus actually told from the perspective of the Starbucks' visitors.

The campaign is a good example of integrated marketing communication. The brand story can be seen on YouTube, in the form of a 6-minute film. A shortened version of this film, a 60-second commercial, was broadcast on television in the United States. The commercial was used by Starbucks in other countries, with variants on this TV spot. Other media used were billboards and displays, and advertisements on different websites. In addition, the Instagram hashtag #HowWeMet was used. Here Starbucks encourages users to take photos showing them who they meet in Starbucks. Twitter and Tumblr are also used for the "Meet me at Starbucks" campaign.

On YouTube, the film also has an interactive element: during the video the viewer can click to mini-documentaries: mini-stories that emphasize certain aspects of the Starbucks story. For example, one such mini-story tells the story of a deaf lady in Honolulu who says she usually feels left out when people talk to each other until she got in touch with a group of deaf friends who meet regularly, at the local Starbucks store. The moral of this story: Starbucks brings people together.

---

www.starbucks.com presents a detailed description of the mission statement of Starbucks

The Starbucks Mission: to inspire and nurture the human spirit – one person, one cup and one neighbourhood at a time. Here are the principles of how we live that every day:

Our coffee

It has always been, and will always be, about quality. We're passionate about ethically sourcing the finest coffee beans, roasting them with great care and improving the lives of people who grow them. We care deeply about all of this; our work is never done.

Our partners

We're called partners, because it's not just a job, it's our passion. Together, we embrace diversity to create a place where each of us can be ourselves. We always treat each other with respect and dignity. And we hold each other to that standard.

Our customers

When we are fully engaged, we connect with, laugh with, and uplift the lives of our customers – even if just for a few moments. Sure, it starts with the promise of a perfectly made beverage, but our work goes far beyond that. It's really about human connection.

Our stores

When our customers feel this sense of belonging, our stores become a haven, a break from the worries outside, a place where you can meet with friends. It's about enjoyment at the speed of life – sometimes slow and savoured, sometimes faster. Always full of humanity.

Our neighbourhood

Every store is part of a community, and we take our responsibility to be good neighbours seriously. We want to be invited in wherever we do business. We can be a force for positive action – bringing together our partners, customers, and the community to contribute every day. Now we see that our responsibility – and our potential for good – is even larger. The world is looking to Starbucks to set the new standard, yet again. We will lead.

Our shareholders

We know that as we deliver in each of these areas, we enjoy the kind of success that rewards our shareholders. We are fully accountable to get each of these elements right so that Starbucks – and everyone it touches – can endure and thrive.

Source: www.starbucks.com, December 9, 2015.

Questions

1. a) The book distinguishes three types of benefits. Which three are these?
    b) Explain to what extent each of these benefits is emphasized in the Starbucks brand story.
2. Create a means-end chain for Starbucks.
3. Demonstrate with the Value Compass which are the core values for Starbucks. Argue whether you consider this a consistent value profile.
4. Is the brand story of Starbucks focusing on mindshare or heartshare? Explain your answer.
5. a) Which four types of positioning are distinguished in the book?
    b) Which of these types match the "Meet me at Starbucks" campaign? Explain your answer.
6. Describe the positioning strategy behind the campaign "Meet me at Starbucks."
7. Create a positioning statement for Starbucks.
8. The book describes storytelling as "The brand story communicates the brand identity and the core values of the brand, and allows the target group to feel all the functional and emotional benefits that the brand represents." Assess whether the Starbucks brand story matches this.

Case 3. Focus Group for a Microbrewery: Maallust[1]

About Veenhuizen

Around 1820, the "Society for Benevolence" was founded in the 1820s near the hamlet of Veenhuizen, in a remote area in the north of the Netherlands. The company bought 30 km² of land to found colonies which would house and provide work for the poor from the large cities of the Netherlands.

Veenhuizen then became a reform housing colony for the poor and homeless from the large cities (like Amsterdam and The Hague). It was founded as a colony, one of the few colonies in this world within a country's own borders.

The structure is still evident in the way the village was set up. The village is made up of roads in a grid pattern with blocks measuring 700 by 700 metres, in a style similar to that of American villages. The difference with the United States is that most of these blocks are still filled in with farmland on which the inmates used to work.

Later in the 19th century the Society for Benevolence filed for bankruptcy and the whole complex/village was taken over by the Department of Justice for use as a penal colony, of which one complex is in use today as the National Prison Museum. The prison buildings that were added around 1900 are still in use today (albeit modernized several times since). The windows of the buildings have educational texts in large sculptured sills on the front, about two stories high to educate the people working in and around them. The texts used to correspond with the intended inhabitant. The headmaster's house said "knowledge is power," and the pharmacist's house said "bitter and sweet."

1 Maallust is used as an example here for creating a focus group. The brand is not available in most countries, but you can organize this focus group for other beer brands, or basically for any kind of product. When adapting the product, take care to adapt the briefing and the script accordingly.

Historic building of the Maallust brewery[2]

About Maallust

For a long time, prison village Veenhuizen was a self-sufficient village. In addition to the prisons, there were also schools, churches, a spinning mill, and farms. Farm products from the area were processed at the industrial complex.

In 2011, brewery Maallust was founded, as an initiative of 25 entrepreneurs. They not only took the initiative to brew beer in Veenhuizen but also to revitalize the dilapidated Maallust complex. In what was once the grain mill, brewery Maallust is now established. After a major refurbishment, the brewery opened its doors in this historic location. Under the old roof trusses and the remains of the drying machines are the copper kettles, in which Maallust brews its delicious beer in a traditional way. Today the Maallust complex is beautiful and the beer is available throughout the Netherlands. Maallust is the perfect addition to a village with a unique history.

2 The photos in this cases were reprinted with permission of the Maallust company.

Maallust: a microbrewery grounded in tradition

The beer

The traditional speciality beers of Maallust are contemporary, but rooted in the past and inspired by old beer types. In the beers one can taste the history of prison village Veenhuizen. The beers from Maallust are traditional, authentic, and brewed with only the best ingredients. Whether it is the Benefactor ["Weldoener"], a hoppy blonde beer, or the Heavy Boy ["Zware Jongen"], a treacherously soft triple, Maallust beers are full of character.

The "Weldoener" the blonde beer of Maallust

The challenge

Maallust is a microbrewery, with an interesting story, but there is a lot of competition in the market. By using a focus group, you should answer the following questions:

- How can Maallust successfully build a strong brand?
- How should Maallust tell its story?

■ And to who? What should be the target audience?
■ In short: how should Maallust successfully position the brand in the market?

Attached to this case is an extensive format for doing a focus group. Use this format as example to organize and execute your focus group.

Script focus group

1. Objectives

Under this header you need to state explicitly the key objective(s) of the focus group, and the research questions the focus group is supposed to answer.

Example:

Key objective

■ Map the decision-making process of the target group, with respect to buying beer.
■ Deliver insight in the perception of Maallust beer, as opposed to competing brands.

Research questions

■ What is the associative network around Maallust beer?
■ What is the perception of Maallust, as compared to competing beer brands?
■ How does the means-end chain for Maallust beer look like?
■ Which hierarchy of effects is most relevant to this type of beer?
■ How does the decision-making process look like with respect to buying a new brand of beer?

2. Activities

State for each research question the activities that should be executed during the focus group to get the answer to the research question. Activities include of course the questions to be asked, but also include appropriate research techniques, demonstration items, stickers that should be put on a whiteboard, etc.

Example:

What is the associative network around Maallust beer?

1. Show a bottle of Maallust, and after examining the packaging, have the respondents taste the beer as well.
2. Have each respondent write three associations on post-it stickers, one association per post-it.

3. Ask respondents to stick their post-its on the whiteboard.
4. Group the post-its in different types of associations.
5. Now, the first-order associations are visible on the whiteboard. As a next step second-order associations could be created by further associating in the form of a discussion. Example: a first-order association could be "strong." A discussion on associations around "strong" could give items like "a lot of alcohol," "for real men," or "vodka."
6. As end result, draw the associative network.

What is the perception of Maallust, as compared to competing beer brands?

1. Bring Maallust and five competing beer brands.
2. Show three bottles of beer, of which one of them is a Maallust bottle.
3. Ask the respondents to compare the bottles, with the help of questions like "Which of these three bottles would you buy? Why?" or "Which of these bottles does not match with the other two?" Comparison can be done based on packaging or based on taste.
4. Continue the comparison with the two bottles that remain, add another bottle, and repeat the question.
5. Etc.
6. Write down the comments from the focus group in each comparison.

How does the means-end chain with respect to Maallust beer look like?

- Etc.

3. Necessities

Based on the overview of activities, determine which objects/items should be present during the focus group.

During the focus group the following should be present:

- Maallust beer
- Four bottles of competing brands
- ...
- ...

Typical necessities include:

- Recording device.
- Laptop.
- List of participants and name tags.
- Coloured post-it stickers.

- Pens/markers.
- Whiteboard or A3-sized paper.

4. Organization and planning

A focus group typically has:

- One moderator.
- One assistant.
- 5–9 participants.

Also, a date and time have to be set. Participants need to be invited, and often get some kind of reward.

5. Detailed script of the focus group

The list of activities should be transformed in a specified script for the focus group. Based on the example used so far, the detailed script could look like:

Introduction	16:30–16:40

- Introduction of participants
- Purpose of the focus group: introduction by the moderator
- Duration of the focus group
- Etc

Associative Network of Maallust	16:40–17:10

1. Show a bottle of Maallust, and after examining the packaging, have the respondents taste the beer as well
2. Have each respondent write three associations on a post-it sticker, one association per post-it
3. Ask respondents to stick their post-its on the whiteboard
4. Group the post-its in different types of associations
5. In this way, the first-order associations are visible on the whiteboard. As a next step second-order associations could be created by further associating in the form of a discussion. Example: a first-order association could be "strong." A discussion on associations around "strong" could give items like "a lot of alcohol," "for real men," or "vodka"
6. As end result, draw the associative network

If necessary and of added value, provide here a detailed task description for both the moderator and the assistant. E.g.:

Assistant:	show bottle
Moderator:	ask respondents to examine the packaging
Assistant:	give three post-it stickers to each respondent
Moderator:	ask respondents to write associations on the stickers, and give respondents 5 minutes to do so

Etc.

Perception of Maallust and competition	17:10–17:30
....	

Means-end chain	17:30–17:45
....	

Hierarchy of effects	17:45–18:00
....	

Decision-making process	18:00–18:20
....	

Closure	18:20–18:30
■ Moderator thanks participants ■ Assistant or moderator gives premium and/or form for compensation of travel expenses ■ Moderator closes session	

Part III

The implementation of the brand positioning strategy

The end result of Part II of this book is a distinctive, relevant brand positioning strategy. Part III illustrates the consequences and implementation of a brand positioning strategy. We start with the relationship between brand positioning on the one hand and marketing and communication on the other (Chapter 7). The emphasis is on the relationship between positioning and communication, because these two elements are strongly linked. We do not devote separate chapters to the other Ps (product, price, and place) because they are sufficiently covered in other marketing books. But we do give specific attention to a couple of strategic choices that are related to the brand positioning strategy:

- the choice and interpretation of the brand architecture (Chapter 8)
- the choice of a brand name and visual design (Chapter 9)

Finally, we outline the relationship between positioning and staffing decisions in Chapter 10. The "P" of personnel may not be a marketing instrument in itself but it has important relationships with brand positioning.

Chapter 7

Brand positioning and communication

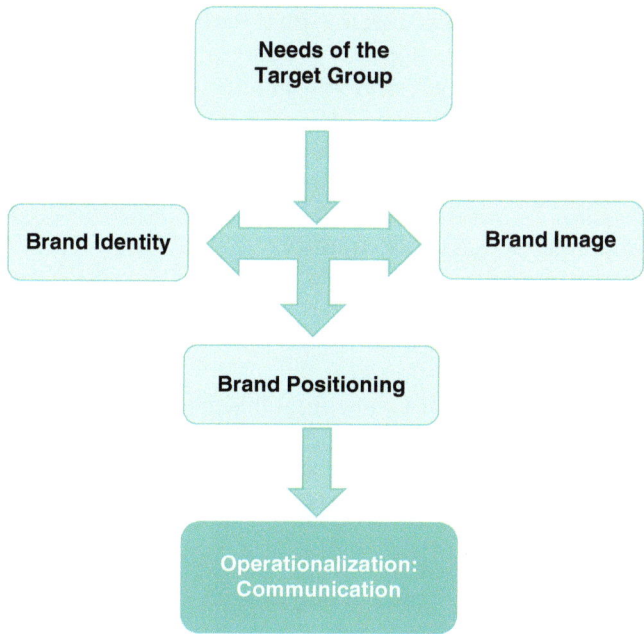

7.1 An introduction to (marketing) communications

The central marketing idea behind this book is that a clear choice for a positioning strategy is necessary before many other decisions can be made. First strategy, then tactics. The subtitle of this book is "Connecting Marketing Strategy and Communications." In Chapter 2 we explained that brand positioning is the core of the marketing strategy and that the four (or five) market instruments are the operationalization of the marketing strategy. This already gives a clear indication of the relationship between marketing and positioning.

This chapter focuses on one of the market instruments: marketing communications. This special attention is needed because of the importance of marketing communications, but also because in many companies marketing communications belong to the domain of two different departments: the marketing department and the communications department. And yet in other companies, marketing and communications merge: the marcom department.

In the professional reality of communications, the link with positioning is often insufficient. Many companies spend a lot of time and money on communications. But important communications choices are not always sufficiently strategically substantiated. "We need to be in the news again." This statement expresses a wish for a tactical way of communicating: "in the news." There can be justifiable reasons. Brand awareness could be low. Or certain brand values are insufficiently known to the target group. But "in the news again" certainly does not have to be the best way to solve this.

For the not always optimal match between marketing strategy and communications we should not blame "the marketers," nor "the communications people." The cause is often the (insufficient) cooperation between these functions, or unclarity about the differences between marketing and communications.

Many books have been published about (marketing) communications. In this chapter we focus on the strategic relationship between positioning and communications. We do this by looking at the elements of a communications plan:

1. communications target group (Section 7.2)
2. communications message (Section 7.3)
3. communications objective (Section 7.4)
4. creation and media resources (Section 7.5)
5. communications budget (Section 7.6)
6. monitoring and evaluation of communications outcomes (Section 7.7)

We put the communications message before the communications objectives. This is because we feel that what a brand wants to communicate generally also should become part of the objectives.

There are many books in which these or similar steps are detailed extensively. We also discuss now each of these steps, but only concise, with specific attention to the relationship with positioning.

We end this chapter with the role of the advertising agency in the communications process (Section 7.8).

7.2 The communications target group

Chapter 2 pointed out that marketing strategy can be summarized as **STP**. This creates a distinction between segmentation and target group choice. The difference between segmentation and target group choice is that segmentation is a matter of research: examining whether groups of (potential) customers can be distinguished. Segmentation divides a possible market into groups of customers. The strategic choice that must then be made is to choose the **target group**: Which segment(s) will the company focus on? Segmenting is dividing. Targeting is choosing.

We need to distinguish here between two types of target groups:

- the **marketing target group**: the customers that actually "consume" the product
- the **communications target group:** the customers with whom the company intends to communicate

These two target groups often overlap, of course, but not necessarily. This depends on the role that people have in the purchasing process. For example, many home furnishing or cooking equipment choices seem to be made by women. However the consequences are also noticeable for men. And when it comes to purchasing toys, parents (also) belong to the communications target group whereas the kids consume. In the healthcare sector, the target audience is often quite difficult to determine (Example 7.1).

Example 7.1 Target groups in healthcare

Consumers in the healthcare industry are the clients. The concern is to help people who are sick or have (other) limitations. But many other stakeholders also play an important role in healthcare. For example, family members are important influencers and therefore very important from the point of view of communications. For instance, information material in the care for the elderly is therefore also intended, and sometimes mainly intended, for the family. In addition to the clients and their families, many different stakeholders play a major role in healthcare such as general practitioners, insurance companies, or in some cases even municipalities (who are responsible for the allocation of part of the care).

Photo 7.1 **The client is just one of the communications target groups. Photo published on Flickr, September 16, 2016 (public domain)**

When defining the communications target group, there is a logical relationship with the marketing strategy: the target group choice is actually already part of the marketing strategy. It is the T of STP.

There is a second strategic link when determining the communications target group. That is related to **accountability**: the desire for quantification. A marketing plan ultimately should provide a good estimate of the results to be achieved. This is important when it comes to defining communications objectives. For the definition of the communications target group, this implies that this target group should be measurable. So how big is the target group? This can only be determined if the target group is described sufficiently clearly. In Chapter 3 a number of criteria were mentioned to describe segments. The advantage of the demographic (and geographical) characteristics mentioned there is that they are often easily quantified. Information is available to determine, for instance, how many men from 20 to 30 live in Amsterdam or any other European city. Quantification is often more difficult when it comes to psychographic and behavioural criteria. There are no general data that will tell you how many people prefer cheaper airlines for their vacations (behavioural), or how many people favour a healthy lifestyle. Complementing general data with specific market research can provide a solution. If behavioural preferences or psychographics are measured by using questionnaires, an estimate can be made of the size of the target group.

7.3 The communications message

Of all stages in the communications process, the relationship between positioning and the **communications message** is the strongest. The positioning is the image that the brand wants to convey. This image has to be expressed in the communications message (or **proposition**) of the brand. The positioning thus does not literally determine the communications message, but it does create the framework for making a proposition.

In this context we should also distinguish the following forms of communications:

1.   thematic communications
2.   action-based communications

7.3.1 Thematic communications

Thematic communications communicate the characteristics of the brand. This is very similar to brand positioning. As long as the positioning is not sufficiently ingrained in the minds of the target group, it has to be repeated with communications. Different aspects of the positioning can be emphasized in a campaign. We have to repeat here that brand positioning emphasizes mindshare, heartshare, or a combination of both. This means that depending on the positioning strategy, there is a preference for a functional or a more emotional message.

7.3.2 Action-based communications

Action-based communications concern temporary changes in the brand's marketing mix, for example the introduction of a new product variant or discount offerings.

The central communications message of action-based communications does not have to be the same as the brand positioning. But communications always have to fit within the positioning strategy. For example, offering a prestige brand on a discount can be a very bad idea.

The positioning of a brand usually has to be more or less established to the target group before proceeding to action-based communications. Suppose a company introduces a new brand; the image of this brand first has to be made known to the target group. Only then additional aspects can be communicated. The reason is that the first impression of the brand is very important for conveying the personality. This phenomenon also happens with people: within a few seconds after being introduced to someone, you already create an image of the person you just met.

7.4 Communications objectives

Objectives, or goals, or targets, generally have different functions:

- They motivate and direct people.
- They can be used as a means of communications to others to show what the plan should lead to and, for example, how much money is needed;
- They serve as check whether plans have succeeded.

The latter function of a target has to do with the so-called **PDCA cycle**: Plan, Do, Check, Act. (Figure 7.1).

Figure 7.1 PDCA cycle

The PDCA cycle has the following stages:

1. Plan: create SMART goals and make a plan. **SMART** means Specific, Measurable, Acceptable, Realistic, Time-bound. Also indicate how and when your goals will be checked.
2. Do: implement the plan.
3. Check the results against the SMART goals.
4. Act: this mainly means adjusting the actions if necessary, so "react."

In stage 1 of this cycle, goals are formulated. These goals are checked in stage 3.

It is recommended to use such a cycle for communications plans. The reason for this is that communications often require direct and visible investments (in media or production) for which budget is needed. In such a case, it is justified to ask the question what the added value of the investment is.

Although it seems to make sense to define and check communications goals, one might ask why this only happens with communications and not, for example, for costs for product development, which also require investments that have to be recovered. In reality, SMART goals are not often formulated, and then there is no "check" on revenues. The reason for this is probably that communications expenses were traditionally seen as costs and less as investments. And it sounds a lot better to cut costs than to stop investing. Keller's point, as outlined in Chapter 1, that brand value is in fact the value of the knowledge that people have of the brand contradicts that premise: communication is an investment that increases and/or maintains the knowledge of a brand. This line of thought also ties in with the findings of Sharp, which show that a brand must always and intensively be visible, both mentally (communications) and physically (distribution).

The question then is which communications goals should be chosen. These goals can vary per campaign. It is clear that there is a direct relationship with the communications message or the proposition. If it is decided that the price image must be improved, the communications target must relate to price image. Because of this relation, we feel that communications objectives should be defined after formulating the message.

A **communications objective** shows what you want to achieve with the communications, with whom, and in which period. For example the goal of campaign Y of brand X is to reduce the percentage of people who think that brand X is "expensive" from 54% to 40%, in the target group of young people up to 25 years, to be realized by the end of 2020.

The attitude models discussed in Section 6.2 are often used as a guideline for defining communications objectives.

In reality, non-measurable communications goals are sometimes formulated. Such as: "On December 31st, 2021, the target group must know that we are the cheapest provider." We believe that such targets are incorrect: no measurable level is indicated and therefore no "check" is possible.

7.5 Creation and media

In this section we first discuss the concept of "creation" for "packaging" the message. Then we will detail the media resources that you can use to deliver the message to the target group. Online media receive separate attention.

7.5.1 Creation

Creation is coming up with an appealing, attention-grabbing, creative, or fun way to tell the message to the target group. A brand can of course choose to "just tell" the message in, for example, print ads or via social media. But the disadvantage is that communications can become dull and then receive little attention. Packaging the message in a creative way is called the **creative concept**, for example the involvement of George Clooney for Nespresso, the use of famous athletes in Nike commercials, the magic in Disney commercials, or the Christmas commercials of Coca Cola. Thinking of a creative way of communicating is usually a task of an advertising agency (or communications consultancy agency). In this context, this is often referred to as the "big idea." We describe the cooperation with such an agency in Section 7.7.

Here, we give an example of the relationship between positioning, communications message, and creative concept. We illustrate these concepts with a campaign of the Axe deodorant brand (Lynx in the United Kingdom): see Example 7.2.

Example 7.2 Positioning the Axe brand

Competing brands such as Nivea focus on functional benefits in their positioning (preventing perspiration smell, soft for the skin, etc.), but Axe used the psychosocial effects of the brand: a transformational positioning in which symbolic and social benefits are central – attraction, seductive looks, impressing women. This positioning was specified in the proposition (promise) of the brand: Axe makes you irresistible for women. This proposition had been creatively translated into the Axe effect by the advertising agency (in this case the British agency BBH). The "big idea" was therefore the Axe effect: it is the way in which the brand expresses that Axe makes the man irresistible.

In 2017, Axe's management adjusted the positioning of the brand, based on the following consumer insight:

> Man up! Quit crying! Don't be such a sissy! These are the type of behaviors 72 percent of guys have been told make them a real man*. The pressures caused by these rigid notions of manhood result in fear, anger and frustration. Moreover, 59 percent of guys believe they should act strong even if they feel scared, and nearly half think they shouldn't ask for help with their personal problems*.
>
> This internal struggle can contribute to bullying, violence and even suicide. As a champion of self-expression, AXE believes there's no one way to be a man and is launching The Find Your Magic Initiative to address this important issue.
>
> Building on the brand's "Find Your Magic" point-of-view that self-expression is key to confidence, this initiative aims to help break the cycle of toxic masculinity by providing guys with resources to live more freely. AXE intends to reach men and women with this message of confidence and individuality to further ignite the growing cultural conversation and create a healthier, more equal world for everyone.
>
> *(Source: Axe press release, May 17, 2017)*

This change has been translated by a new agency (creative agency 72 and Sunny Amsterdam) into a new creative concept with the slogan "Find your Magic."

7.5.2 Media resources

With media resources we mean the combination of all possible media and other means to get the communications message to the target group. Table 7.1 contains an overview.

In this book we do not detail any of these media tools, but we refer to specialized marketing communications literature.

It is possible to distinguish between three types of media:

- paid media such as TV and print.
- owned media such as a folder or a website.
- "earned" media: media attention when people spontaneously talk about you (word of mouth (WOM) through journalists, blogger, social media, etc.).

Especially this last category has received a lot of attention in recent years, illustrating the rising importance of WOM. In our opinion, the essence of social media for marketing is that they enable an extremely fast form of WOM. Wouldn't it be great if the marketing of a brand is done "automatically" through real **ambassadors**. In categories where involvement is high, such as in healthcare, it is certainly recommended to encourage consumers to spread the word about the quality of your products or services by means of so-called "**9+ experiences**." The emphasis here is on *relevance* (Section 6.3). Unfortunately, many other product categories deal with low involvement. And then *dominance* (high visibility) is an important goal in communications.

Table 7.1 **Media resources**

Brand elements

1. Brand name and name URL
2. Design and logo
3. Packaging and location communications

Communications when providing services

4. Face-to-face communications by service employees

Communications for promotional purposes

5. Advertising
   - Print (newspapers, magazines)
   - Television (spot and non spot), radio, cinema
   - Outdoor (on buses, in bus stops or metro stations, etc.)
6. Sales promotions
7. Sales
8. Direct marketing communications (telephone, mail, e-mail)
9. Public relations (PR) (brochures, website, press releases)
10. Sponsoring and events
11. Online communications ("online marketing")

The choice of media resources depends on different criteria such as:

1. target group
2. reach
3. contact frequency
4. timing
5. market area
6. speed
7. budget
8. communicative ability
9. creative idea
10. activities of the competition

The relationship between target group choice and choice of media is a trade-off of three criteria: target group, reach, and market area. Which media or sources of information does the target group use? Where and how can we reach the target group? Those types of questions must be answered.

The relationship between positioning and choice of media resources has to do with communicative ability and creative idea. For example, an "old-fashioned" TV commercial has a very strong communicative capacity with both image and sound. Social media are more directly applicable and cost virtually nothing, but have a limited and less manageable communicative capacity. An advantage of outdoors media is visibility. Each communications plan requires a specific consideration of the best media mix. There is never one best solution. Each option has its own advantages and disadvantages.

Because of the novelty of online communications and its specific potential, we devote specific attention to online communications including social media. We do this because these (partly earned) media lend themselves perfectly to increasing the involvement of consumers (*relevance*). At the same time, these media channels can be used as well to "send."

7.5.3 Online communications

We mentioned that sometimes marketing and communications are not always clearly distinguished. In the case of online marketing and communications this problem is perhaps even bigger. The concept of online marketing is often used. Mostly this is about things such as search engines, conversion, and social media. But we would like to highlight that the name *online marketing* is very remarkable in itself. This is because online channels are regular communications channels, just like print or TV. Apparently, they are considered so important that the name "online marketing" is chosen, but then there should also be something like "television marketing," or "print marketing," or "outdoors marketing." But they don't exist. Therefore, we believe it makes more sense to talk about **online communications** as long as it is about communication. On the other hand, we do accept that online marketing exists but then one should talk about all stages of marketing planning, so marketing research, marketing strategy, and all four marketing instruments, and not only communication. The special thing about the channel "online" is that it has consequences for the other marketing instruments as well. Examples include:

- product: cocreation with customers to involve them in new product innovation (related to communication)
- place/channel: online shopping
- pricing: dynamic pricing, so different prices over time depending on supply and demand

In this chapter we focus on online communications. Which forms of online communications then exist? There are different ways to categorize types of online communications. Based on a study of several of these formats we come to the following categorization:

- analytics
- search engine advertising (SEA)
- search engine optimization (SEO)
- display and affiliate marketing
- content marketing
- conversion optimization
- e-mail marketing
- social media

We discuss these forms below and end with a couple of more general conclusions.

Analytics

Analytics are about analyzing internet data. This point is in line with what has already been discussed in Chapter 1 about big data. How do you get relevant brand information out of your data? Is it possible, for example, to monitor your brand image by following (and analysing) how your brand is discussed on social media? The advantage of expressions on social media is that they are available without expensive market research activities. They are, as it were, free market research data.

Search engine advertising (SEA)

Search engine advertising is that you can show ads when a keyword appears. The best example of this is Adwords. Advertisers can enter search terms into Adwords and indicate how much money they are willing to spend for a click to their site. If a consumer types in that search term, the paid (mini) advertisements appear above or next to the "regular" links. Only if a consumer clicks on this commercial link, costs are incurred (PPC: pay per click). When the advertiser is willing to pay more for a click, the paid advertisement is higher in the list. Increasingly finding a site using your voice is possible, meaning that a website should also be optimized for 'voice'.

Search engine optimization (SEO)

Google places websites in a specific order when someone enters a search term. These are called **organic search (engine) results**, in contrast to the aforementioned paid search results. Obviously, the higher you are with your site in that list, the sooner you will be found. Every owner of a site wants to make his site so that it is placed high by Google. And it is "more reliable" to be organically high than paid high. But being high on the list of search results is not that simple because Google does not state exactly on the basis of which criteria and how those rankings take place. Of course, the search term itself plays an important role. If "cheap beer" is offered on a site, it is logical that it counts whether the "cheap beer" label is in the name or the URL and also how often it is mentioned on the site. But it is not that simple. It involves a lot more such as the number of links from other sites to your site (backlinks), the number of times the site has been liked on social media, the structure of the site, and so on. What also plays a role is whether the site is "responsive," which means that the layout adapts to the device on which the site is displayed. That if you click a site on your mobile, you do not literally get the same homepage in a small font but in a good and easily readable layout. Trying to get your site as high as possible in organic search results is **SEO**.

Display and affiliate marketing

Display marketing means that as a site owner you have an ad (display) placed on another site. For example, if you click on Booking.com, you will see an advertisement for a Samsonite suitcase. **Affiliate marketing** is very similar; the big difference is that the advertiser only has to pay if someone actually clicks on that ad (just like Adwords) or if this leads to an application.

Content marketing

In **content marketing** you make content that is really relevant and interesting for readers. This in contrast to advertising that generally seems less interesting to a reader. It is therefore serious content which is mainly associated with online applications. Examples include a blog (for instance with a relevant opinion published on a site), a white paper (a type of article that you can download, often after leaving your e-mail address, so that you can later be contacted by the producer of the white paper), a video (for example a vlog of a famous person on YouTube in favour of your brand), an infographic (a beautifully designed piece of content with pictures and figures), a podcast (a radio broadcast on your site), and so on. It is clear that this type of content can be nicely adjusted to the positioning of your brand. For instance, Pampers can use content marketing to publish all kinds of information about babies. This information is relevant for mothers, but Pampers also uses this information to profile the brand in a positive way.

Conversion optimization

Conversion optimization implies that the site is organized in such a way that people who take a look at it actually make the desired action (= conversion). For example, it is important that the "landing page" (the page where someone ends up when, for example, you visit the site via Google) is clear and inviting.

E-mail marketing

E-mail marketing is a form of direct marketing (DM) communications that uses e-mail addresses. Nowadays this is often only legally allowed in an **opt-in** context: people must explicitly give permission to approach them by e-mail; otherwise the advertiser is punishable.

Example 7.3 Crowd sourcing Lay's/Walker

Lay's, or Walker in the United Kingdom and a few other countries, frequently solicits new flavours through its "Do Us a Flavour" promotions. In these promotions, consumers are encouraged to come up with new flavours. In a nationwide competition, the most popular flavours are selected and then produced by Lay's. This resulted in new variants such as Pulled Pork in sticky BBQ sauce (United Kingdom), Mastana Mango (India), Jalapeño Mac N' Cheese (Canada), or Fried Green Tomato (United States). This type of crowd sourcing stimulates customer engagement with the brand.

Photo 7.2 Lay's/Walker uses crowd sourcing to create new tastes. Source: istockphoto.com.

Social media

Social media are hot. **Social media** are platforms like Facebook, LinkedIn, YouTube, Snapchat, and Instagram, which people use to exchange their own experiences, feelings, pictures, and so on with others. This also means that these channels are seen as the channels of consumers themselves and not as platforms for promotion. But of course companies and brands can also be active on social media, often aimed at increasing the involvement of consumers. A well-known form is **crowd sourcing**: actively engaging the public with your brand. We have already mentioned that the involvement of consumers is often low, so if you can increase it, that is a nice bonus. Brands can also use social media by paying an 'influencer' (e.g. a famous vlogger) to talk about your brand ('influencer marketing'). A brand can hope to stimulate the creation of a **brand community**. Brands can use social media to create a platform for the community. Obviously, the brand that manages such a platform must ensure that such a platform radiates dynamism and actually becomes a place where admirers of the brand feel at home, share information about the brand, and organize joint activities. In itself, setting up a platform, such as a Facebook site for your brand, does not create a vibrant brand community. Important things to take into account when creating a platform for a brand community on social media include:

- Choose carefully a target group that matches the overall target group of the brand.
- Place interesting content that is in line with the brand positioning. Fitbit, producer of wearable activity trackers, offers examples to keep yourself fit on its Facebook page.
- Communicate with the customer: a Facebook page offers the possibility to communicate directly with the customer.
- Create interaction between members of the community. For example, a brand like Fitbit can encourage people to compare their daily activity level.
- Organize competitions or – if the brand allows – real activities where users can meet. For most fast moving consumer goods, a national user day may be a little too high, but a photo contest where users show what they do with the brand is often possible. In that case, preferably take care of activities that are distinctive compared to competing platforms.
- Consider what you will do with negative reactions. Especially if a brand receives negative publicity, it is important that a crisis communications plan is in place for the social media platform to counter the negative publicity around the brand.

Conclusions on online communications

The different forms of online communications can be combined. For example, content marketing on YouTube with a famous person or opinion leader may lead to millions of followers. There is a strong link with the marketing strategy: the use of online channels should match the behaviour of the target group and the positioning of the brand and the category. Categories such as fashion and perfume are examples of categories with a strong social media presence, but communication about diapers or soft drinks might be more effective by using other channels. So the reaction that "Our brand has to be on Facebook because everybody does" is not necessarily correct. The positioning strategy of the brand determines the content. Online communications channels, by nature, require continuous attention. A brand community on Facebook, for instance, requires an administrator. The administrator has to ensure that the brand community develops in a direction that is in line with the brand positioning. But there is a danger here as well: precisely because social media are "earned" media and therefore cannot be managed, the use of online communications is a challenge.

A final warning is necessary. The growth of online communications sometimes leads to the suggestion that offline is old school. This suggestion is just as wrong as the announcement of "the end of mass marketing" in the nineties of the last century. Experience shows that media are added but that they will never completely replace others. And Sharp's push for the necessity of dominance in communications calls for the use of mass media, with a strong offline component. In the end there is always a balance.

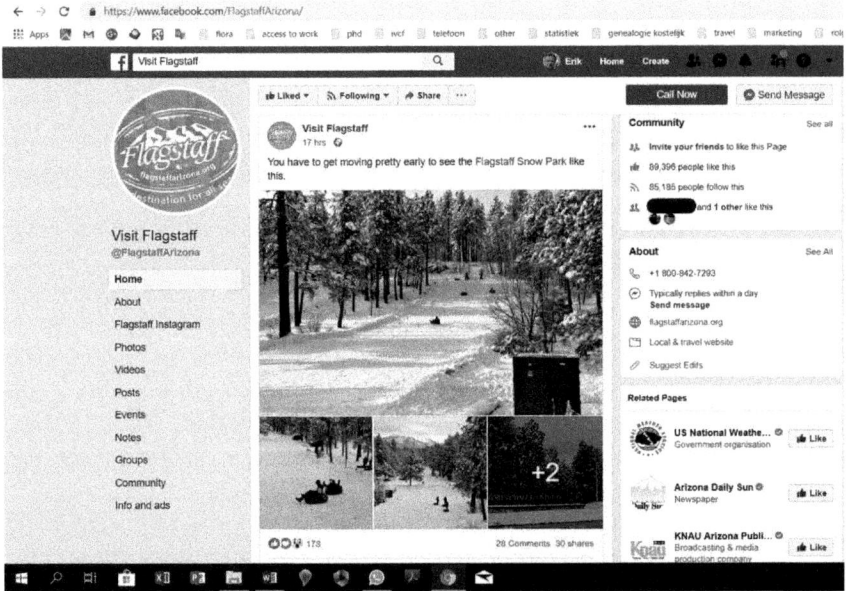

Photo 7.3 The city of Flagstaff (Arizona, United States) uses social media for city marketing. Screenshot provided with permission of the Flagstaff Convention & Visitors Bureau

7.6 Communications budget

Communications costs money. And as mentioned earlier, communications expenses are often considered as costs (Section 7.4). For this reason, a budget must often be set and approved. In organizations such as Unilever or Procter & Gamble (P&G), this usually happens annually as part of a marketing plan. For example, the brand manager of P&G's Pampers diapers must make a marketing year plan and submit it to the category manager "baby care." And the category manager must then give approval (or not) based on the plans and expected results. Subsequently, the brand manager is responsible for effectively spending the approved budget during the course of the year.

However, not all organizations have a clear annual cycle with plans. In that case, a plan for a campaign will be made on an ad hoc basis but approval is still required to implement this.

In both situations, determination of the **communications budget** is important. The size of this budget is closely related to the communications objectives: ambitious goals cost a lot of money. The literature mentions various methods to determine a communications budget. A well-known discussion here is whether the communications budget should go up or down when things go bad. Many budgeting methods, such as the **percentage-of-sales method**, lead to a lower budget in bad times. If a company makes less profit, it is easy to cut down on communications. This can lead to a strengthening of the downward trend. The alternative is a **counter-cyclical** budget policy, in which the level of the budget is determined in such a way that fluctuations in turnover are avoided as much as possible: if things get worse, more is spent on communications in order to turn the trend back in the right direction. Of course, this is often not reality.

Although this discussion is justified and counter-cyclical budgeting seems more sensible, it is still not clear how the budget should be determined. In reality, the **objective-and-task method** makes most sense. This means that first the goals are set in the communications plan; then the budget is calculated to realize these goals. For example, a new campaign is created that will be repeated three times a year. On the basis of reach figures it is possible to calculate how many people can be reached how often through which media channels. Next, an assessment must be made of what is needed to meet the communications objectives. The media plan then specifies which media should be used how often, and then the costs can be determined. For example, the use of X magazine ads costs Y euros. Such costs, together with the creative costs (of making a commercial or ad or designing a social media platform), then determine the budget.

It is difficult to determine which additional expenses are included in a communications budget. For example, almost all organizations have someone responsible for communications. Is the income of this person part of the communications budget? One would say yes, but the reality is often that this communications employee needs a budget to actually carry out communications. You have to think of the costs of using media, and of making and producing communications material. If the costs of hiring the communications manager are not included in the communications plan, then they also do not show up in the communications budget.

7.7 Monitoring and evaluation of communications

The evaluation of communications activities is the C (check) in the PDCA cycle mentioned in Section 7.4. This stage is closely related to the stage in which the (quantitative) communications goals have been set. And the communications goals have been set in line with the positioning.

The purpose of **monitoring** is to check whether the objectives have been achieved. This requires research. Ideally, a baseline measurement is already available. In the example in Section 7.4 the purpose of campaign Y for brand X is to reduce the percentage of people in the target group of young people up to 25 years who think that brand X is "expensive" from 54% to 40% in 2020. Then the baseline percentage is 54%. This could have been established in a survey among the target group that included a question such as:

Specify which of the following characteristics match with brand X:

- *young*
- *quality*
- *expensive*
- *and so on*

In 2019, apparently, 54% of the respondents indicated that "expensive" matches with brand X. The campaign objective is that this has to go down to 40%. Whether the campaign was successful can then be checked by repeating the same study a year later and looking at the outcomes.

7.8 Agencies and briefing

Organizing the communications can be done entirely within the company. But that is often not the best way. This is because professional marketing communications requires specific skills. Implementation without the necessary professional support does not produce the desired quality. We can refer, for instance, to the following skills:

- the development of the creative concept
- planning and scheduling the best media mix
- "smart" purchase of media space.
- the professional development of communications tools such as brochures and a website
- website maintenance and SEO

Larger companies, therefore, hire an **agency** for their marketing communications. Agencies can be specialized in advertising, online communications, sponsoring, and so on. Here we focus on advertising agencies. In organizations where advertising is less common (e.g. non-profit organizations or smaller companies) it is less normal to hire an agency. We now focus on the role of the advertising agency. In the introduction to this chapter we outlined the following stages in the communications process:

1.   communications target group
2.   communications message
3.   communications objective
4.   creation and media resources
5.   communications budget
6.   monitoring and evaluation of communications outcomes

In these stages, the **division of roles** between the client (often the marketing or communications department of the brand) and the advertising agency is important. Broadly speaking, the advertising agency implements stage 4. From our point of view, the brand management is responsible for the other steps. The choice for the communications strategy, and therefore the translation of the positioning into a message, is a strategic choice that should not be outsourced to an external agency.

In the coordination between client and agency, e.g. prior to a campaign, important matters should be specified in a **briefing**: a description of what is expected from the agency. The marketing manager (or brand manager) is primarily responsible for creating a clear briefing. After consultation and discussion with the advertising agency, the agency must also agree with the briefing. The components of a briefing are summarized in Table 7.2.

The background section gives key data about the company, the brand/product, the properties, technical data, and so on. Furthermore, it includes the objectives and brief content of the marketing mix: product, price, location, and promotion/communications (if these have already been determined). A description of the strengths, weaknesses, opportunities, and threats (SWOT) analysis provides the framework within which the campaign is developed. In addition to the core elements of the SWOT, the perceptions of the target group are of great importance. Then the core problem highlights the issue that the campaign needs to solve; this often has to do with a difference between image and identity.

The campaign essentials form the heart of the briefing. First the communications target group is described. The next section includes the proposition (with possible evidence) and the brand personality/brand values. Communication objectives are also made explicit in the briefing: what does the manager want to achieve for that target group? Often, a provisional budget is already mentioned here. The budget mentioned in the briefing can sometimes be adjusted later on, based on creative ideas from the agency.

Table 7.2 Components of a briefing

Marketing background

1. Key data about company and brand/product
2. Marketing environment:
   - Summary of SWOT analysis
   - Current image (brand as perceived by the target audience)
   - Core problem (image versus identity)

Campaign essentials

3. Communications target group
4. Proposition and brand personality/brand values
5. Measurable communications objective and budget

Conditions

6. Media or other resources that should be used or avoided
7. Planning
8. Other preconditions (such as style, required font, etc.)

The conditions section includes specific desires of the advertiser. Often, advertisers have specific preferences with respect to the choice of media or possible sales promotion tools (e.g. DM and internet). Some advertisers even specify a budget allocation for the media choice (for example, percentage offline versus online), while others do that less specific or leave it entirely to the agency.

Other preconditions include necessary elements in the campaign (visual design, use of logos, etc.), the use or non-use of humour, statutory regulations, and so on. Finally, the time schedule should also be specified.

A clear and well-defined briefing is of great importance to an advertising agency. Advertising agencies often complain that advertisers cannot write good briefings. Advertisers sometimes simply ask an advertising agency to "design something that results in higher sales." But it also happens that clients ask advertising agencies to develop a positioning strategy! This can be the result of a lack of knowledge and skills of the client. But it is also because many advertisers cannot make a choice. They want too much. This creates very generic and therefore vague briefings. A vague briefing gives inadequate guidance, which means that the advertising agency can move in all directions with the campaign. Then brand consistency is no longer feasible. The consequence might be that the campaign moves in a different direction than was actually the intention, but there is also the risk that afterwards much more work has to be done: if the briefing is not specific the result is often not according to the ideas of the client resulting in a higher probability that many creative designs are rejected by the advertiser. A good advertising agency will therefore refuse to approve an insufficiently completed briefing.

We conclude by stressing the importance of "classical" branding in combination with multi-channel communication. Advertising agencies can have their role, and online agencies as well. The task of the manager is to integrate all communications within the framework of a well-defined marketing strategy.

Summary

Communications planning is based on the following stages:

1. communications target group
2. communications message
3. communications objective
4. creation and media resources
5. communications budget
6. monitoring and evaluation of communications outcomes

There is a clear relationship between positioning (and target group choice) and the stages of communications planning. The positioning frames the content of the communications message; it is sometimes even the core of the message. Communications goals must be SMART and in line with the positioning and target group. Any creative concept must match the brand values. The media resources have to match with the information search behaviour of the target group. The budget is determined, among other things, by the campaign goals. Monitoring and evaluation checks whether the desired identity sufficiently matches the image. Within the media mix online communications (in all its different forms) become increasingly important. The result is also that more data become available for research: "big data." But the use of online communications should always be in balance with "classic" offline communications. An ad agency can offer support in various stages of communications planning support, but a clearly outlined positioning strategy is key input for the briefing.

Chapter 8

Brand positioning and brand architecture

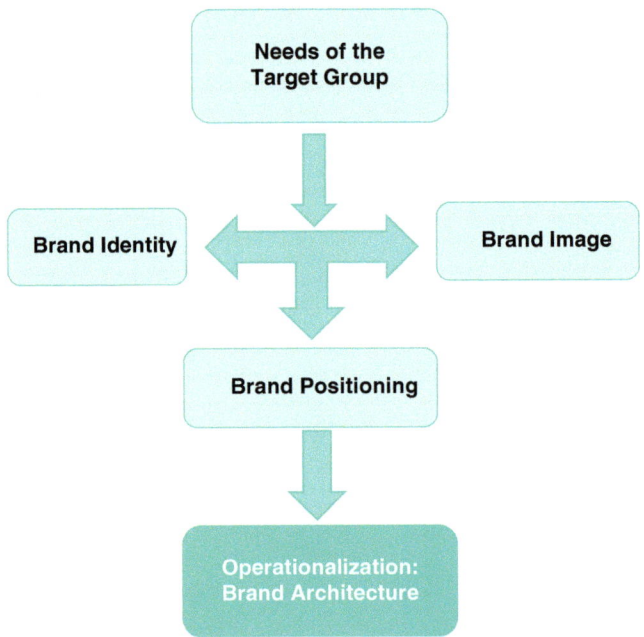

8.1 An introduction to brand architecture

We now address the relationship between positioning and brand architecture. **Brand architecture** is the choice of an organization for a certain combination of brand names. This choice can vary from simply one brand name for all products and services in the product portfolio (e.g. Philips) to a large number of different names for all kinds of products with or without the addition of the name of the parent company (e.g. Procter & Gamble).

The choice for a certain brand architecture depends on various factors. In this chapter, we first discuss the levels of branding in a company in Section 8.2. We also highlight a number of variants that exist in the choice of which levels are used and how. Then in Section 8.3 we indicate which factors determine the choice for a certain brand architecture and which guidelines can be followed. We also discuss here the relationship with brand positioning. We end the chapter with recommendations with respect to choosing a brand architecture.

8.2 Levels of branding

In this section we specify possible alternative with respect to levels of branding and brand architecture. But first, we discuss line and brand extensions.

8.2.1 Extensions

A company often brings multiple products or services onto the market: a **portfolio**. These products can be more or less comparable or still differ greatly. There are possible differences or similarities on two dimensions:

- The positioning of the product within the same category. For example FMCG producer Unilever markets various types of detergent products (and brands) while each separate brand has its own specific attributes, hence a specific brand positioning.
- The type of product itself, i.e. the category to which the product belongs. Unilever not only produces detergents but also food and personal care products.

The reason why a company markets a portfolio of different products is usually growth. A company can, by definition, grow in four ways, depending on the "newness" of the activities with which growth takes place. A familiar classification at this point is the **Ansoff matrix** that distinguishes four growth strategies (Table 8.1). These strategies are ordered by the degree to which the strategy is aimed at activities that are novel to the organization:

1. Market penetration: the company tries to grow with existing products among existing target groups (called "markets" by Ansoff). This therefore means an increase in the market share of a product with a specific target group.
2. Market development: growth by selling the same products to other target groups.

Table 8.1 Growth directions for a company ("Ansoff matrix")

Product Target group[a]	Existing	New
Existing	Market penetration	Product development
New	Market development	Diversification

a Ansoff distinguishes products and markets. We replaced the word "market" by "target group."

3. Product development: a company tries to create new products targeted at its existing target groups to achieve growth. Often these are product varieties: products that are very similar to what the company already produces but just a bit different.
4. Diversification: bringing new products to the market for new target groups.

The growth strategies mentioned under points 3 and 4 can be summarized as "product innovation": the development of a new product for the company.

If a company has decided to grow and market a new product, the question automatically pops up: how shall we label this product? And then we are not talking about the name of the product itself (that is the subject of Chapter 9), but the question whether a different brand name should be used at all. If a new product is labelled under an existing brand name of the company, this is by definition an extension. An extension is therefore a new product of a company with an existing brand name. Another option is to choose a different brand name for a new product (there is no separate term for this).

Within extensions (so when using an existing brand name of the company), a distinction can be made between:

- **Brand extensions** (sometimes called category extension). This is when a company uses the existing brand name for new products in a different product category. An example would be a manufacturer of watches that starts to sell cars.
- **Line extensions**. These are extensions by using the existing brand name within the original category. This involves the introduction of so-called varieties. For example, a beer manufacturer that introduces a different taste variant.

Companies have to make the choice under which brand name to market the product. There are several advantages and disadvantages of choosing an existing brand name; we discuss this in Section 8.3.

8.2.2 Levels of branding

Brands and brand names exist at different levels. Table 8.2 contains an overview with examples.

Table 8.2 Levels of branding

Level	FMCG*	Durables	Services
Corporate brand	Unilever	Volkswagen Audi Group	Deutsche Post DHL
Umbrella brand (family brand)	Axe/Lynx	Volkswagen	DHL
Individual brand	Axe deodorant	Volkswagen Golf	DHL Express
Type or variety	Axe deodorant Dark Temptation	Volkswagen Golf GTI	DHL Express Parcel Services

* Fast moving consumer goods

The **corporate brand** refers to the corporation that offers the brand. This corporation is sometimes part of a larger organization. A company can choose whether they use the company name or not in their positioning. In the insurance industry, for instance, corporate names are increasingly being used as a source of trust. This has to do with the expectation that consumers find it increasingly important to know who is behind the brand. Also, the company's social behaviour (Corporate Social Responsibility (CSR)) is becoming increasingly important. A good reputation is therefore of great importance.

An **umbrella brand** or **family brand** is a brand that is used for different product categories. A family brand can differ from the corporate brand.

An **individual brand** is limited to one product category. An individual brand is often offered in various types or variants (e.g. bottle size for cola, taste variants for potato chips).

The division into levels is sometimes arbitrary. The difference between type and individual brand can be difficult to make (see Example 8.1).

Example 8.1 Difference between type and individual brand

Some brands in the car industry use type numbers (Peugeot 308, Mercedes A, B, or C). These type numbers can sometimes also be considered as individual brands. There is a big difference between a Mercedes A-class (relatively small) and a Mercedes C-class (large). In the same car industry, there is an increasing tendency to use "real" individual brand names (Ford Fusion, Ford Mustang, Volkswagen Golf, Volkswagen Passat).

Photo 8.1 Toyota Prius: an example of an individual brand. Photo used with permission of Toyota

There is often a relationship between the brand level and the attributes that are used in the brand's positioning. In Chapter 3 we introduced the means-end chain in which a distinction is made between attributes, consequences (benefits), and values. The relationship with brand levels is that on higher brand levels, brands profile themselves with aspects higher up in the means-end chain. In other words at lower brand levels, functional properties are communicated (the size of the cola bottle, the flavour of the potato chip) whereas emotional benefits and brand values are communicated to differentiate the brand at higher levels. For example, Unilever increasingly stands for sustainably produced food.

Photo 8.2 **The CEO of Unilever takes the social responsibility of the brand seriously. Photo used with permission of Unilever © DFID – UK Department for International Development, June 8, 2013 (cc-by-2.0). Paul Polman stepped down as CEO in 2019. The current CEO of Unilever is Alan Jope. Unilever's commitment with respect to social responsibility has remained unchanged of course**

The choice of brand levels relates to the brand architecture. Brand architecture is the combination of brand names and brand levels of a company. There are three possibilities:

1. A corporate brand architecture, also called **monolithic brand** or branded house: the corporate name is used as a name for all products.

Photo 8.3 Siemens is an example of a monolithic brand. Photo used with permission of Siemens; © Siemens PLM Software (cc-by-nd/2.0)

2. An **endorsed brand architecture** uses two brand levels: the corporate level in combination with the individual brands. Sometimes the endorsing corporation is profiled very visibly, but it can also be more on the background.

Photo 8.4 Ralph Lauren endorses its individual brand Polo. Source: istockphoto.com.

3. An **individual brand architecture** uses only the individual brands. This is also called a **house of brands**. Procter & Gamble is the classic example of a brand that only uses the individual brands towards consumers. Procter's house of brands includes brands such as Head and Shoulders, Pampers, Tide, Always, Gillette, and Oral B. Other examples include Unilever, Mars, and Nestlé.

Photo 8.5 We associate Mars, Inc. with candybars, but the company is also home to brands such as Uncle Ben's (rice) and pet food like Whiskas, Pedigree, and Royal Canin. Source: istockphoto.com.

Sometimes an architecture is used that seems to lie between the possibilities mentioned earlier. For some years now, Unilever shows the Unilever logo small but visibly on its brands. And after more than 150 years of invisibility of the organization for the consumer, even Procter & Gamble developed a corporate brand promise during the 2012 Olympic Games. Commercials are aired on television around a message thanking all the "moms." In addition, each of their products is associated in advertisements with the brand "PG." Officially this is an endorsed brand structure. But some find the use of Unilever or PG only so limited that they prefer to call it an individual brand architecture.

Photo 8.6 When you look for it, you will find the Unilever logo somewhere (photos provided with permission of Unilever).

When a company uses multiple brand names, the combination of all brands is called the **brand portfolio**. Companies such as Procter & Gamble and Unilever have a large brand portfolio. But also, companies that are frequently associated with only one brand, like Pepsico, sometimes have a quite large brand portfolio. In the case of Pepsico we expect the company to be a branded house (just one brand: Pepsi), whereas actually it is a house of brands.

Photo 8.7 **A collection of brands from the product portfolio of Pepsico.** © **Erik Kostelijk**

Brand architecture relates to the combination of brand levels within a company. But brands can also be combined between companies. Brands can also visibly co-operate with other brands. If both brands are explicitly mentioned in such a collaboration, this is called **co-branding**. Co-branding implies that two brand names (from different companies), or a combination of them, are visible on one product. The Smart is an example. This car started as a co-production of Mercedes-Benz and Smart; the word "Smart" stands for Swatch Mercedes ART.

Photo 8.8 **The Smart: Swatch Mercedes ART. Photo Mike Bird, Pexels.com**

The advantage of co-branding is that brands can use each other's strengths. Research has shown that in co-branding the weakest of the two brands generally benefits the most in terms of brand image.

A specific form of co-branding is **ingredient branding**. This occurs when a brand is communicated as part of a product of another brand. *Intel inside* is a typical example.

Photo 8.9 Intel inside: example of ingredient branding. Source: Commons Wikimedia (public domain)

8.3 Advantages and disadvantages of the various brand choices

Two dilemmas surround the choice of a brand architecture:

1. The brand architecture can generally be chosen only once. In any case it is a long-term strategic decision, not something that can be changed annually. Situations that call for a change in brand architecture are, for example, mergers and acquisitions. In such a situation, what becomes the new brand architecture?
2. Do you choose a new or an existing brand name for new products?

We will discuss both choices in this section. But first we outline two important principles when choosing the brand portfolio.

8.3.1 Key principles for the choice of brand architecture

When choosing the brand architecture, there are two important principles:

1. The first principle is **simplicity**: not too many levels or combinations of names. The simple reason: multiple names are difficult to remember for customers. The most radical solution would be to work only with individual brands. But both "below" and "above" individual brands there may be reasons to add another name. Individual brands are often offered in variants. And individual brands can sometimes be grouped under an umbrella, often part of a larger organizational unit of which the brand is part together with a number of other brands. Then there are reasons to link the name of this parent organization to the umbrella brand.
2. The second principle plays an important role in extensions. This principle says that a brand name can only have **one identity**. A brand is like a person: it has its own DNA and its own personality. And that cannot, and should not, behave very differently according to one or the other situation. So, if the umbrella brand unites brands with different profiles, they have to have different brand names. Note in the execution there can be differences between different products with the same brand name. Like with people someone will often behave differently during a job interview than with friends at home. But the underlying motives and personality remain the same.

The latter principle means that if a company markets products with a different positioning (and probably also a different target group), then it cannot choose for only one brand name. Unilever is a producer of various brands of personal care products. Each brand has its own positioning. Axe helps guys to look, feel, and smell great. Dove is committed to helping women realise their personal potential for beauty by engaging them with products that deliver real care.

8.3.2 Relevant factors for choosing a brand architecture

The choice for a brand architecture is a strategic long-term decision. Once chosen for a certain structure, it is difficult to change it, unless there are compelling reasons.

Emphasizing the corporate brand in the communication has the following advantages:

1. *Sign of quality.* Showing that the brand is part of a larger entity creates an extra feeling of security and quality for the customer. The fact itself that a brand belongs to a larger corporation generally gives additional confidence.
2. *Strengthening the corporate brand.* The reverse of the previous also applies: strong individual brands have a positive influence on the parent brand.
3. *Impact on stakeholders.* Every company has to deal with multiple stakeholders. In addition to customers, there are competitors, suppliers, current employees, future employees, the government, possible shareholders, and so on. When in the communication to customers the parent brand is always used; this also has

an effect on the other stakeholders, for the simple reason that they can also be customers. In any case they will be confronted with communication with customers. It is a misunderstanding to think that communication to one group of stakeholders can be completely separated from communication to other stakeholders. For example, a Lay's commercial on TV (aimed at consumers) will be seen by everyone, including Pepsico shareholders and health activists. By letting the parent brand piggyback in the customer-oriented communication of the individual brands, the brand image in other target groups is also influenced.

4. *Cross-selling*. Another advantage of showing the parent brand is that it makes cross-selling easier. **Cross-selling** is selling other products of the company to existing customers. A guy using Dove Men + Care might be more open to buying Axe shower gel, if he knows that they both come from the same barn (in this case: Unilever). If a company knows the names of its customers, it can directly engage in cross-selling: for example, sending an email with an offer for a different product. Unilever could even choose to become an online supermarket itself by offering all its brands online.

Linking the parent brand to the individual brands also has disadvantages.

1. *More complex*. As stated, an important rule in branding and communication is to keep it simple. Every additional name that needs to be remembered makes it more difficult for a customer. Keep it as simple as possible.
2. *Extra risk*. An additional risk is that if there is a problem with one of the individual brands, this can be reflected on the parent brand and therefore on the other individual brands.
3. *More expensive*. Having multiple brands on the market requires more marketing expenses than when there are fewer brands.

8.3.3 Relevant factors in the choice of extensions

A decision that will occur more often than the redesign of the entire brand architecture is the labelling of a new product. From the principle that a brand can only have one positioning, it is therefore important to find out whether a new product, in terms of target group and positioning, fits the profile of the **parent brand**. So here we look at the fit between extension and parent brand.

A great deal of research has been done in academic literature about the acceptance of extensions. One reason for this is perhaps that such research can be organized relatively simple: experimental research. Extensions can be presented to different groups of consumers and then they can be asked a number of questions such as the willingness to buy, but also the degree of (perceived) fit with the parent brand. For example one group will receive a (non-alcoholic) soft drink labelled Heineken and the other a pair of jeans with a Heineken brand label. The main conclusion that emerges from such research is that the fit of the extension with the parent brand significantly influences the success of a new product (Völckner & Sattler, 2006). In short if people do not feel that a product fits with what they are used to from the brand, then the new product will be less successful.

Fit can be established at different levels: at the level of attributes, benefits, or values. A fit on attributes means that the new product, in terms of ingredients or functions, fits the mother brand. For example Tropicana brings out a new taste of fruit juice. But even if there is no functional fit, there can still be a fit at value level. Especially with lifestyle brands such as Tommy Hilfiger, all kinds of products are possible that functionally are very different from the original product of the brand: in the case of Tommy Hilfiger, for instance, fashion, perfume, shoes, or watches. It still works since the values of these products match the values of the core brand.

The various studies on brand extensions also show the following:

- heavy marketing support positively influences success
- acceptance by the retailer (if applicable) is important
- extra communication helps to improve the perceived fit

8.4 Recommendations and step-by-step plan

There are two situations in which a review of aspects of the brand architecture is important:

- acquisitions or mergers of brands
- product development

8.4.1 Brand architecture and acquisitions

If a company can take over a brand, this is by definition an existing brand with its own reputation and image. There are two possibilities regarding the place of this brand in the brand portfolio:

1. The old name is maintained.
2. The brand is integrated in the existing brand architecture.

Maintaining the old brand name seems the most obvious. After all, with an acquisition you also buy the reputation and strength of that brand, including the existing customer base. We illustrate this with an example from the elderly care market (see Example 8.2).

Example 8.2 Brand architecture and acquisition

In the care for the elderly there are all kinds of retirement homes. These are often known under the local name of the house, for example Silver Springs. Now these local homes often work together in a group context, as part of a healthcare provider. Suppose this healthcare provider is called Carat and also has two other houses: Desert Flower and Romanus. Then Carat has the organizational structure as shown in Figure 8.1.

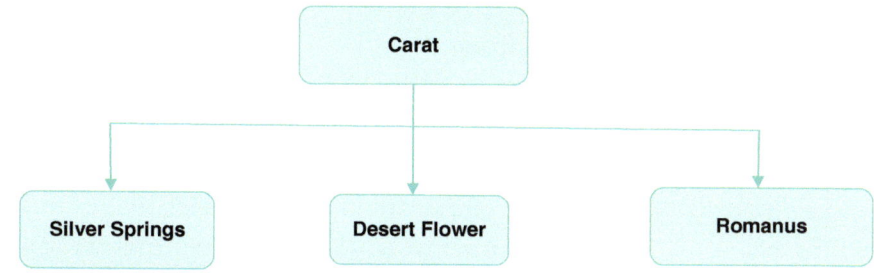

Figure 8.1 **Organizational structure Carat**

Now the question is which brand architecture is communicated to the public. This communicated structure does not have to be equal to the real actual organizational structure. For example, Carat could have a department that researches comfortable living for the elderly, so that there is a Knowledge Centre in the Carat Group. This does not have to be communicated externally.

There are the following possibilities for the brand architecture (with increasing visibility of the parent brand) (Figures 8.2–8.5).

Figure 8.2 **Individual brands**

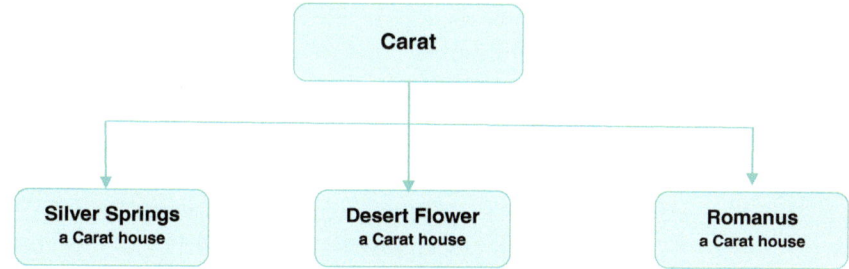

Figure 8.3 **Endorsed with the individual brand name first**

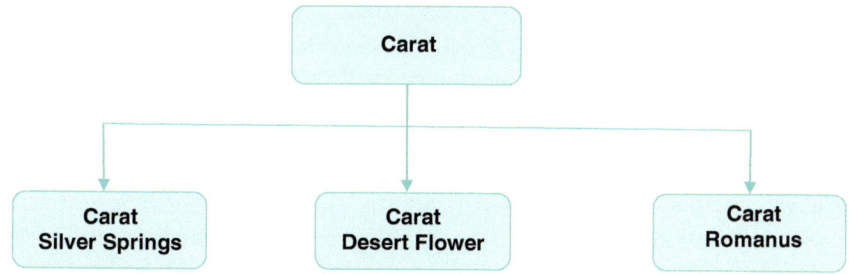

Figure 8.4 **Endorsed with the parent brand name first**

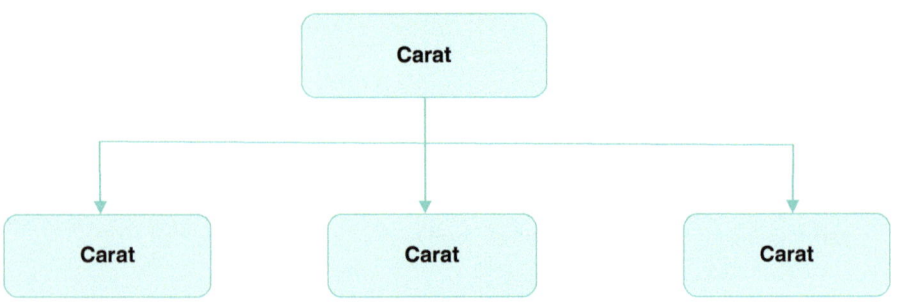

Figure 8.5 **Corporate branding: the local name disappears**

The last option in the example seems strange in the healthcare market, but in the retail it is very normal: all Walmart stores are called Walmart.

With acquisition of brands, the choice for a structure depends on:

- the differences in positioning between the parent brand on the one hand and the newly acquired individual brand(s) on the other
- the differences between individual brands
- the weight that management assigns to the advantages and disadvantages of the various options, as mentioned in Section 8.3.2

The simplest solution is corporate branding: everything is called Carat. Yet this is not that easy because by rebranding everything in Carat, the brand equity of the existing homes is thrown away. And moreover, it probably causes resistance among staff members and the elderly living in the homes. Another aspect is to what extent there are differences in the positioning of the homes. It is perfectly conceivable that there are differences just as Unilever's Dove promises something else than Unilever's Axe (Lynx in the United Kingdom). Assuming that the management of Carat does not simply want to throw away the brand associations and brand equity of the individual brands, then the question is to what extent the parent brand needs to be added. If the parent brand is a well-known brand, then endorsement results in a quality image. If the parent brand is not well-known, the individual brands will not benefit much, but there is an effect vice versa: the parent brand can be loaded with the image of the individual brands. What is crucial is the extent to which the DNA of the parent brand actually comes back in the individual brands. Suppose Carat is known for its great expertise in care. That would have to translate in the care levels in all her homes when there is an endorsed structure. Finally, there is also the question to what extent the parent brand must be visible: mentioned first, or behind the individual name. Important is then again the extent to which there are differences between the homes, and the importance of the original names of the homes for the target group. In the practice of elderly care, the option "individual brands" is usually chosen and increasingly in combination with "endorsement with the parent brand last."

In the (fictional) example, we should note that the house Romanus itself differs quite a bit from the other two names. That does not have to be a problem if this home is also quite different from the other homes.

The step-by-step plan for the **choice of the brand architecture** then becomes:

1. Visualize each alternative: this helps to imagine the new architecture. There can even be made a logo to see how the different options work out. Also consider what the choices mean for communication, for example for the person answering the telephone in the company's contact centre.
2. Discuss each alternative on the basis of the differences between the positioning of the brands.
3. Determine how strong the brands are and how necessary it is for the parent brand to support the individual brands, or vice versa.
4. Draft a decision.
5. Operationalize this decision by creating a positioning statement for each brand (in one sentence), and then assess whether the architecture logically fits with the positioning. Does the parent brand fit in well with the individual brands and vice versa? Can an employee, and certainly an employee in the front office, easily explain the differences and relationships between brands?
6. Make a final decision.

8.4.2 Brand architecture and product development

The second relevant situation in rethinking a brand architecture is that in which new products are developed. Should the new product receive a new brand name or can it be marketed under the umbrella of an existing name? In the case of a line extension mostly a type name is added such as "0.0" in the alcohol-free beer of Heineken: Heineken 0.0. In case of a brand extension it depends.

The most important question is whether there is a fit between the target group and positioning of the new product and the existing brand. In order to establish this, the image of the existing brand should first be known, and also the desired associations with the new product. The question then is whether there is sufficient overlap between these two. The overlap in associations can be functional or more on an emotional level. If this is not clear, a simple test among a group of customers can give a conclusive answer. If the new product is too far away from the parent brand, a new name has to be developed.

Summary

The brand architecture is the combination of levels of branding and brand names of an organization. The choice depends on the positioning of the corporate or umbrella brand and possible individual brands. That is because a new product for a brand (an extension) must logically fit the brand name under which the product will be marketed. Academic research demonstrates that extensions without fit with the parent brand often fail and are also harmful to the parent brand. We showed that if a new product does not logically fit under the existing brand name, a new name must be chosen. Also, with mergers and acquisitions, it should be very well considered to what extent the positioning of the brands matches. At the same time there are also other considerations such as what kind of power relation must be communicated after the merger or acquisition.

Chapter 9

Brand positioning, brand names, and visual design

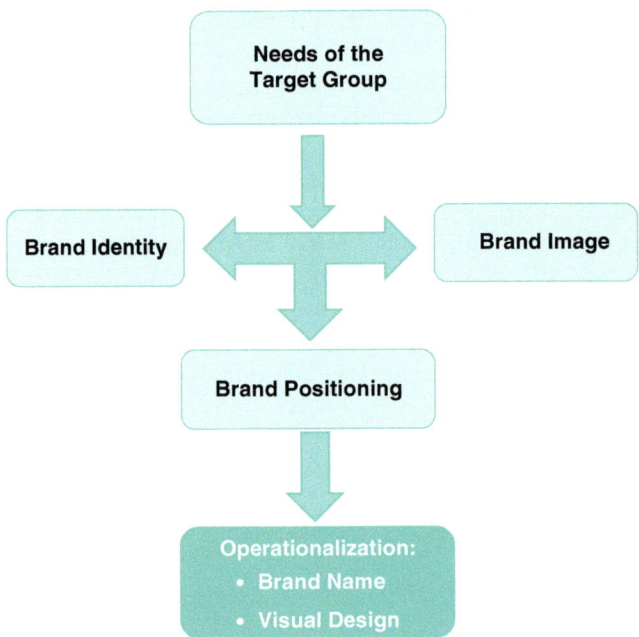

9.1 An introduction to the choice of a brand name

"The most important marketing decision you can make is the name that you give to your product," according to Trout and Rivkin (2010). That makes sense. After all, the brand name carries all associations. And also for Sharp, who places a strong emphasis on awareness and availability, something similar applies: awareness is linked to the name.

Yet we need to put this in some perspective because the associations to a brand name are by definition learned. And "learning" has a time element. People learn about brands through continuous communication. If the link between a brand name and the desired associations is communicated long enough, those links will become automatic, practically independent of the name. Just consider: what's the logic of thinking about computers and mobile phones when we hear the word Apple, and not simply about apples?

But research shows that certain associations are easier to learn when associated with certain types of brand names. So there is some connection between associations and the name.

In reality, it doesn't happen too often to have the opportunity to create a new name. But sometimes, as with new product introductions, a new brand name can be chosen. Also in mergers and acquisitions, when there is often a necessity of name change, the question is which name or names should be used afterwards. Nevertheless, in spite of the great importance, a name is often chosen in an imprudent manner, which makes it more difficult to "load" the brand.

First, in Section 9.2, we look at different types of brand names and their advantages and disadvantages. In Section 9.3 we discuss the requirements for a good name. Section 9.4 describes the process of creating a new name. Section 9.5 discusses the situation in which an enterprise wishes to change a name (rebranding). Finally, Section 8.6 is not about brand names but about a different brand element: visual identity.

9.2 Requirements for a brand name

A **brand name** literally carries the identity and positioning of the brand. At the same time, we have already established that every name can theoretically be loaded with a multitude of associations, as the example of Apple shows: the brand has succeeded in associating "Apple" with computers and not with apples. The condition for creating such associations is that it should be sufficiently consistent.

Because a random name can, theoretically, receive any kind of association, there are only a few basic requirements that a "good" brand name must meet. These are guidelines, however. In order to determine which requirements a brand name must meet, we first look at the basic function of the brand: creating mindshare and heartshare.

- Mindshare means familiarity and relevance. The brand name should facilitate this as much as possible: a brand name should actually be chosen so that this name can easily be recognized by the consumer, and a name that the consumer can easily remember whenever he feels a certain need. Think for example of the name "Bob the Builder": this is certainly remembered more easily than "Robert the Builder" or "Carl the Builder."
- Heartshare relates to the creation of relevant and unique associations. This essentially forms the basic idea of positioning.

How do these basic functions translate into **guidelines for brand names**? In our opinion, there are the following guidelines:

1. be distinctive
2. be legally protected
3. associations can be easily attached
4. no wrong or negative connotations
5. availability and findability online

9.2.1 The name is distinctive

A name must be distinctive in order to make it as easy as possible to see the brand as different from competing brands. Interestingly, recognizability also increases with a distinctive name. After all, recognizability relates to recognizing the brand in the midst of competing brands and other environmental influences. A brand name that is not distinctive is by definition difficult to trace back to a specific supplier.

9.2.2 The name is legally protected

In connection with the previous point, a name should also be legally protected. This requirement goes a step further than distinctiveness in itself. A name can in fact be quite distinctive in the category, but this does not imply necessarily that the name can be protected. In the legal sense, the proof of the pudding is whether a name, within the category for which it is intended, does not lead to confusion with another brand. If the judge believes that confusion can occur, then the name cannot be used. It is important to check this thoroughly in advance; otherwise this might cost a lot of money (see Example 9.1).

Example 9.1 A wrong new name chosen: Hunkemöller and Seza

In 2004, lingerie chain Hunkemöller considered changing the name. The newly chosen name became Seza. The acceptance of this name was tested favourably in various stores across Europe. But what Hunkemöller had overlooked was the existence of an existing lingerie store with almost the same name: La Senza in Canada. La Senza objected successfully. La Senza was already a well-known brand in England and Ireland. And the lingerie chain had a so-called European Community registration. Sense (margarine), Senseo (coffee makers), and Senz (umbrellas) never got in trouble with La Senza, as they obviously had not registered in the category lingerie.

9.2.3 Associations can be easily attached

A name should not be too difficult to **load with associations**. This applies not only to a functional positioning but also to a more emotional positioning. The latter is difficult for names that are an abbreviation without being a word: it is more difficult to develop a feeling with an abbreviation. But it is not impossible: the Dutch airline KLM has become a strong brand, but that brand has also existed for a long time. Also, the name should preferably support the desired brand associations. An organization that wishes to radiate values such as friendliness, for instance, should preferably not choose an aggressively sounding name. Research shows that names that have a meaning of their own are easier to load with associations than names without meaning.

9.2.4 No wrong or negative connotations

A name or word can have very different meanings in another language. This becomes relevant when the brand is sold in different countries. Before a name is chosen, a check is needed whether it leads to unwanted associations in other languages (Example 9.2).

Example 9.2 Unlucky choice of brand names for Ford

Years ago, Ford introduced a new type of car: the Ford Pinto. But in Portuguese, "pinto" means "small dick." Ford did not learn from this wrong choice. A couple of years later, the Ford Caliente was introduced. But in Mexican slang, Caliente translates into "street hooker." And when the Ford Fiera was introduced, the company had to discover that "fiera" in Spanish means violent person, or ferocious animal. And the SUV Ford Kuga was problematic in Croatia, where "kuga" stands for "the black plague."

9.2.5 Availability and findability online

A brand name should be easy to find on the internet. The easiest way is if the brand name is available in combination with the most logical extension (.com, .co.uk, .fr, etc.). If that is not available, alternatives such as .eu could be tried, but are less logical. If a certain URL is not available, another solution is possible, namely changing a letter in the name, so that a non-existent word arises with apparently a spelling mistake. Like *focuz* instead of *focus*. Another popular "spelling mistake" is using the q instead of the k.

9.3 Types of brand names

As we already noted in Section 9.1, to a certain extent, associations can be linked to any name. This suggests that a new name, of itself, has no meaning yet. This is often the case with brands. Because now we know for example what Disneyland is, we have associations with it, but in the dictionary you will not encounter the word. When the name Disney was introduced, it was in fact nothing more than a family name.

But names can also have meaning in themselves. This can be done in two ways: via the phonetic properties of the name (sound, length, or letters; a name can, for example, sound Italian) or via acquired meanings. The ease with which it is possible to associate a name to a brand therefore depends partly on the type of name.

Brand names can be classified in different ways. Different formats can be found in literature. It is important to be clear about the criteria that are used. An important criterion is to what extent the name of itself already says something about certain brand properties (meaningfulness). The **meaningfulness** of a brand name is, according to various studies, of great influence on the speed with which the name is accepted. We can distinguish the following types of brand names:

1. Abstract names: these do not contain information about the brand.
2. Functional names: these contain information about the category of the brand.
3. Associative names: these say something about the positioning of the brand.

Next to this classification, another aspect of choosing a name is whether the name is an already existing word.

9.3.1 Abstract names

An **abstract name** is a name or word that says nothing about the brand. This includes different types of names. First, we can distinguish word names. These are existing words that say nothing about the brand. Examples: Apple, Jaguar, Diesel. A different kind of abstract names are invented names: words that have no meaning yet and do not say anything about the characteristics of the brand. Examples include Twix, Doritos, Gillette. People's names also fall under abstract names, because personal names have no meaning at all for others who do not know the person. Examples include founders of the company such as Heineken or Disney, or a combination of names of the founders: Adidas. Also, ancient Greek or Latin names or words from less familiar languages are abstract for many people, because they have no association with them: Nike (Greek goddess of victory; the swoosh is the flame of the goddess), Google (googol is a huge number: a 1 followed by 100 zeros), or Samsung (three stars in Korean).

9.3.2 Functional names

A **functional name** refers to the category in which the brand is active. For example, many organizations in healthcare have something with the word "care" in their name. Other examples of functional names are: University of Groningen, Amsterdam Airport Schiphol, *Journal of Marketing*, *The New York Times*. Abbreviations are often included here such as KLM or BBC.

Functional names can be existing words, as in the earlier examples, but also made-up words, where a link is made with the category. Examples include Ryanair and Volkswagen.

9.3.3 Associative names

An **associative name** provides some information about the characteristics and perception of the brand. Here too, existing words can be used such as After Eight, Dove, Head & Shoulders, and Playboy. But new words can also be created such as Microsoft, EasyJet, and Aquafresh.

Table 9.1 summarizes types of brand names.

The different types of brand names all have advantages and disadvantages. We deal with these on the basis of some of the criteria mentioned in the previous section.

Table 9.1 Types of brand names

	Abstract name, no information about brand	Functional name, information about category	Associative name, relates to brand positioning
Existing word	Apple, Shell, Jaguar, Diesel	*The New York Times*, British Broadcasting Corporation (BBC), Amsterdam Airport	Head & Shoulders, Dove, After Eight
Invented word, or name	Twix, Google, Nike, Disney, Heineken	Ryanair, Volkswagen	Aquafresh, Microsoft

An advantage of a functional name with an existing word is that it creates immediate associations: it is completely clear what the brand is (unless it is an abbreviation). Research also shows, as we saw at the beginning of this section, that meaningful names are accepted faster than non-meaningful names. The opposite applies to abstract names: whether an existing or a new word is used, it is (at the beginning) completely unclear what the brand stands for, even the category is not clear. The latter is reason for many organizations to explain their name. But when we look at the top 100 strongest brands, it appears that the majority has an abstract name. The reason is that abstract names are much more distinctive than functional names. And with the right communication, stakeholders quickly learn that Twix is a candybar and not a car brand. In short the more descriptive the name, the less distinctive. Here is a kind of contrast between the criteria "easy to load" and "distinctive." And ultimately, the latter is the most important in brands.

The associative names are a bit between the abstract and functional names. These do not necessarily say something about the category but rather about the positioning of the brand. The advantage of these names is that they are somewhat meaningful but also distinctive.

As far as the criterion "easy to load" is concerned, we observe that functional names and certainly abbreviations are difficult to associate with emotional values. Abbreviations of themselves already have a kind of business-like association. The use of abbreviations as name is therefore strongly discouraged. Yet brand names often result from abbreviations. If that leads to a new word, then it is not bad. Because then a new, abstract name arises. IKEA, for example, is an abbreviation of the initials of the first and last names of the two founders. But that does not matter anymore. The brand is the word IKEA, an abstract word and a very strong brand.

9.4 The brand naming process

Two methods are often used to arrive at the choice of a new brand name:

- *Internal brainstorm.* This is the fastest and costs the least, but generally yields the worst names. The problem is that managers often do not get away from their own situation and do not fully understand how the name comes across to the customer. What can also go wrong is that a name has already been used elsewhere and then legal issues arise.
- *Brand name contest among staff and/or customers.* The big advantage is that support is created for the name or the name change. Staff members and customers have to accept and to propagate the name, and then it is wise to involve them. The disadvantage is that generally only obvious names pop up. To stimulate involvement, a company can issue a competition, but then it should be explicitly stated that none of the submitted names will be chosen immediately, but that they will be submitted to a jury or professional agency for assessment.

Of course, both methods are not necessarily bad. In the past, when there were no special brand name agencies, young entrepreneurs always invented the name themselves. The name Apple was also a creative impulse of Steve Jobs himself.

But if a manager wants a systematic and fresh approach when choosing the name, then a third method is recommended:

■ *Hiring a brand naming agency.* There are various agencies that can do this. Examples are Tungsten Branding and Globrands, but there are many more to choose from.

For the creation of a brand name with a naming agency the same applies as for the development of an advertising campaign: first a briefing must be drawn up with as main points: the vision of the company, the product, the target group, and the brand positioning. If there is no clarity about this, no name should be created. The reason for this is that the possible associations with the name must fit with the positioning.

A **brand naming agency** often works according to the following steps:

1. A briefing is requested. Next to clarity about the items mentioned earlier, also the brand architecture and the international use of the name should be specified.
2. Consider a large number of (approximately 50) names. These are presented to the client. Based on this long list, the agency finds out what the client does or does not like. The list may also include names from competing brands.
3. A smaller quantity of names is presented to the client, including names from the previous list and new names. According to the same process, one tries to arrive at a list of three names.
4. The three names are tested with the target group. This is not necessary, but is recommended if the client considers fast acceptance important.
5. The three names will be subject to a connotation check and legal investigation. A **connotation check** intends to check whether a particular name in other countries does not generate unwanted associations. This way the problems that Ford encountered in Example 9.2 can be avoided. A legal investigation checks whether the name has not already been used elsewhere (or has been deposited) and whether the associated website www.name.ext (where "ext" is the country's extension) is still available.
6. The client selects a name.

9.5 Rebranding: changing the brand name

Changing the brand name is referred to as **rebranding**. This is a narrower definition of the word rebranding than in some other publications, where rebranding also means repositioning, i.e. changing the positioning of the brand, without changing the brand name.

Changing a brand name is a rare phenomenon, and rightly so, because it means a lot if you do that. The brand name is the main carrier of the brand knowledge that people have. And all accumulated brand knowledge is precisely the strength of a brand. That is what Keller also says: the fact that people have all sorts of associations about the brand when they hear the name is the **brand equity**. That is in fact the value of all knowledge and associations that people have about a brand added together. If you then change the brand name, it is not that the brand knowledge suddenly disappears, but the most logical link with the brand knowledge is gone. In short by changing a brand name, part of the brand equity disappears (see Example 9.3).

Example 9.3 The name of the Dutch mail delivery service

The Dutch mail delivery has had problems with its name: it was an abbreviation (which is difficult to load) that continuously changed. For years, the name was PTT: Postal, Telegraph and Telephone Services. The first T has disappeared as a phenomenon already for a long time. Then, after privatization, it was changed to KPN Post. KPN is the abbreviation for Koninklijke PTT Nederland (Royal PTT Netherlands). Subsequently, the postal services division was acquired by the Australian company TNT and the abbreviation of TNT Post Group was chosen: TPG Post which was switched in 2005 to simply TNT. But with all the changes, who still knows the real name? Many people still use the familiar name PTT. And even the completely independent Dutch phone company KPN is sometimes referred to as PTT.

If you read Example 9.3, you may wonder what the reasons are to change the name. We will look at that in Section 9.5.1. Then in Section 9.5.2 we answer the question of what the best way is to organize the rebranding process.

9.5.1 Reasons to change the brand name

The reasons for changing the brand name are as follows:

- mergers and acquisitions
- legal issues
- a crisis
- efficiency

A goal of **mergers and acquisitions** is often to work more efficiently. A consequence is that brands can disappear. An example is the merger between Dutch banks ING and Postbank. For a long time both brands existed but in 2010 Postbank was completely gone. This was a form of rebranding because Postbank has become ING (see also Example 9.4).

Example 9.4 Postbank switched to ING

The acquisition of the Dutch Postbank by ING and consequently the rebranding of Postbank into ING went neither gradually nor in one go, but somewhere in between. The first announcement took place in the Summer of 2007 and afterwards the people were slowly prepared for the change in various campaigns. Thus the blue lion (Postbank) and the orange lion (ING) were presented together in commercials and the blue lion literally slowly converted into orange. In the course of 2008, cash dispensers were also gradually converted.

In the end, the Postbank brand disappeared completely in 2010. Whether this major change with two different brand images woven together into one resulted in a loss of customers is something we will probably never know exactly.

We already referred to **legal problems** earlier. These are generally a consequence of shortcomings in preparatory research.

The third reason for rebranding is the most difficult one: **a crisis**. There may have been such a blemish on the brand that the brand decides to change the name. In a number of countries, Foster Parents Plan was changed to Plan International after all sorts of bad publicity. Another example was Malaysia Airlines that faced the issue of name change after two major tragedies in 2004.

A fourth reason for rebranding is a push for **efficiency**. This often has to do with internationalization. At Frito-Lay, for instance, a number of local brands were placed under the name Lay's chips. In the Netherlands, for instance, the old name Smiths disappeared and was replaced by Lay's (see Example 9.5). The "historic" switch from Raider to Twix in 1991 was even an international operation: the name change happened simultaneously in a number of countries in mainland Europe.

Example 9.5 Smiths becomes Lay's

The taste was already internationalized, but then the brand name Smiths, which had been used since 1958, disappeared in 2001 from the snack aisles to make way for the international name Lay's.

This was a remarkable decision for a brand that had a brand recognition of 99% and a market share of more than 60%. The parent company Frito-Lay, part of Pepsico, followed the trend of reducing the number of brand names, similar as to what for instance Unilever has been doing as well for some time already with cutting in the spectrum of dairy brands.

The replacement of the crisp packagings with the old brand name took around six weeks. To make the change more gradual, the old name, Smiths, was still printed on the bags for some time. Meanwhile, the manufacturer extensively advertised to introduce the new brand name.

9.5.2 Organizing a rebranding operation

What is the best way to organize a rebranding operation? To answer this question, we first look at some research in this field. Research into the acceptance of brand names shows that meaningful names are accepted earlier than brand names with a non-meaningful name.

The acceptance of a non-meaningful name appears to be faster with the help of communication. Research into the acceptance of extensions without an obvious fit (Völckner & Sattler, 2006) also shows that communication increases the perceived fit and thus the acceptance. Although research into the acceptance of changed brand names is still scarce, it seems reasonable to assume that a name change must be accompanied by strong and clear communication externally, and internally with a clear motivation, and a clear vision and ambition, in short with good communication and explanation.

Photo 9.1 The classic example of a major international rebranding operation: Raider became Twix in 1991. Photos used with permission of Mars Wrigley Confectionery UK Limited. Photo Raider: © Gaspar18, May 27, 2018 (cc-by-sa/4.0). Photo Twix: Photo Pxhere.com. CC0 public domain

Then two transition paths are possible:

- *Gradually*. For example, the new name is first put in small print on the packaging (Twix) next to the existing old name (Raider). Over time, the format of the new name becomes stronger and eventually the old name vanishes. The advantage of this is that the target group slowly gets used to the new situation; the disadvantage is more (marketing) costs because of a temporary double situation and perhaps also some confusion when two names are used.
- *In one go*. With a "big bang" the company is clear: the name has changed.

Finally, another comment is appropriate about the disadvantages of rebranding. They are of course big. In any case, it costs a lot of money to teach the target groups the new name. But there are plenty of examples that show that the rebranding was ultimately not a problem. See, for example, Lay's chips. There might be a greater danger if a brand actually disappears and is included in another brand such as in the Postbank example. Then there is the risk that customers disappear. However, Sharp's studies give the impression that true brand loyalty is a rare phenomenon. And that brands are mainly about visibility. This confirms the need to invest heavily in communication during rebranding and perhaps also to do it preferably in one go so that it is clear to everyone what is happening.

9.6 Visual identity

Many different terms are used around the subject of visual identity such as house style, (corporate or brand) design, logo, trademark, and brand symbols or brand elements. Sometimes even the term brand decisions is used for matters concerning visual identity. Then the branding is mainly concerned with advice on logos or other aspects of the visual identity.

Chapter 5 described how Birkigt and Stadler (1986) define **(corporate) identity**:

1. personality, the core of the identity
2. behaviour
3. communication
4. symbols

In our view, the corporate identity mainly relates to the first element, the personality of the organization. The (desired) positioning is close to that. From the personality, a certain style or symbolism is derived. It is just like with people. A person's personality determines how he dresses, not the other way around.

What is **corporate design** then? Is that the same as visual identity? That depends on whether you choose a broad or limited definition of corporate design. Some authors choose a broad definition of corporate design and state that it is the same as corporate identity, therefore consisting of behaviour, communication, and symbolism. This seems to us to be a non-logical definition.

We would opt for the narrow definition of corporate (or brand) design, and refer to it as the visual identity of the brand or the company. In this narrow definition, **visual identity** is the visual aspect of branding that companies create in order to evoke the desired feelings and experiences with the brand. It includes anything visual that the brand produces such as logo design, fonts, photos, and any other visuals that are used to communicate the brand. It therefore only concerns the *symbolic* part of the brand identity.

Then we are not there yet because there is also disagreement about what is to be considered as **brand symbols**. Of course, there are all visual choices such as logo, use of colour, shapes, and fonts. And that applies to all forms of communication such as print and online. But some also consider the choice of a brand name a form of symbolism and thus part of the visual identity. We do not consider that a logical choice again.

Much confusion may arise from the legal definition of a brand. Legally, brands are often defined with mainly symbolical references. For instance, according to US Trademark Law, "a brand is a trademark. A trademark is a word, phrase, or logo that identifies the source of goods or services." The UK uses a similar legal definition: "A trade mark can be a name, word, phrase, logo, symbol, design, image, sound, shape, signature or any combination of these elements."

The legal definition focuses on the components of a brand that can be legally registered in the context of trademark law. The word **logo** is often used in this context. In legal terms, a logo is a design or image with or without a name. This includes the specific way in which the name is written as the design of the name Coca-Cola with "long C's."

Photo 9.2 The Coca-Cola logo has remained virtually unchanged since 1886. Source: Commons Wikimedia (public domain)

Brand design is used in this book as a synonym for house style, visual identity, or brand symbols. By this we mean the design of all graphic brand elements: drawings, prints, stamps, letters, numbers, forms of products or packaging, and all other graphic signs that serve to distinguish the products or services of the company.

In addition to this definition, it is important to mention that in the retail sector the symbolism applies to the entire organization: that is the house style and design of the store itself! The house style then concerns the total combination of colours, decoration, interior, and so on. The design of a store largely determines the experience that customers feel. An interesting example is the successful Dutch Marqt store concept, which started in 2008 in Amsterdam. Marqt offers fresh products, produced in a responsible way, and opened its fifteenth store in 2015. Founder Quirijn Bolle then stated that "in retrospect the interior of our first stores was too 'designed'. Partly as a result, a high price image has emerged. We now have to get rid of that image again" (NRC Next, October 2, 2015).

9.7 Guidelines for visual design

The most important guideline is that the visual design is always a consequence of the brand personality and positioning. This seems logical, so logical that we would expect that this is often done in practice. Yet that is not the case. In reality, visual design decisions are often taken too lightly. It is often said that a certain logo is "no longer up to date" or "not appealing enough" and that the visual design must be adjusted accordingly. A new logo is then designed and if the management likes the logo, a new visual design is born. However, this method ignores the function of the brand design as a carrier of the brand identity. For example, a new logo can only be designed if a discussion has first taken place about the brand identity: what does the brand or company stand for?

A good example can be found in Australia: the logo used by the Melbourne City Council is a capital M in a dynamic modern font, consisting of fragments of different shades of matching colours. The font is an expression of the corporate identity of Melbourne as a vibrant progressive city, where its culturally diverse population joins to create an innovative, liveable, and sustainable unity.

Photo 9.3 The City of Melbourne logo. Photo provided with permission of the Melbourne City Council, © City of Melbourne

With more abstract logos, the natural associations of a certain form or image must be taken into account. For example, round logos have different associations than angled. Colours also have their own associations: blue is seen as mild, red as spicy and bright, etc. Colours are important for brands. For example, colours play an important role in the recognition of coffee varieties (red label, gold label, silver label, etc.).

For visual design more or less the same applies as for brand names: it helps brand recognition when the intrinsic characteristics of the visual design tie in with the positioning, but at the same time sufficient communication stimulates a lot of "learning" for the stakeholders in terms of associations and familiarity. It is also important to be intensive and consistent in communication.

Another comment concerns the method of developing a visual design. There, too, a comparison is possible with brand names. Namely that hiring an external agency develops the opportunity for an innovative but appropriate visual design. The Melbourne logo, for instance, was developed by the American branding company Landor Associates. But hiring external expertise is not always necessary. Nike illustrates this. The Nike logo, the "Swoosh," was once developed by a student. He never seems to have received anything for it. But it is now one of the most well-known logos, easily recognized even without a brand name.

Photo 9.4 **The Nike Swoosh. Source: Commons Wikimedia (public domain)**

There is a difference with respect to the development of brand names. Occasionally a redesign is necessary. Visual designs can simply go out of fashion. What could look like a beautiful website a few years ago can now be old-fashioned and user-unfriendly. Even more than with a brand name, a visual design should keep a contemporary look and move with the times but always based on the brand personality. The previously shown logo of Coca-Cola did not undergo any major changes since 1886. On the other hand, Starbucks has changed its logo recently (see the picture).

Photo 9.5 **Starbucks changed its logo in 2011. Source: istockphoto.com**

Photo 9.5 (Continued) **Source: istockphoto.com.**

Visual design includes more than logos. Product packaging often shows the specific features of the overall design of the brand. The typical Coca-Cola bottle is a good example. Especially with retail stores or restaurant, the design often extends to all details of the store. The appearance of most McDonald's restaurants, for instance, is so typical that they are recognizable as McDonald's even without the iconic golden arches of the McDonald's logo.

Photo 9.6 **The typical features of a McDonald's restaurant. Source: McDonald's Multimedia Library**

Summary

The choice for a new brand name occurs with new products and with name changes ("rebranding"). Those are the moments when the choice for a new name is important. One reason for the importance is that acceptance of a new name is easier if the name already includes a reference to the brand positioning. Yet that is not the main reason. People can learn to link associations to any word or combination of letters and symbols. Besides acceptance, there are four other requirements for a brand name. First of all a brand name has to be distinctive. Functional names consisting of existing words are the least distinctive. Functional names also often do not meet two other requirements: online availability and the possibility to create legal protection. Finally, a name should not generate the wrong associations, for example in another language. Hiring a brand naming agency increases the probability of finding a suitable name. This certainly also applies to the choice of visual identity: the use of an external agency is usually preferred. When hiring an agency, it is important to have a clear positioning and thus make a clear briefing: the design that is created should fit well with the desired identity of the brand.

Chapter 10

Brand positioning and employees

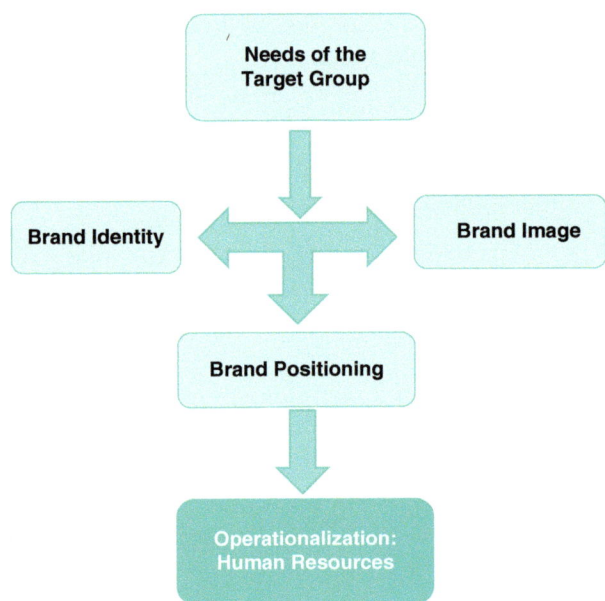

10.1 Brand positioning and the employees in the organization

The marketing strategy guides the implementation of the well-known four Ps (product, price, place, and promotion/communication), plus issues such as brand architecture, brand name, and visual identity. The previous chapters detailed these relationships. We conclude this book with a chapter in which the relationship between positioning and staffing is highlighted. The P of personnel is sometimes referred to as the fifth P of marketing. But some modesty at this point is necessary: human resource management (HRM) is not part of marketing. However, there is an important relationship between marketing and staffing. In this chapter we investigate the relationship between brand positioning and staffing. This involves two different aspects:

1. What is the link between brand positioning and aspects of HRM?
2. How should marketing and communication be organized in the organization?

10.2 Core values and HRM

In Chapter 5 we emphasized the importance of distinctive core values. This is important in order to create a clear brain position of the brand towards external target groups. But in order to realize the brand's promises, it is essential that those who are responsible for it, the employees, actually propagate the brand values. This brings us to **internal branding**: ensuring that all employees are sufficiently aware of the core values of the organization and behave accordingly (see Figure 10.1).

The latter could suggest that top-down management efforts are necessary to realize the desired behaviour. But if all works out well, that is only needed to a limited extent. This is because, normally, the core values should have been determined after analyzing the culture of the organization. The relation between brand positioning and staffing is a two-way relationship:

■ A brand positioning results from a careful analysis of target group needs and brand image, *in combination with* an analysis of the culture and DNA of the organization, in which the employees are an important element.
■ After the positioning has been determined, all organizational behaviour (including the employees' behaviour) has to be in line with the positioning.

This does not mean that core values are completely static. If the organization desires to change its organizational culture, **change management** is of great importance. An organization with a strong supply-oriented approach, for instance, can be turned into a customer-oriented organization, although that will not go without a struggle.

Lee (2004) gives a vivid description of internal branding at Disney (see Example 10.1).

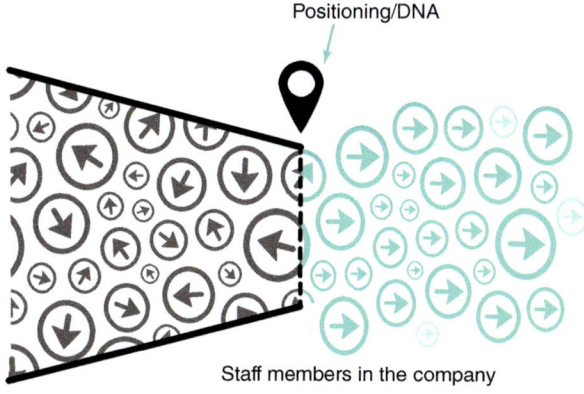

Figure 10.1 **Internal branding**

Example 10.1 Internal branding at Disney

Photo 10.1 **The magic world of Disney. Photo with permission of Disney; © Disney**

Every new employee at Disney will see a video showing Disney's culture. Among other things, that includes that everyone always greets each other on a first name basis. That is also made easy: everyone receives a big badge with his or her name on it. Furthermore, customers must always be positively addressed. A small number of employees quit after the video. That is considered a good thing: they apparently do not match the core values of Disney. Customers who come to Disney for the first time also receive a badge stating "first visit." When entering attractions, staff then cheerfully asks: "Do you like your first visit?" Although this might seem artificial, it certainly does make it easier for both employees and customers to feel good. According to Lee, for example healthcare institutions could learn something from this culture.

Chapter 5 highlighted that the company's core values should preferably relate to the culture within the company. We also emphasized that the core values must be distinctive and not generic. It is important to be different than competitors. But here we want to add another important point: core values should be translated into the **job description** of employees (see Example 10.2).

Example 10.2 Translation of the core values into job descriptions

An educational institution chooses as one of the core values: top education. How is this "value" translated into guidelines for staff? That is very difficult. Of course, it can play a role in the recruitment and selection of personnel, but it offers few starting points for managing incumbent staff. Another educational institution profiles as down-to-earth. Down-to-earth says something about the way of communicating with students as well as what attitude of the students is expected. This can be translated into guidelines for HRM and for recruitment. This also has consequences for labour market communication.

In short when defining core values, a manager should realize that they have implications for the people working in the organization.

10.3 The organization of marketing and communications

In Chapter 1 we made a distinction between three levels of marketing: marketing as culture, as strategy, and as tactics. The tactical level requires that many activities have to be carried out: everything must be visible in the five Ps. To do this effectively and efficiently, marketing must be well organized. Another organizational question is which departments have to work together to implement strategies effectively. We will discuss this in this section: Section 10.3.2 is devoted to the organization of marketing and communication, because these two functions determine to a large extent the brand image.

But first we need to highlight that before everything else, marketing should be accepted as culture throughout the organization; this is given in Section 10.3.1. We conclude the chapter with a brief discussion of the relationship between marketing and communications (Section 10.3.3).

10.3.1 The part-time marketer

Many years ago, marketing scientist Gummesson (1987) introduced the concept of the **part-time marketer**. This idea means that marketing is only properly secured in an organization if everyone in the organization thinks and acts as a marketer. A recent survey among thousands of marketing managers, published in the *Harvard Business Review* (De Swaan Arons Van den Driest & Weed, 2014), also shows this as a key issue: everyone should be aware of the need to put the customer first. This certainly applies to service companies but it is also essential for organizations that manufacture products such as a car-producing company because even then the whole process is aimed at making cars that meet the wishes of customers. Customer orientation must have penetrated in all operations of the organization. If all employees in a company have acquired such an attitude, the principle of the part-time marketer is met: everyone in the organization is a bit of a marketer besides his professional work!

The principle outlined here also means that if a company has a marketing department, but the marketing idea is insufficiently permeated in the organization, there cannot be any successful marketing. In fact, having an official marketing department is sometimes a nice excuse in organizations for not having to deal with it yourself. Customer orientation is therefore a matter for the entire organization. The reverse is also true: a customer-oriented organization does not necessarily have to have a separate marketing department. Especially smaller organizations often have no marketing department, while such an organization can be very customer-oriented.

Nevertheless, having marketing knowledge in a company is often a necessity to enable the strategies and activities discussed in this book. This is also because marketing also entails a number of specific activities, such as market research or marketing communication, including the control of online communication, for which someone must be responsible. We will now go into the way in which this can be organized.

10.3.2 Marketing tasks

Marketing should be top-of-mind for everybody working in an organization, but besides that marketing must also be explicitly represented in the organization. Then the question is: how and where in the organization? In Chapter 1 we argued that marketing exists on three levels:

- Marketing as a culture: the marketing idea (focus on brand identity and customer) is represented in the hearts and minds of everybody in the organization.
- Marketing as a strategy: a sound analysis should lead to make focused, distinctive, and relevant choices about target group and positioning.
- Marketing as tactics: an integrated marketing mix, in which all activities with respect to the five Ps are derived from the marketing strategy.

What does this mean for the **marketing function** in an organization?

1. The marketer is primarily responsible for the marketing strategy.
2. In addition, he is in charge of the implementation of marketing activities.
3. He provides the organization with sufficient information from marketing research.
4. He is responsible for creating the connection between marketing, top management, and the corporate strategy.
5. He has to cooperate with departments such as sales, finance, HRM, R&D, and communication.

At this location it is interesting to highlight the most important results of the aforementioned study published in the *Harvard Business Review* (De Swaan Arons & Vermeer, 2014). Table 10.1 summarizes these results.

Table 10.1 **What is different in better performing companies?**

Percentage of companies that:	Well-performing company (%)	Lesser-performing company (%)
Uses data and analytics	52	35
Includes a "societal" element in the brand positioning	56	46
Connects marketing to the corporate strategy	52	38
Inspires employees by referring to the brand identity	61	46
Measures brand performance (uses metrics)	67	47

Source: De Swaan Arons & Vermeer, 2014.

Table 10.1 demonstrates that successful companies base themselves more on analysis and research, apply a well-integrated positioning strategy that includes "societal" elements, and provide a strong link between brand, top management, and employees. Example 10.3 illustrates some of these principles.

Example 10.3 The CEO of Bayer refocused the company

In a time frame of six years, Bayer's CEO Marijn Dekkers reorganized the company from a general chemical company to a specialized life-sciences company.

Dekker "*Bayer always had good researchers. But the company was less equipped in translating brilliance in the lab into a commercial success. That was the focus of my attention in the past six years. Marketing and customer research, and an additional billion euros for R&D. People might say that a good product sells itself, but this is really not the case.*"

Interviewer: "You made Bayer more specialized. Doesn't that imply that you have become independent of one market?"

Dekker: "Diversification is not that much in the company as it is in the group of customers served. If I have a bakery near a school and I only sell my cookies to school kids, I don't earn anything during the holidays. But when entire families are my customers, then I have diversified my customers. We always sell molecules, but we sell them to doctors and to farmers. They don't have a lot in common. If farmers don't sell well, that does not really impact the doctor and vice versa."

Interviewer: "When you started, there was resistance among Bayer employees. How could you take their fears away?"

Dekkers answers with a smile: "With a lot of patience. And by continuously repeating that Bayer exists by the grace of innovation, not administration. So that's where the money had to go, and we could save on overhead expenses."

Source: Het Financieele Dagblad, October 16, 2015

10.3.3 The relation between marketing and communications

For the internal organization, we emphasize the importance of a strong **relation between marketing and communication**. Creating a strong brand position is primarily a task and responsibility of marketing. It is not called the marketing strategy for nothing. At the same time, there is a strong relation with (marketing) communications. In organizations where different people are responsible for marketing and communications, it is therefore important that they work well together. The marketing person has to provide the input for the communications professional. This must be clearly specified. Of course, this does not have to be done separately. Actually, it seems wise to involve communication professionals in building the brand positioning. The advantage of involving a communications officer is that he (or she) can correctly assess the translation of the brand positioning into a proposition. Top management should also be involved in creating a brand positioning strategy. Its importance is so great that it cannot be developed within the marketing function alone. The brand positioning follows from the DNA of the brand, and also closely matches the vision and mission of the organization.

Another point about the internal organization is whether marketing as a function has to be present in the organization at all. This is normal in bigger companies. But in smaller companies or organizations that are less profit-oriented, such as government institutions, healthcare providers, or utility companies, the marketing function is not always explicitly present while the communication function is almost always represented. Without an explicit marketing department you run the risk that such an important strategic topic as brand positioning does not receive the necessary attention. And then, the organization becomes a ship without control.

Summary

The relationship between positioning and HRM runs along different lines. First, a solid brand positioning can only be created after an extensive analysis of the culture of the organization. Only then the desired positioning can be decided. Second, the chosen positioning then becomes a guideline for the behaviour of staff members (internal branding). The goal is ultimately to realize "part-time marketers": that everyone in the organization is customer-oriented. Third, the marketing department also has to be explicitly present in an organization. The marketer has tasks such as using the right set of "metrics" and analyze marketing data, creating and safeguarding a functional, emotional, and often also a societal dimension in the brand positioning, and ensuring proper alignment of marketing activities on all levels in the organization. Collaboration between marketing and communication is essential, especially in the realization of the brand positioning.

Case material
for Part III

Case 1. Häagen-Dazs is reinventing its brand for the Instagram generation

It does not matter if you source the best ingredients or create the most luxurious taste, if millennials think your product is something their mum would buy it's the "kiss of death" for any brand, according to Jennifer Jorgensen, vice-president and global brand director of Häagen-Dazs. Especially for a brand that's supposed to live in the "super premium luxury space."

"To have the younger generation saying 'that's for older people', that's not good news," she states. Even though they describe the brand as the jewel in parent company General Mills' crown, Jorgensen and her team interpreted this consumer reaction to Häagen-Dazs as a "rallying cry" for a brand revival, firmly focused on capturing the attention of a millennial audience.

The brand aims to refresh its image, and is going to roll out a revamped packaging, communications strategy, and in-store experience across its more than 800 ice cream shops worldwide.

New visual identity

Häagen-Dazs's vision is to be the most desired ice cream brand in the world. While it currently sits behind Unilever's Magnum in second place, Jorgensen explains that the business is going after the number one slot with "really tight messaging" across its branding, communications, and packaging.

The plan is to deepen its presence in key ice cream markets around the world. Jorgensen argues that to be a global name you need to be iconic and generate brand love while on a local level consumers need to feel like you understand them. Therefore, the brief for the new visual identity was "Instagrammable," a term the Häagen-Dazs team talk about constantly. From reimagining the logo to streamlining the interiors of its ice cream shops, all aspects of the new brand are designed to chime with an Instagram-friendly millennial aesthetic.

Recognising that with any repositioning there's a risk, Jorgensen says the team understood there was a possibility of alienating its existing consumers, but the brand had to make a move regardless. "First of all, you never want to be the outdated brand, so we've got to modernise and this millennial generation is a huge generation coming through. If we miss that we won't have a business in the next 30 years," she explains. "We tested the packaging and the advertising with the millennial consumer, but we also tested it with the older consumer and it works for both. It's a little bit like there's a millennial inside everyone."

It was also crucial to decipher what young people look for in luxury today. Häagen-Dazs believes it is less about bling and overtly branded products, and more about experience, indulgence, and craftsmanship. When people want that emotional escape they look for Häagen-Dazs. Taking this insight on board, the aim was to retain the desire and emotion the brand evoked when it first arrived on the market, but apply this aesthetic in a modern way.

In the 1990s, Häagen-Dazs was known for its seductive black and white adverts featuring good looking couples sharing a tub of ice cream. Jorgensen describes these adverts as "iconic" creative that set the standard for luxury at the time and pushed the boundaries by being brave. "It was on the offence versus being on the defence, like here are all the million reasons why we're so great. It was just like boom, here we are; take it or leave it, which really changed the tone," she recalls. "Reuben Mattus our founder started this whole 'ice cream for adults' thing, so it launched with a very adult positioning, then justified the price point and why it's so premium."

Despite having a true appreciation for those adverts, the Häagen-Dazs team recognised that the luxury cues that worked in the 1980s and 1990s are not what young people look for today. This thinking also applies to the brand's desire to deliver a premium experience in its ice cream shops. Realising that the brand associations had become out of date and were resulting in a declining footfall in some markets, Häagen-Dazs has begun rolling out a refreshed in-store identity, starting on the French Riviera. The interior design takes inspiration from the new-look packaging design, mixing the brand's signature burgundy shade with white walls and vibrant graphic patterns. This scheme is paired with natural woods and cues to the brand heritage such as neon wall mounted quotes from founder Mattus and pendant chandeliers made from milk jugs. The brand has also decided to completely revamp the way ice cream is sold, swapping the generic tubs for containers designed to look like giant ice cream pints.

Riding the wave of disruption

"You don't want to be unattainable and I think that's where we got to a little bit in the past," Jorgensen says. "A little bit too unapproachable and unattainable luxury that lacked that personal connection with the new generation."

Part of creating this personal connection has meant shifting the focus from mass communication to more one-to-one social strategies. Jorgensen explains that whereas when she started working on the brand in 2014 it was almost 100% focused on TV advertising, the team recognised the brand needed to come alive on social and mobile if it was to transition from a mid-40s consumer to a 25- to 35-year-old demographic. As a consequence, Häagen-Dazs is also putting influencer marketing at the heart of its business but it has strict criteria about when to invest.

> We needed a new business model that had to be really targeted, precise and laser-focused. We are speaking to a new age consumer who is digital first. It was necessity that influencer marketing was a touchpoint. We had to embrace it fully and commit to it,

explains Arjoon Bose, head of marketing in Europe for New Ventures, General Mills' natural and organic business.

General Mills, the parent company of Häagen-Dazs, is investing a third of its digital spend in influencer marketers. To ensure authentic and effective influencer marketing, General Mills has six simple criteria: the three Ts – truth, transparency, and trust – and the three Rs – reach, relevance, and resonance. Despite these clear criteria, Bose admitted there are "many ways to skin a cat" when it comes to deciding how to pick the correct influencer. However, he believes being able to hand over control is key. He explained: "The best content and storytelling authenticity [comes from] letting go of control and letting your influencer be their own creative director."

Bose was candid about the lack of knowledge around influencer marketing and said General Mills is on a "journey." Bose admitted that "initially it's a more expensive investment" but that "the line flattens out" over time. As influencer marketing is still a relatively new discipline, deciding how much to pay influencers can be complex but General Mills' Bose asks three questions. He explains:

> It's the who, how and the what. How much would it cost me as a brand to produce that piece of content with an agency or anyone else? How many people do I want to get that message out to? That's how we would arrive at an ROI and then apply index, whether there's a one off or a long-term benefit to it.

"It really depends on what metric you are seeking whether it's engagement or conversion but the best influencer marketing is where you go all the way down the funnel to advocacy."

Bose believes that influencer marketing will become important in a range of industries, not just obvious areas such as beauty or fashion: "Industries like beauty are going to lead the way but we're going to see it across every brand and touchpoint. People don't just buy products, they buy benefits, values and passion points."

Sources: Marketingweek.com

■ https://www.marketingweek.com/2018/08/23/haagen-dazs-brand-revival/, August 23, 2018

■ https://www.marketingweek.com/2019/05/16/general-mills-influencer-marketing/, May 16, 2019

Questions

1. The book distinguishes four levels of branding
   a) Which four levels are these?
   b) On which level is the brand Häagen-Dazs defined? Explain your answer.
2. The book distinguishes between three types of brand names.
   a) What type of brand name is Häagen-Dazs?
   b) How do you think the name Häagen-Dazs had been chosen?
3. The book distinguishes between brand extensions and line extensions.
   a) Define a brand extension for Häagen-Dazs.
   b) Define a line extension for Häagen-Dazs.
4. The case describes a redesign of the visual identity of Häagen-Dazs. Do you think that this redesign also changes the identity of Häagen-Dazs? Explain your answer.
5. Use the Value Compass to describe the core values of Häagen-Dazs. Does the redesign of the visual identity create a change in the core values of the Häagen-Dazs brand? Explain your answer.
6. Hägen-Dazs uses influencer marketing as one of its touchpoints.
   a) Illustrate with an example how influencer marketing works.
   b) Do you think that influencer marketing is a powerful tool for Häagen-Dazs? Why (not)?
   c) Which other touchpoints are used by Häagen-Dazs in the visual identity redesign described in the case.

Case 2. Moxy: Lifestyle in the hotel business

The first Moxy

Most hotels focus on a certain kind of people: travellers. And not Baby boom travellers, or Generation X travellers, or millennial travellers – but all travellers. However, Moxy promises to do it differently. This new hotel chain is specifically "designed to capture the rapidly emerging millennial traveller," according to a press release. Moxy therefore focuses on the "millennials," roughly young people between 18 and 35. "Every hotel will be lively, uncompromising and young at heart," according to the press release.

The first Moxy hotel opened its doors in September 2014 in Milan. Moxy is a Marriott brand. Marriott is a company operating in the hospitality industry, owning – next to the Marriott brand – several mainly luxury hotel concepts such as Ritz-Carlton and Sheraton. And, since 2014, also Moxy.

For the first hotel in Milan, Marriott cooperated with IKEA. When the hotel chain opened, the media reported on "IKEA's first hotel." However, the reality of the hotel seems different. There is no IKEA furniture or IKEA branding: modern stylish furniture, trendy designs, but no yellow and blue IKEA house style, and certainly no Billy bookcases. The only thing that actually reminded of IKEA in the beginning was the Swedish meatballs in the hotel's self-service bar.

But the IKEA expertise is used. The rooms are pre-fab units produced by Ikea-owned company Inter Hospitality. Due to the modular structure, a hotel of 300 rooms can be built in six months. The smart solutions in construction and design are directly derived from IKEA's ideas about furniture. The rooms are so cleverly arranged that the modules are connected to the hotel with a single plug. That saves money. The room rates are between €68 and €95, although the bed, the showers, and the Apple TV are super trendy.

In the hotel itself everything is geared towards the specific target group. Tina Edmundson, brand manager at Marriott: "Moxy is the essence for the new generation of travellers. Because millennials are so dependent on technology, we provide them with super-fast internet." It sounds a bit cynical: if there is internet, the millennial is satisfied. But target group thinking involves more than access to the digital highway. "Millennials choose the hotel 'for its attitude'; most economy hotels are anonymous and hardly leave any impression, but we try to do it differently," according to Edmundson. Moxy wants to be hip, creative, and online and intends to achieve maximum experience with minimal resources. For example, visual artists and other creative minds were challenged to participate in the "blank canvas challenge," and thus earn a place as the home artist of the first Moxy in art city Milan.

This resulted in a number of playful elements that should be cool for the target group. Imagine an elevator with a shower head inside, so that it looks like a bathroom. Or room-wide images of bearded hipsters with tattoos. Or the "do not disturb" signs at the door where a man in underwear is depicted, completely covered with lipstick. Yes, you must love it; but the idea is that it fits in with the target group. And this has been extensively tested with these "savvy travelers who thrive on self-service and embrace new technology." And furniture with an IKEA look does not fit in with this concept.

But cheap it is. The IKEA method of modular construction keeps prices low, but also in other ways costs are pushed back. The millennial no longer wants to pay for unnecessary extras. There are no certainties that older generations need such as front desk staff, room service, or meeting rooms. According to the press release, the millennial is "wildly self-sufficient." Consequently, everything can be arranged online, but the millennial has to manage without service or staff once he arrived in the hotel.

"Unnecessary space" has also been cut back. At the hotel in Milan, most of the rooms are no more than 17 square metres, equipped with only the strictly necessary for the target group: 42-inch flat-screen TVs, super-fast internet,

USB connections in the wall, and sound-proof walls so you won't be bothered by the multimedia experiences of the neighbours.

The ground floor also reflects target group thinking. It is divided into three parts. First of all, there is the "library and plug-in" zone, where people can connect with the rest of the world. In addition, there is the 24-hour self-service bar, with Swedish meatballs, but without staff. Finally, there is the lobby, which looks more like a lounge area. "This is where the buzz lives," according to Moxy's press release. Industrial style, with lots of visible copper and a concrete floor, a DJ booth, and a huge screen with a live *#attheMoxy* Instagram newsfeed should encourage guests to post their selfies and share with others. Because of all this, the lobby gives the look and feel of a nightclub, with DJs, loud music, purple lighting, and cocktails waiting for you in their bottles.

A final striking aspect of the hotels is the location. Both of Milan's Moxy hotels did not open in a hipster downtown place, but right next to the two Milanese airports of Malpensa and Linate. Is this where the millennial wants to be? Maybe not, but you have to do something to keep the prices low.

The Moxy Logo (public domain. Commons Wikimedia)

Moxy to New York

When Mitchell Hochberg, the president of New York-based real estate company Lightstone, was trying to find a new hotel concept to bring to the United States, he found himself at a bit of a dead end. He and his team had been searching everywhere for an innovative hotel concept that would be of added value to the New York hotel scene. But when Hochberg found himself at the Malpensa Airport in Milan in 2013 and saw an "under construction" sign for a Marriott brand he'd never heard of before, he knew he'd found his answer.

At the time, there were no Moxy hotels in the United States. This new brand from Marriott was marketing itself as offering the "bare maximum" for cost-conscious millennials, and for that very first Moxy in Milan, Marriott had even collaborated with Ikea to develop prefabricated modular room components to cut back on costs.

This "fun" micro-hotel concept, Hochberg thought, might just work in the United States. So, in 2017, the first Moxy hotel in New York City opened its doors, on Times Square. "If people are happy being in a 175-square-foot room in Europe, why couldn't you design a 175-square-foot room in the United States that people would be happy with?" Hochberg asked. "We felt that if we could make the room size a third to 50 percent smaller than it usually is, we could charge less and be a very attractive, affordable alternative."

Before bringing the Moxy brand to New York, Lightstone tweaked Moxy's "bare maximum" select-service model in Europe to make sure it would appeal to US audiences by investing more in the design, and adding food-and-beverage venues where there weren't any before. "We felt that the brand needed to be somewhat fine-tuned for the American consumer, from what the brand was evolving in Europe," Hochberg said. "The brand was established on a complete select-service chassis in Europe, whereas we felt that food and beverage was an important component to have if the brand were in a major gateway city like New York, Los Angeles, or Miami."

New York City isn't a place that's known for relatively affordable hotel accommodations, either to stay in or to build, so developing Moxy's cost-consciousness here required some thought. The Moxy Times Square hotel has nightly rates that range anywhere from $150 to $279. A select number of 120-square-foot rooms, called Crash Pads, go for $99 a night all year-round. Those 19 rooms account for 3% of the hotel's total 612-room inventory. Compared to other Manhattan-based hotels, the price is relatively affordable.

While New York City hoteliers can demand relatively high average nightly rates and expect to have nearly fully booked hotels, they've also had to deal with the impact of the popularity of home-sharing and an influx of new hotel supply that makes it a challenge to compete.

Hochberg said that brands like Moxy are "a very compelling alternative to someone who's considering Airbnb." For example, he said, even if it costs $279 a night to stay in the Moxy Times Square, and $179 a night for an Airbnb listing in Queens, the guest who stays in the Moxy eventually wins out in terms of the overall experience. "If you're in Queens, you've got to take two subway rides, walk down a dark street, walk into a building that you've never seen before, and hope that everything is OK," he said.

> Whereas if you're staying at the Moxy Times Square, you're in the middle of everything. You know what you're going to get. You get your Marriott Rewards points. You're going to have security, nightly maid service, and five restaurants and bars to choose from just within the hotel.

Hochberg said that customer response to Moxy Times Square has been "overwhelmingly positive" and that the performance of the hotel in just five months "has exceeded our underwriting."

"Today's guest needs are rapidly evolving, and I think the industry has been playing catch up," Hochberg said.

> Consumers are beginning to acclimate themselves to the fact that if they want an affordable product, they're going to have to sacrifice something, and if you can give them an overall experience which they enjoy, then the size of the room — particularly in an urban environment — is something that they're willing to sacrifice.

The exhibits below highlight the different ways in which the "traditional" Marriott and the Moxy profile themselves in the New York market. Feel the difference by reading the exhibits.

Moxy's profile
(http://moxy-hotels.marriott.com/hotels/nyc-times-square, 16/05/2019)

Fearlessly imagined for fun hunters, Moxy Times Square is your launch pad into the city that never sleeps. Fresh design, immersive social spaces, and vibrant restaurants make this hotel your ultimate playground. From stylish guestrooms and flexible meeting rooms to our bustling brasserie and lively bars, you can eat, drink, connect, play, and chill out to your heart's content. The cherry on top is Moxy's enchanting indoor-outdoor rooftop lounge and bar, the biggest and baddest in NYC, offering epic skyline and Empire State Building views, light bites, and decadent cocktails.

Each of our 612 design-driven rooms gets you an uncompromisingly cushy bed, a massive walk-in rain shower you'll never want to get out of, and free wifi plus personal screen casting – YouTube, Hulu, Netflix, Pandora, and more.

Located just south of Times Square, Moxy sits at the electrifying epicentre of the city – where Uptown and Downtown collide, a New York minute from wherever you want to go.

Marriott's profile
(https://www.marriott.com/hotels/travel/nycmq-new-york-marriott-marquis/, 16/05/2019)

There is no city quite like New York City, and no hotel quite like New York Marriott Marquis. Set in the heart of Times Square on West 46th Street and Broadway, our iconic Manhattan hotel lets you experience all the magic of NYC from the moment you arrive. Feel the energy all around you, both within the hotel and as soon as you step outside. Inside our towering hotel, you'll find some of New York City's largest hotel rooms and suites and multiple restaurants, including the only revolving restaurant in the city and a popular outdoor lounge. Event planners have more than 120,000 square feet of versatile meeting and event space to work with and an expert staff ready to help you design an anything-but-ordinary event. And our knowledgeable staff is always ready to help hotel guests navigate this expansive and ever-changing city. Whether visiting for a family vacation, a Broadway show weekend, or attending a conference, New York Marriott Marquis is truly the perfect hotel for your stay in New York City.

Sources: www.ft.com, September 14, 2014
www.skift.com, the-inside-story-behind-marriotts-moxy-led-invasion-of-manhattan, August 24, 2018.

Questions

1. Four types of segmentation variables are mentioned in the book.
   a) Which types are these?
   b) Which variable is central to the segmentation of Moxy?
2. Products and services provide the consumer with certain benefits through the product characteristics (attributes) that make up the product or service.
   a) Which benefits do you think are essential for the Moxy concept?
   b) Which attributes are used by Moxy to realize these benefits?
   c) Which values characterize the Moxy concept? To which value types from the Value Compass do these values match?
3. Personas are frequently used to design target group descriptions. Create a persona that fits the target audience of Moxy.
4. Define the communication objectives that Moxy could have had when the brand was introduced in 2014. Use an appropriate attitude model to define your objectives.
5. An advertising agency was used to shape the introduction campaign for Moxy. Write a briefing that could have been used by Moxy.
6. Explain how Moxy tries to stimulate WOM via social media. Do you think that this is effective?
7. The book discusses four growth strategies. Explain which growth strategy was used by Marriott Hotels when the Moxy concept was created.
8. From the point of view of Marriott Hotels, is Moxy a line extension or a brand extension? Explain your answer.
9. The book explains the various forms of brand architecture.
   a) Explain which form of brand architecture has been chosen by Marriott Hotels.
   b) Why is the Moxy brand not endorsed by Marriott?
10. The book distinguishes between different types of brand names.
   a) What type of brand name is Moxy?
   b) How do you think the name Moxy had been chosen?

References

Aaker, D. A. (1991), *Managing brand equity: Capitalizing on the value of a brand name*. New York, NY: The Free Press.

Aaker, D. A. (1995), *Building strong brands*. New York, NY: The Free Press.

Aaker, D. A., & Keller, K. L. (1990), 'Consumer evaluations of brand extensions', *Journal of Marketing*, 54 (January), 27–41.

Aaker, J. L. (1997), 'Dimensions of brand personality', *Journal of Marketing Research*, 347–356.

Aaker, J. L., Benet-Martinez, V., & Garolera, J. (2001), 'Consumption symbols as carriers of culture: A study of Japanese and Spanish brand personality constructs', *Journal of Personality and Social Psychology*, 81(3), 492.

Aggarwal, P., & McGill, A. L. (2007), 'Is that car smiling at me? Schema congruity as a basis for evaluating anthropomorphized products', *Journal of Consumer Research*, 34(4), 468–479.

Alsem, K. J. (2019), *Applied strategic marketing*. Abingdon, UK: Routledge.

Alsem, K. J., & Klein Koerkamp, R. (2012), *Zorg met liefde en lef*. Groningen: New Publishers.

Alsem, K. J., & Kostelijk, E. J. (2013), *De onderscheidendheid van waarden in de zorg*. Groningen: Hanzehogeschool Marklinq.

Anderson, J. (1983), 'A spreading activation theory of memory', *Journal of Verbal Learning and Verbal Behavior*, 23, 261–295.

Bagwell, L. S., & Bernheim, B. D. (1996), 'Veblen effects in a theory of conspicuous consumption', *The American Economic Review*, 86(3), 349–373.

Balmer, J. M., & Greyser, S. A. (2002), 'Managing the multiple identities of the corporation', *California Management Review*, 44(3), 72–86.

Birkigt, K., & Stadler, M. M. (1986), *Corporate Identity, Grundlagen, Funktionen, Fallspielen*. Landsberg am Lech: Verlag Moderne Industrie.

Borg, I., & Groenen, P. J. (2005), *Modern multidimensional scaling: Theory and applications*. New York, NY: Springer Science & Business Media.

Bryson, J. M. (2004), 'What to do when stakeholders matter: Stakeholder identification and analysis techniques', *Public Management Review*, 6(1), 21–53.

Carroll, B. A., & Ahuvia, A. C. (2006), 'Some antecedents and outcomes of brand love', *Marketing Letters*, 17(2), 79–89.

De Swaan Arons, M. V. F., van den Driest, F., & Weed, K. (2014), 'The ultimate marketing machine', *Harvard Business Review*, 92(7), 54–63.

Dijksterhuis, A. (2007), *Het slimme onbewuste*. Amsterdam: Bert Bakker.

Eden, C., & Ackermann, F. (1998), *Making strategy: The journey of strategic management*. London, UK: Sage Publications.

Edson Escalas, J., & Bettman, J. R. (2005), Self-construal, reference groups and brand meaning', *Journal of Consumer Research*, 32, 378–389.

Floor, J. M., Van Raaij, W. F., & Bouwman, M. Y. (2015), *Marketingcommunicatiestrategie*. Groningen/Houten: Noordhoff Uitgevers, 7e druk.

Fombrun, C. J., Gardbert, N. A., & Sever, J. M. (2000), 'The reputation quotient: A multi-stakeholder measure of corporate reputation', *Journal of Brand Management*, 7, 241–255.

Freeman, R. E. (1984), *Strategic management: A stakeholder approach*. Boston, MA: Pitman.

Gummesson, E. (1987), 'The new marketing – Developing long term interactive relationships', *Long Range Planning*, 20(4), 10–20.

Gutman, J. (1982), 'A means-end chain model based on consumer categorization processes', *Journal of Marketing*, 46(2), 60–72.

Hallahan, K., Holtzhausen, D., Van Ruler, B., Verčič, D., & Sriramesh, K. (2007). 'Defining strategic communication'. *International Journal of Strategic Communication*, 1(1), 3–35.

Hanssens, D. M. (2015), *Empirical generalizations about marketing impact*. Cambridge, MA: Marketing Science Institute.

Hillebrand, B., Driessen, P. H., & Koll, O. (2015), 'Stakeholder marketing: Theoretical foundations and required capabilities', *Journal of the Academy of Marketing Science*, 43(4), 411–428.

Holbrook, M. B., & Hirschman, E. C. (1982), 'The experiential aspects of consumption: Consumer fantasies, feelings, and fun', *Journal of Consumer Research*, 9(2), 132–140.

Keller, K. L. (1995), *Strategic brand management: Building, measuring, and managing brand equity*. Upper Saddle River, NJ: Prentice Hall, 1st ed.

Keller, K. L. (2012), *Strategic brand management: Building, measuring, and managing brand equity*. Upper Saddle River, NJ: Prentice Hall, 4th ed.

Kostelijk, E. J. (2016), *The value compass: The influence of values on consumer behaviour*. Oxford, UK: Routledge.

Kotler, P., & Armstrong, G. (2008), *Principles of marketing*. Upper Saddle River, NJ: Pearson, 12th ed.

Kotler, P., Kartajaya, H., & Setiawan, I. (2010), *Marketing 3.0*. Hoboken, NJ: Jon Wiley & Sons, Inc.

Kumar, V. (2018). 'Transformative marketing: the next 20 years'. *Journal of Marketing*, 82(4), 1–12.

Laforet, S. (2010), *Managing brands: A contemporary perspective*. New York, NY: McGraw Hill Education, 1st ed.

Lee, F. (2004), *If Disney ran your hospital, 9½ things you would do differently*. Bozeman, MT: Second River Healthcare Press.

Levitt, T. (1960), 'Marketing myopia', *Harvard Business Review*, 38 (July–August), 45–56.

Mark, M., & Pearson, C. S. (2001), *The hero and the outlaw: Building extraordinary brands through the power of archetypes*. New York, NY: McGraw Hill Professional.

Maslow, A. H. (1954), *Motivation and personality*. New York, NY: Harper & Row.

Muniz, A. M., & O'Guinn, T. C. (2001), 'Brand community', *Journal of Consumer Research*, 27(4), 412–432.

Nederstigt, A. T. A. M., & Poiesz, T. B. C. (2014), *Consumentengedrag*. Groningen: Noordhoff Uitgevers, 6ᵉ druk.

Omondi, G. (2013), *Tell me a story: Storytelling as platform for reputation management*. Groningen: Hanze University of Applied Sciences Groningen (Master dissertation).

Park, W. C., Jaworski, B. J., & MacInnis, D. J. (1986), 'Strategic brand concept-image management', *Journal of Marketing*, 50(4), 135–145.

Pauwels, K., & Van Ewijk, B. (2013), 'Do online behavior tracking or attitude survey metrics drive brand sales? An integrative model of attitudes and actions on the consumer boulevard'. *Marketing Science Institute Working Paper Series*, 13(118), 1–49.

Petty, R. E., & Cacioppo, J. T. (1986), *The elaboration likelihood model of persuasion*. New York, NY: Springer.

Pine, J. B., & Gilmore, J. H. (1999), *The experience economy: Work is theatre & every business a stage*. Boston, MA: Harvard Business Review Press.

Porter, M. E. (1980), *Competitive strategy*. New York, NY: The Free Press.

Porter, M. E. (1985), *Competitive advantage: Creating and sustaining superior performance*. New York, NY: The Free Press.

Prahalad, C. K., & Hamel, G. (1990), 'The core competence of the corporation', *Harvard Business Review*, 68(3), 79–91.

Reichheld, F. F. (2003), 'The one number you need to grow', *Harvard Business Review*, 82(6), 1–11.

Reinartz, W., N. Wiegand, M. Imschloss (2019), 'The impact of digital transformation on the retailing value chain', *International Journal of Research in Marketing*, 36, 350–366.

Reynolds, T. J., & Gutman, J. (1988), 'Laddering theory, method, analysis, and interpretation', *Journal of Advertising Research*, 28(1), 11–31.

Ries, A., & Trout, J. (1981), *Positioning: The battle for your mind*. New York, NY: McGraw Hill, Inc.

Roberts, K. (2005), *Lovemarks: The future beyond brands*. New York, NY: Powerhouse Books.

Rokeach, M. (1973), *The nature of human values*. New York, NY: The Free Press.

Rokeach, M. (1979), *Understanding human values, individual and social*. New York, NY: The Free Press.

Rossiter, J. R., Percy, L., & Donovan, R. J. (1991), 'A better advertising planning grid', *Journal of Advertising Research*, 31(5), 11–21.

Scheibehenne, B., Greifeneder, R., & Todd, P. M. (2010), 'Can there ever be too many options? A meta-analytic review of choice overload', *Journal of Consumer Research*, 37, 409–425.

Schwartz, S. H. (1992), 'Universals in the content and structure of values: Theoretical advances and empirical tests in 20 countries'. In M. P. Zanna (Ed.), *Advances in experimental social psychology* (Vol. 25, pp. 1–65). New York, NY: The Free Press.

Sharp, B. (2012), *How brands grow: What marketers don't know*. South Melbourne: Oxford University Press.

Sheeran, P. (2002), 'Intention-behavior relations: A conceptual and empirical review', *European Review of Social Psychology*, 12(1), 1–36.

Treacy, M., & Wiersema, F. (1993), 'Customer intimacy and other value disciplines', *Harvard Business Review*, January–February, 71(1), 84–93.

Trout, J., & Rivkin, S. (1996), *The new positioning*. New York, NY: McGraw Hill.

Van Rekom, J. (1997), 'Deriving an operational measure of corporate identity', *European Journal of Marketing*, 31(5/6), 410–422.

Van Riel, C. B. (2010), *Identiteit en imago*. Den Haag: Academic Service, 4ᵉ druk.

Veldhoen, B., & en Van Slooten, S. (2010), *De 9+-organisatie: Van marketshare naar mindshare*. Culemborg: Van Duuren Management.

Verhoef, P.C. & T.M.A. Bijmolt (2019), 'Marketing perspectives on digital business models: A framework and overview of the special issue", *International Journal of Research in Marketing*, 36, 341–349.

Völckner, F., & Sattler, H. (2006), 'Drivers of brand extension success', *Journal of Marketing*, 70, 18–34.

Voss, K. E., Spangenberg, E. R., & Grohmann, B. (2003), 'Measuring the hedonic and utilitarian dimensions of consumer attitude', *Journal of Marketing Research*, 40(3), 310–320.

Webster, F. E. (1992), 'The changing role of marketing in the corporation', *Journal of Marketing*, 56(10), 1–17.

Webster, F. E. (2005), 'Back to the future: Integrating marketing as tactics, strategy and organizational culture', *Journal of Marketing*, 69 (October), 4–6.

Wernerfelt, B. (1984), 'A resource-based view of the firm', *Strategic Management Journal*, 16, 171–180.

World Commission on Environment and Development (1987), *Our common future.* Oxford, UK: Oxford University Press.

Zaichkowsky, J. L. (1985), 'Measuring the involvement construct', *Journal of Consumer Research*, 12, 341–352.

Illustration references, with links to original material

Figure

- **Figure 3.2** Maslow's need hierarchy (illustration © J. Finkelstein (cc-by-sa/3.0)). https://commons.wikimedia.org/wiki/File:Maslow%27s_hierarchy_of_needs.svg

Photos

- **Photo 1.1** Red Bull stands for extreme performance (stock photo purchased at istockphoto.com).
- **Photo 1.2** Coca-Cola. Happiness, Cozy, Christmas (stock photo purchased at istockphoto.com).
- **Photo 1.3** Heineken has high brand awareness (photo © Moktarama (cc-by-3.0), with permission of Heineken). https://commons.wikimedia.org/wiki/File:Heineken_-_Can_-_Canette.jpg
- **Photo 3.1** Lifestyle is often a better indicator for behaviour than demographics (age). Photos released under Pixabay license: free for commercial use, no attribution required. young travellers: https://pixabay.com/photos/adventure-backpack-backpacker-2610258/; old travellers: https://pixabay.com/photos/senior-elderly-people-couple-3336451/
- **Photo 3.2** Gucci: a brand with symbolic benefits (photo made by Godisable Jacob, released under Pexels license: free for commercial and non-commercial use). www.pexels.com/nl-nl/foto/afro-amerikaanse-vrouw-blauw-buiten-buitenshuis-1024036/
- **Photo 3.3** Two different benefits of using toothpaste: healthy teeth and sparkling white teeth healthy teeth (photo CC0 public domain). https://pxhere.com/en/photo/1445997 sparkling white teeth: Photo CC0 public domain. https://pxhere.com/en/photo/496707
- **Photo 3.4** Conspicuous consumption: expensive brands give status (photo CC0 public domain). https://pxhere.com/nl/photo/1508059

- **Photo 3.5** Fashion helps to make people feel beautiful (photo © Garry Knight (cc-by-2.0)). www.flickr.com/photos/garryknight/8377862576/
- **Photo 3.6** Iceland inspires for stimulating holidays (photo CC0 public domain). https://pxhere.com/en/photo/1370111
- **Photo 3.7** Coca-Cola: the pleasure of a moment for yourself (stock photo purchased at istockphoto.com).
- **Photo 3.8** The intimate relation between parent and child is often used for brand positioning purposes (photo released under Pexels license: free for commercial and non-commercial use). www.pexels.com/photo/love-sweet-face-portrait-38535/
- **Photo 3.9** Christmas: important for people that value care & affection (photo © Sigismund von Dobschütz (cc-by-sa/4.0)). https://de.wikipedia.org/wiki/Datei:Geschenke-2007.JPG.
- **Photo 3.10** Many companies include social responsible values such as CSR, circular economy, or sustainability, in their corporate identity (photo released under Pixabay license: free for commercial use, no attribution required). https://pixabay.com/illustrations/nature-earth-sustainability-leaf-3294632/
- **Photo 3.11** Honesty is a core value for Fairtrade products (photo © Juliamh123 (cc-by-sa/4.0)). https://commons.wikimedia.org/wiki/File:Fairtrade-m%C3%A4rkta_bananer.jpg
- **Photo 3.12** Insurances are important for people that value security (photo © Money, July 30, 2014 (cc-by-2.0)). www.flickr.com/photos/pictures-of-money/17121703798
- **Photo 3.13** The *L. casei* bacteria in Danone Actimel are supposed to be good for us (photo used with permission of Danone Actimel).
- **Photo 3.14** Elon Musk's Tesla symbolizes innovation (photo used with permission of Tesla; © Maurizio Pesce, October 1, 2011 (cc-by-2.0)). www.flickr.com/photos/30364433@N05/8765031426
- **Photo 4.1** An emotional brand response: Disney aims for heartshare (photo with permission of Disney; © Disney).
- **Photo 4.2** The carefree jester as archetype: Pringles (photo released under Pexels license: free for commercial and non-commercial use). www.pexels.com/nl-nl/foto/berg-bomen-buiten-buitenshuis-1450480/
- **Photo 4.3** Facebook uses the "thumbs up" symbol to express "likes" (illustration used with permission of Facebook, Inc.).
- **Photo 4.4** An expression of brand love for Starbucks (© Erik Kostelijk – photo created by the authors, in compliance with INTA nominative fair use of trademarks: www.inta.org/TrademarkBasics/FactSheets/Pages/Fair-Use-of-TrademarksNL.aspx#).
- **Photo 4.5** The Facebook community of Harley Davidson has almost eight million likes. www.facebook.com/harley-davidson/?epa=SEARCH_BOX, retrieved January 7, 2019 (screenshot provided with permission of Harley-Davidson, Inc. and with permission of Facebook, Inc.).
- **Photo 4.6** "Hello Kitty" stimulates brand engagement (stock photo purchased at istockphoto.com).
- **Photo 5.1** Samsung is a good example of a product leader (photo © Hans Olav Lien (cc-by-sa/2.0), with permission of Samsung). This Samsung store is in the

shopping mall "SM Aura Premier" in Bonifacio Global City, Metro Manila, The Philippines. https://commons.wikimedia.org/wiki/File:Samsung_in_SM_Aura,_Bonifacio_Global_City.jpg

Photo 5.2 McDonald's is a good example of operational excellence. Photo taken from the McDonald's multimedia library; all materials here are free for editorial use: https://news.mcdonalds.com/press/multimedia-library/

Photo 5.3 Amazon.com uses individual preferences to create personalized offers (logo reprinted with permission of Amazon.com).

Photo 6.1 Cheers with Maallust beer: An appeal to the affective component (photo with permission of Maallust Beer).

Photo 6.2 Family time at Center Parcs (photo used with permission of Center Parcs).

Photo 6.3 Perfume and make-up: shopping goods with high symbolic value (photo CC0 public domain). https://pxhere.com/nl/photo/722591

Photo 6.4 Laundry machines: a shopping good with mainly instrumental benefits (photo CC0 public domain). https://pxhere.com/nl/photo/670071

Photo 6.5 HEMA, since 1926 (photo © Jordy Schaap (cc-by-sa/4.0), with permission of HEMA). https://nl.wikipedia.org/wiki/Bestand:HEMA_at_London_Stansted_Airport.jpg

Photo 6.6 The New Zealand Story (photo provided with permission of New Zealand Story Group).

Photo 7.1 The client is just one of the communication target groups (photo published on Flickr, September 16, 2016 (public domain)). www.flickr.com/photos/68716695@N06/29609195382

Photo 7.2 Lay's/Walker uses crowd sourcing to create new tastes (stock photo purchased at istockphoto.com).

Photo 7.3 The city of Flagstaff (Arizona, United States) uses social media for city marketing (screenshot provided with permission of the Flagstaff Convention & Visitors Bureau, and with permission of Facebook, Inc.).

Photo 8.1 Toyota Prius: An example of an individual brand (photo used with permission of Toyota).

Photo 8.2 The CEO of Unilever takes the social responsibility of the brand seriously (photo used with permission of Unilever © DFID – UK Department for International Development, June 8, 2013 (cc-by-2.0)). Paul Polman has stepped down as CEO in 2019. The current CEO of Unilever is Alan Jope. Unilever's commitment with respect to social responsibility has remained unchanged of course. https://commons.wikimedia.org/wiki/File:Paul_Polman,_CEO_of_Unilever_(8987490357).jpg

Photo 8.3 Siemens is an example of a monolithic brand (photo used with permission of Siemens; © Siemens PLM Software, May 16, 2017 (cc-by-nd/2.0)). www.flickr.com/photos/31274959@N08/34316629450/in/photostream/

Photo 8.4 Ralph Lauren endorses its individual brand Polo (stock photo purchased at istockphoto.com).

Photo 8.5 We associate Mars Inc. with candybars, but the company is also home to brands such as Uncle Ben's (rice) and pet food like Whiskas, Pedigree, and Royal Canin (stock photo purchased at istockphoto.com).

- **Photo 8.6** When you look for it, you will find the Unilever logo somewhere (photos provided with permission of Unilever).
- **Photo 8.7** A collection of brands from the product portfolio of Pepsico (© Erik Kostelijk – photo created by the authors, in compliance with INTA nominative fair use of trademarks: www.inta.org/TrademarkBasics/FactSheets/Pages/Fair-Use-of-TrademarksNL.aspx#).
- **Photo 8.8** The Smart: Swatch Mercedes ART (photo Mike Bird, Pexels.com, attribution not required) www.pexels.com/photo/grayscale-photo-of-smart-fortwo-217722
- **Photo 8.9** Intel inside: example of ingredient branding. Public domain: Commons Wikimedia (https://commons.wikimedia.org/wiki/File:Intel_Inside_Logo.svg).
- **Photo 9.1** The classic example of a major international rebranding operation; Raider became Twix in 1991. Photos used with permission of Mars Wrigley Confectionery UK Limited. Photo Raider © Gaspar18, May 27, 2018 (cc-by-sa/4.0)). https://commons.wikimedia.org/wiki/File:Relief_3_Twix.jpgPhotoTwix. Photo CC0 public domain. https://pxhere.com/nl/photo/794500
- **Photo 9.2** The Coca-Cola logo has remained virtually unchanged since 1886. Public domain. Commons Wikimedia (https://commons.wikimedia.org/wiki/File:Coca-Cola_logo.svg). Use of logo in compliance with INTA nominative fair use of trademarks.
- **Photo 9.3** The City of Melbourne logo (photo provided with permission of the Melbourne City Council, © City of Melbourne).
- **Photo 9.4** Nike Swoosh. Public domain. Commons Wikimedia (https://commons.wikimedia.org/wiki/File:Logo_NIKE.svg). Use of logo in compliance with INTA nominative fair use of trademarks.
- **Photo 9.5** Starbucks changed its logo in 2011. Left the old logo; right the new logo (stock photo purchased at istockphoto.com).
- **Photo 9.6** The typical features of a McDonald's restaurant. Photo taken from the McDonald's multimedia library; all materials here are free for editorial use: https://news.mcdonalds.com/press/multimedia-library/
- **Photo 10.1** The magic world of Disney (photo with permission of Disney; © Disney).
- **Photo Cases Part II** Historic building in Veenhuizen (photo © Baykedevries (cc-by-sa 4.0)). https://creativecommons.org/licenses/by-sa/4.0. The other photos were printed with permission of Maallust.
- **Photo Cases Part III** Moxy logo. Public domain. Commons Wikimedia (https://commons.wikimedia.org/wiki/File:Moxy_Hotels_logo.svg)

Index